Just South of Zion

JUST SOUTH OF ZION

The Mormons in Mexico and Its Borderlands

Edited by

Jason H. Dormady and
Jared M. Tamez

UNIVERSITY OF NEW MEXICO PRESS • ALBUQUERQUE

Library of Congress Cataloging-in-Publication Data
Just south of Zion : the Mormons in Mexico and its borderlands / edited by Jason H.
Dormady and Jared M. Tamez.
pages cm
Includes index.
ISBN 978-0-8263-5181-4 (cloth : alk. paper) — ISBN 978-0-8263-5182-1 (electronic)
1. Church of Jesus Christ of Latter-day Saints—Mexico—History. 2. Mormon Church—
Mexico—History. I. Dormady, Jason, 1975– editor. II. Tamez, Jared M., 1981– editor.
BX8617.M4J87 2015
289.3'72—dc23
2014049523

Cover photograph: *Two Sister Missionaries*,
courtesy of the Museum of Mormonism in Mexico
Book Design: Catherine Leonardo
Composed in Minion Pro 10.25/13.5
Display type is Avenir Lt Std

For Isaac, Oliver, and Helen

For Jesus Tamez, Leonor Tamez, Angie Allred, Grant Allred, Manuel Bueno Sr., Mary Bueno, Eliodoro Tamez, Linda Tamez, Aileen Tamez, Laura Tamez, Joseph Tamez, and Hyrum Tamez

Contents

Acknowledgments

THIS COLLECTION STARTED as a round-table presentation at the Rocky Mountain Council for Latin American Studies conference in Park City, Utah, in 2012. We would like to acknowledge the reassurance we received from those who attended that session (particularly Ken Mills of the University of Toronto) as well as the 2012 RMCLAS committee that allowed us the time and space to begin this conversation. We would also like to acknowledge the support of Clint Christensen of the Archives of The Church of Jesus Christ of Latter-day Saints, who served as a member of the round table but is not included in this collection. And of course, we wish to thank the University of New Mexico Press and Editor-in-Chief Clark Whitehorn, who encouraged us at that 2012 conference to pursue this project.

Just South of Zion is the product of a collective enterprise by a diverse range of scholars—established and new, traditional and independent, historians of Mormonism, Mexico, and the borderlands—willing to venture into what for many readers will be controversial territory. The nonconfessional discussion of the recent history of Mormonism draws the ire of both faithful Mormons who feel academic histories are possibly heretical and critics of the faith who are convinced that any history that is not openly condemnatory is "pro-Mormon." As such, we appreciate the scholarly attitude and collegial enthusiasm displayed by the authors contributing to this collection.

We would like to offer particular thanks to the institutional support of Central Washington University and the University of Texas at El Paso. In addition, we are grateful to the occasionally grudging but always helpful support of Fernando Gómez of the Museum of Mormon Mexican History with locations in Provo, Utah, and Mexico City, and we appreciate the limited but fruitful access to the museum's photographic collection.

In addition, we would like to thank the following people for their support and comments regarding this volume: Ernesto Chávez, Samuel Brunk,

Charles Ambler, Yolanda Leyva, Sandra McGee Deutsch, Paul Edison, Manuel Ramírez, Kristopher Klein, Michael K. Bess, Carolina Monsiváis, Cynthia Rentería, Joanna Camacho, Melanie L. Rodríguez, Jessica DeJohn Bergen, Lina María Murillo, Dennis Aguirre, Mario Villa, Aarón Margolis, Susie Aquilina, Gene Morales, Juana Moriel Payne, Heather M. Sinclair and Samuel Alva. In addition, conversations from the late 1990s with Ken Lockridge, Pamela Voekel, and Bethany Moreton served as motivation to take seriously the role of religion in the private and public lives of people as it played out in both their sacred and secular communities.

Finally, we would be remiss if we did not mention the support of our respective spouses and children, who put up with missed holidays and violated vacations as we worked through this time-consuming but rewarding project.

The Mormons in Mexico

JASON H. DORMADY

THE FIRST MORMONS in Mexico came both as refugees and as conquerors.

Perhaps as early as 1832 the founder of the movement now known as the Church of Jesus Christ of Latter-day Saints, Joseph Smith Jr., identified the Rocky Mountains—then squarely located in the northernmost reaches of Mexico—as an optional location for the religion, which was first established in New York State in 1830.[1] Just two years into the official existence of the church, protest—at times violent and at times lawful—from Protestants and local governments in New England and in the mid-Atlantic states had driven the group nicknamed Mormons to Ohio and Missouri.[2] But as scholar Val D. Rust argues, the early converts to Mormonism were used to existing on the fringes of American society. Most Mormon convert families descended from early Puritan migrants to the British New England colonies who chose to engage in protest and subversive so-called seeker traditions such as Anabaptism, Quakerism, or Gortonism.[3] Joseph Smith spent his childhood amid the religious upheaval of western New York during the Second Great Awakening, and his new religion was born at the same time as groups like the Seventh-day Adventists and Campbellites.

By 1839 Smith's group invited resistance from neighbors because of its economic and social communitarianism, adoption of non-Biblical texts, growing political influence, polygyny, and belief in Smith as a prophet of God. In Missouri, Governor Lilburn Boggs issued Executive Order 44 for the extermination of Mormons, forcing thousands to flee. In addition, financial problems and schisms in Ohio moved the group to seek refuge on the banks of the Mississippi in Nauvoo, Illinois. While there, Mormons first began discussing concrete plans to enter Mexico, naming the Great Basin, or the Great Salt Lake, as their preferred destination. The Masonic Lodge of Nauvoo even hosted meetings of Mormon leaders where they sketched out a map of the West on the floor and planned their travels from Illinois into the extreme north of Mexico. Joseph Smith, not long before his death, fled the city of Nauvoo for the Great Basin before turning back and submitting to an arrest warrant that landed him in a jail in Carthage, Illinois, where he was shot by a mob in June 1844.[4] By spring of 1846 the group's new leader, Brigham Young, finalized the decision to settle the area surrounding the Great Salt Lake, citing the area's extreme isolation. Though never referring to it as such, preferring instead to use the terms "Rocky Mountains" or "Great Basin," tens of thousands of New England Yankees chose Mexico as their destination for religious liberty.

The declaration of war by the United States against Mexico in 1846 rendered Mormons invaders as well as refugees as they prepared to leave their temporary camps for the Great Basin. As Mormons in Iowa and Nebraska awaited their exodus to the West, the US government saw the imminent westward movement of the group as an opportunity to occupy and hold northern Mexico, and so Stephen W. Kearny's Army of the West recruited over five hundred Mormon soldiers for the invasion of New Mexico and then California. As the US military expressed in their orders to Kearny,

> It is known that a large body of Mormon emigrants are en route to California, for the purpose of settling in that country. You are desired to use all proper means to have a good understanding with them, to the end that the United States may have their co-operation in taking possession of, and holding, that country. It has been suggested here that many of these Mormons would willingly enter into the service of the United States, and aid us in our expedition against California. You are hereby authorized to muster into service such as can be induced to volunteer; not, however, to a number exceeding one-third of your entire force.[5]

Between 1846 and 1849, Mormon soldiers marched into Mexican towns from Santa Fe to San Diego under the Stars and Stripes but with minimal armed conflict. Once the war ended with Mexico's defeat and the ceding of territory, the Mormon soldiers were discharged, with many seeking work in California to earn money to join their family near the Great Salt Lake in the Great Basin. While in California, many contracted to do lumber work in Sutter's Mill, where they were among those who discovered gold. Perhaps considered at the fringe of American society, they still retained US citizenship and engaged in the implementation of Manifest Destiny and the extension of US authority over the Mexican north. Such history is not lost on modern Mexican Mormons. As one such Mormon told scholar F. LaMond Tullis in Tullis's confessional history of Mormons in Mexico, "The Mormon Battalion offends all of Latin America. Fortunately, the Battalion had no battles. Had it done so the church would never have been allowed to enter Mexico."[6]

Despite the Mormons' usefulness in subduing the West, the relationship between the United States and the LDS Church remained strained. In 1857 President James Buchanan (1857–1861) became convinced of the possible rebellion of Mormons in the newly gained desert West and dispatched an army to put down the alleged threat. Although curbing the power of Brigham Young and his followers may have been Buchanan's top priority, the chance to once again use Mormons to seize additional Mexican territory may have become another consideration. According to Sir William Gore Ouseley, British envoy and confidant to Buchanan, the president saw the possibility of driving Young and the Mormons south to Sonora, Mexico, where they could then be used to sever that state from Mexico.[7] At first glance it may seem puzzling that Buchanan entertained the idea that Young and the Latter-day Saints would remain loyal to the United States after being driven from Utah, but this scenario does fit Mormon patterns of allegiance to the Union after two decades of forced removals.

Although nothing came of the Buchanan intrigues and armies did not drive Mormons south into Mexico, changes in the enforcement of existing US laws did. Possibly as early as the mid-1830s under Joseph Smith, a small portion of LDS men (first secretly and then openly after 1852) engaged in the practice of plural marriage, or polygyny.[8] Though the Morril Anti-Bigamy Act became law in 1862 to stop the Mormon practice, the LDS presence in the courts and on juries in Utah Territory made application of that law difficult—and Mormons largely felt immune from enforcement of anti-bigamy laws since they viewed their marriage practices as the free exercise of religion. In 1874, however, Congress passed the Poland Act, which put the prosecution and trial of plural marriage laws into the hands of non-Mormons. An 1876 test case saw the Utah Territorial Supreme Court rule against polygyny as a religious freedom, and the case headed to the US Supreme Court where the justices upheld the lower court's opinion. It is little wonder that amid this legal uncertainty the attention of Brigham Young turned to Mexico once more.

In June 1874 the Mormon prophet approached Spanish speakers Daniel Webster Jones and Henry Brizee about translating the Book of Mormon into Spanish so that they could take it south for missionary work in Mexico. According to Jones, "there were millions of descendants of Nephi in Mexico and we were under obligation to visit them."[9] The theological reason for the mission of Jones and Brizee (that Mexicans were "descendants of Nephi") makes reference to the LDS scripture known as the Book of Mormon. Adherents believe the book is a record kept by ancient inhabitants of the Americas, which Joseph Smith translated after being guided to its hidden location in New York State by an angel. The Book of Mormon states that around 600 BCE several families fled the destruction of Jerusalem, arriving in an unspecified location in the Americas. These families soon divided into two groups, the Nephites and the Lamanites, who alternately mixed and fought for centuries. The book teaches that after the resurrection and ascension Jesus Christ visited the Americas to teach these Nephites and Lamanites because they were a "remnant of Israel."[10] Eventually, both sides abandoned their belief in Christ, with the Lamanites destroying the Nephites as a cohesive political group and almost completely as a people. According to LDS belief, the Lamanites and Nephites are the ancestors, either in whole or in part, of American Indians.[11] For Brigham Young and Daniel Jones, it was their duty to return Christianity (as revealed to Joseph Smith) to the indigenous of the Americas via this book that, in the Mormons' view, the indigenous themselves had written, hidden, and lost. For many LDS leaders, the people of Mexico, with their mixed racial heritage, represented the descendants of the people who appear in the Book of Mormon.

From 1874 to 1875, Jones worked with a former Spanish army officer and LDS convert, Melitón Gonzáles Trejo, to translate the Book of Mormon and have one hundred copies printed. Finally, in 1875, Jones departed with a party of six for an exploration of Arizona and a mission to Mexico, crossing the border at El Paso in January 1876. They entered after the victory of secular liberalism in Mexico, and the Mormons reported that strong denunciations of them by the Catholic priest in El Paso del Norte (present-day Ciudad Juárez) piqued the curiosity of the population. Said Jones, the attacks by the priest "gave us an opportunity to explain our mission and principles to many that would not have listened had it not been for the padre's talk."[12] Jones notes a similar positive reception in the Guerrero district of Chihuahua.

While Daniel Jones does not list colonization explicitly as his reason for exploring Mexico, he learned of the situation there regarding emigration, which he reported to Brigham Young: colonial-era land grants and private titles tied up most arable land, leaving only uncultivable parcels for colonists. Nevertheless, Jones's group took note of the few possible locations for settlement, making sure to inquire as to the ownership of land and any possible conflicts regarding water.[13] Later, after visiting Guerrero, Tomosachic, and Namiquipa, where they distributed Books of Mormon and gave several sermons, the missionaries went on to say that only colonization could advance the "great work" of conversion in Mexico.[14] In fact, Jones participated in the early colonization of Chihuahua and Sonora by Mormons. And while Jones himself eventually returned to Arizona, his descendants in Mexico left their legacy: his great-great-grandson, Jeffrey Jones, grew up in the Mormon colonies, became a prominent politician in Chihuahua, and finally served as assistant secretary of agriculture in President Felipe Calderón's administration (2006–2012).

Long before colonization could begin, the slow work of establishing contacts and converts took priority. By capitalizing on Catholic distrust and building a respectable saddle business, the travelers secured a reputation in El Paso del Norte as respectable citizens and consequently secured letters of reference from the local *jefe político* that they could use as an introduction to the governor of Chihuahua. As Webster put it, "There were two parties in Mexico, the Catholics and the liberals. We kept our eyes open for the latter as we were always safe with them."[15] Jones sent Books of Mormon to liberal civic leaders throughout Mexico, receiving confirmation from intellectual, jurist, and author Ignacio Altamirano that he had received a copy. A note from the father of Mexican socialism, Greek-born Plotino C. Rhodakanaty, stated that he had subsequently received a "vision showing him the truth of the Book of Mormon."[16] Indeed, Rhodakanaty was visited and baptized by a second Mormon mission to Mexico in 1879.[17]

Nevertheless, the relationship between Rhodakanaty and the US missionaries rapidly deteriorated, particularly considering Rhodakanaty's desire to see his socialist vision fulfilled by a revival of Mormonism's communitarian past. In addition, as Mormon apostle Moses Thatcher despaired at missionary efforts in central Mexico, the first people contacted by Jones in the vicinity of Guerrero in Chihuahua still had not been approached about baptism, years after they expressed a desire for membership in the LDS church.[18] In short, initial efforts to proselytize Mexicans lacked organization and focus. Although conversion efforts eventually grew rapidly in the region between Amecameca in Mexico State and Cuatla, Morelos (already an area of growing Protestant conversion and a zone of traditional peasant unrest), for the time being the effort to colonize northern Mexico with Anglo Mormons seemed to meet with greater immediate success than baptizing Mexicans.

The group of LDS missionaries who baptized Plotino Rhodakanaty also met with highly placed members of the Porfirio Díaz administration to discuss Mormon colonization efforts: Manuel Fernández Leal, minister of development and colonization; Julio Zárate, foreign minister; and Carlos Pacheco, minister of war.[19] Díaz himself commented that hardworking colonists benefited Mexico, as long as they respected the prohibition of settlement within twenty leagues of the Mexican border.[20] And, unlike the Mormon settlers in Canada, who were also seen as tools for the "civilizing" of border regions, Mexico did not seek to directly impose norms of monogamy on Mormons as a condition of their permanent settlement.[21]

By the spring of 1885 the extensive application of anti-polygamy laws in Utah convinced many of the church's Quorum of the Twelve Apostles and its highest authority—the president of the LDS Church and his two counselors, who were known as the First Presidency—to flee to Mexico, even before they secured land. The tendency for families in the highest ranks of church leadership to settle in Chihuahua had far-reaching consequences:

> The self-selection of some of the church's most able families to participate in this particular colonization effort virtually assured that the communities would be well organized, purposeful, and solid. Indeed, between 1885 and 1895 six of the Mormon Church's twelve apostles lived in the colonies, most of them in Juárez. Having fled America because of their way of life, the colonists wanted one thing—to preserve that way of life. They had the leaders and the practical skills to do it.[22]

They also expended considerable effort to maintain as foremost their identity as members of what they considered the Kingdom of God on earth, often culturally isolating themselves from their Mexican neighbors. Of this isolation and focus on perfecting a Mormon culture within the eight colonies in Chihuahua and Sonora, Tullis writes, "Not surprisingly, in succeeding generations the colonies produced a striking number of Mormon leaders who became General Authorities [high-ranking clergy] of the [LDS] church."[23]

Meanwhile, missionary efforts in central Mexico proceeded apace, with particular success in the rural areas of Mexico State near the small towns of Ozumba and Atlautla. As Stuart Parker and Jared M. Tamez demonstrate in chapters 6 and 4 respectively, tension existed between the indigenous converts to Mormonism and the Anglo missionaries who introduced them to Mormonism, often because the missionaries privileged the desires of LDS headquarters in Salt Lake City over the demands of Mexican Mormons. Despite this tension, Tullis points out that a clear pattern of interaction occurred between Anglo and Mexican Mormons and soon-to-be Mormons in the events preceding the Mexican Revolution. First, the Mormon colonies in the north generated Spanish-speaking missionaries capable of effectively communicating with the local population. Second, increasingly, Mexican converts led the smallest LDS congregations (known as branches) as well as the Relief Society—the women's charitable aid auxiliary of the LDS Church. With these positive signs, the leadership in Salt Lake City paid closer attention to Mexico: after 1902 "numerous apostles made one or more visits" with one even spending a month to organize "Sunday schools and [teach] local members basic music skills."[24] Being a Mormon required more than just having a set of beliefs, but included the performed cultural practices that missionaries from the Anglo colonies and the United States brought with them. Nevertheless, Mexican members did not consider conversion to Mormonism as synonymous with gringo-ization.

The 1910 Mexican Revolution proved a watershed moment for Mormons in both the north and center of the country. In the north, thousands of Mormons dotted the landscape in colonies in Chihuahua and Sonora. By 1910, the Anglos that had come to Mexico twenty-five years earlier as penniless refugees now flourished through cooperative labor, and their growing prosperity found a mixed reception from locals and politicians as political tensions within Mexico grew. As historian John Mason Hart asserts, "The Americans were good customers, reliable, and relatively rich—perhaps too rich. They had earned the respect of some Mexicans. . . . Some thought the Americans were arrogant. Many believed the Mormons lived on usurped land and prospered by exploiting them."[25] In addition, Mormons often invested in or worked for unpopular US businesses in northern Mexico. In a period of growing distrust of the international businesses drawn to Mexico by Porfirio Díaz's policies, such associations could only serve to heighten the perception of Mormons as outsiders and not Mexicans.

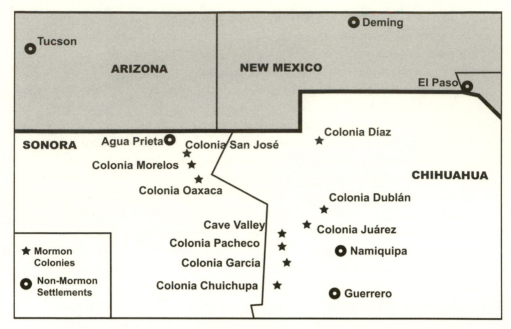

Map of Mormon colonies in Chihuahua and Sonora, Mexico. Map by Jason Dormady.

Resource allocation caused the most contention between Mormons and their neighbors. As historian Friedrich Katz points out, land taken from villagers by Enrique Creel, governor of Chihuahua (and son-in-law to Chihuahua's largest landowner), often benefited Mormons.

> In the Galeana District, unlike the rest of Chihuahua, Mormons rather than members of the oligarchy were the main beneficiaries of the expropriation of village lands resulting from Creel's land law of 1905. In Casas Grandes, the largest town of the district, the Mormons controlled most of the medium-sized and large enterprises. Five of the seven lumber factories were in their hands, as were most of the food-processing enterprises. . . . Economic conflicts, as well as cultural, religious, and nationalist tensions, contributed to opposition to Mormons.[26]

Often, as Katz points out with some irony, Mexican radicals trained in the United States as members of the Industrial Workers of the World (IWW) persecuted the Mormon colonists as representatives of foreign capital. From the other end of the ideological spectrum, Mormons also drew criticism from publisher Silvestre Terrazas during his time as editor of the *Revista Católica* for invading Mexico with foreign ideas.[27] Such interactions are ripe for further scholarly investigation, not (as has been the case to this point) as a look at Mormons in Mexico, but as a study of Mormons as a factor in the unrest of the nineteenth-century foothills of the Sierra Madres.

By July of 1912 the Mormons in the colonies—both Anglos and many Mexicans—chose to evacuate to the United States after followers of Revolutionary leader Pascual Orozco, under the command of José Ines Salazar, killed two Mormons. The forced exodus of the LDS is further complicated by the fact that Pascual Orozco was himself an evangelical Protestant—raised with the beliefs of Methodism in Chihuahua.[28] While one can only speculate about the antagonism from Orozco because of his Methodist distaste for Mormonism, it seems an area of investigation that merits further research to round out our understanding of the multiple reasons for tension between Mormons and non-Mormons in Chihuahua. Whatever the reasons for conflict, the retreat of the Mormons had long-lasting consequences for both Mexico and the United States, as Daniel Herman demonstrates with his reflection on Mormon violence in Arizona in chapter 7: Arizona's most powerful conservative and anti-immigration Mormon families are descendants of the refugees from the Chihuahua colonies. In addition, the 1910 Revolution and so-called exodus from the colonies in northern Mexico saw the flight of many non-Anglo Mormons to Texas, Arizona, and Utah, eventually leading to the creation of the first Spanish-language LDS congregations in the United States.

While the 1910 Revolution disrupted the lives of Anglo Mormons, it played only marginal importance in the lives of LDS Mexicans in central Mexico. Unlike the Protestants who supported revolutionaries like Zapatistas José Trinidad Ruiz and Otilio Montaño, early revolutionary Pascual Orozco, or Carrancistas like Aarón and Moisés Sáenz, Mormons from central Mexico have few heroes from the armed phase of the revolution that they championed. With the exception of two possible martyrs—Rafael Monroy and Vicente Morales of Hidalgo—the revolution seemed to have passed with the LDS remaining as noncombatants or at least unnoticed combatants for much of the conflict.[29] This peripheral involvement, however, wasn't for the lack of trying on the part of some. LDS businessman Hubert L. Hall did attempt to wrangle the Zapatista leadership into joining him in land deals and to act as a United States agent in Mexico (all of which came to naught); however, though future research might indicate otherwise, few Mormons appear to have connections with the armed phase of the revolution.[30]

Although the number of Mormons directly involved in the conflict is unknown, what is understood is that the 1910 Revolution had long-lasting consequences on the practice of the faith in central Mexico. Because of the fighting in the revolution and then the restrictions in the 1917 constitution that barred foreign clergy from serving in Mexico as clerics, Mormons in central Mexico found themselves increasingly isolated from the leadership in Salt Lake City. Relying increasingly on Mexican-born, non-Anglo leadership and missionaries, the Mexican-led LDS Church saw increased success in their missionary efforts. After the revolution, when the 1917 constitution denied foreign-born clergy the right to preach, the Mormons in central Mexico followed the same pattern found in Protestant denominations and grew steadily more self-reliant.[31]

In 1936 the growing division between Salt Lake City and Mexico City came to a head, when members of the LDS congregations in central Mexico gathered in the third of a series of meetings to decide their future. At the convention they expressed their displeasure with one of the few Anglo representatives from Salt Lake City with authority in Mexico, the president of the Mexican Mission, Harold Pratt. Non-Anglo members in Mexico City and the surrounding area felt that Pratt, a Mexican citizen of Anglo descent from the Mormon colonies in Chihuahua, ignored the needs of the members in central Mexico. The Mexican members demanded leadership by a Mexican from central Mexico. In addition, Pratt had distributed a circular in April 1936 rejecting a book by Margarito Bautista, a convert from Atlautla, Mexico State, who extolled the virtue of the Mexicans as descendants of the Lamanites in the Book of Mormon—a popular idea among members of the LDS Church in Mexico. Indeed, the popularity of the book prompted Pratt to proclaim that it was "not in any way church doctrine," an attempt to warn members away from the work.[32] Although Anglo LDS authorities may have seen the book as heretical, the writings of Bautista formed a successful bridge between Mormon theology, popular notions of Mexican history, and the ideology of the Mexican Revolution for many of the Mexican Mormons.

Pratt timed his offensive against Bautista's book poorly, for in April 1936 as Mexican Mormons gathered in the capital at their convention, they clamored for a mission president of "raza y sangre" (of Mexican race and blood).[33] They assumed that Salt Lake City lacked awareness of the résumés of qualified Mexicans, and they debated over the names they could send to Utah as suggestions (including Margarito Bautista, though he later withdrew his name from nomination).[34]

The movement known as the Third Convention spent the following year engaged with Harold Pratt in a series of negotiations in which both sides grew gradually more entrenched in their positions. The increasing tensions included a letter from J. Reuben Clark Jr., a member of the First Presidency of the LDS Church, stating that the convention ran counter to the centralized LDS chain of authority. The letter from Clark probably deepened the anti-US feelings, as Clark's résumé included undersecretary of state for Calvin Coolidge and ambassador to Mexico from 1930 to 1933 for the Hoover administration. In May 1937 the mainline LDS Church excommunicated the leaders of the Third Convention, and as a result one-third of the nearly three thousand members in central Mexico formed their own independent congregations.[35] The convention eventually returned to the mainstream church in 1946 after ten successful years of growth and stability. The reconciliation came after intense negotiations, which culminated in a rare visit from LDS Church president George Albert Smith, who traveled to Mexico to arrange the reunification. Smith also met with President Manuel Ávila Camacho (1940–1946), who lauded the Mormon colonies' contribution to the Mexican economy and said of Smith, "the Mexican People have a friend in him."[36]

For Margarito Bautista and others, however, after the Third Convention the break from the church in Utah became final. Bautista withdrew to a plot of family land in Ozumba, Mexico, where he established his own polygynous colony known as Colonia Industrial / Nueva Jerusalén. In this community the citizens owned property communally (with some success), a practice based in early Mormonism.[37] Similarly, Lorenzo Cuautli created his own community, with roughly the same beliefs as Bautista's, in San Gabriel Ometoxtla in Puebla. Though small, both still exist—and they weren't alone when it came to fundamentalist colonies of Mormons who sought autonomy in Mexico. With increased pressure from both the US federal government and the LDS Church, which sought to purge practitioners of plural marriage from its ranks, US Mormons who practiced polygyny sought refuge in Mexico in the mid-twentieth century. Families with names like Musser, LeBaron, and Allred—all key in the founding of groups like the Fundamentalist Church of Jesus Christ of Latter-day Saints—spent time in or colonized in Mexico. Indeed, in northern Chihuahua, not far from the first Mormon colonies, lies Colonia Lebaron, a farming and ranching town where fundamentalist Mormon polygynists continue to thrive and struggle against the narcotics violence surrounding them in the twenty-first century.[38] The history of these fundamentalists is one area that deserves more scholarly investigation within the context of Mexican history.

Oddly, another area that seems little explored is the period of Mormon history when it saw the most success—the explosion of growth of the LDS Church in Mexico after the reunification of the Third Convention with the mainline church. In particular, the LDS church reversed its position on refusing to fund services like schools in Mexico (they did not want the appearance of buying converts) and began a vigorous expansion of Mormon schools in Mexico. Starting in 1959, the LDS Church established a series of elementary, secondary, and preparatory schools throughout Mexico, as it had in other nations like Chile, Peru, and the Philippines.[39] The LDS Church's Mexican Education System drew not only from the local population of LDS students, but at times served as boarding schools for students coming in from distant locations. In 1981, however, the LDS Church underwent a retrenchment in education, closing thirty-four primary schools in Mexico and choosing to withdraw from most of their global education holdings. This decision, it seems, caused no shortage of dismay and anger among Mexican Mormons, as the schools were popular with both Mormons and their non-LDS neighbors.[40] Applications far outstripped the ability of the schools to provide space—even with strict religious demands and supervision by school and church authorities.

Most recently, June 2013 saw the final graduating class of the flagship educational facility of the LDS church, the Centro Escolar Benemérito de las Américas (CEBA), founded in 1964.[41] LDS officials closed the school to convert the large campus into a new training center where missionaries from Mexico and those from outside of Mexico called to serve in Spanish-speaking missions are trained in their ecclesiastical duty. With the closure of the CEBA, only the first LDS school founded in Mexico remains open—the Academia Juárez in Colonia Juárez, Chihuahua.

Even though the LDS hierarchy thought the time had come to close the school, CEBA had long retained a reputation among Mormons as the church's "vanguard school in Mexico." A 1999 article from the LDS newspaper Church News (written by the school's public relations director and intended for the English-language LDS audience of the paper), says about CEBA,

The preparatory school celebrated its 35th anniversary this year with a large reunion of students and teachers. It is through the thousands of former students such as these that Benemerito's influence continues to grow. Much of this influence is within the Church, with fifty-five percent of the students having filled missions and seventy-five percent having remained active in the Church. But the influence also goes beyond Church circles. Some eighty percent have attended university-level education, and Benemerito is believed to be the preparatory school with the most students enrolled at the Universidad Nacional Autonoma of Mexico (UNAM), the largest university in Mexico.[42]

The article then goes on to interview alumni of the school now employed in managerial positions at places like IBM or Otis Elevator Company. With over two thousand students on campus, CEBA wasn't just building better Mormons, but also Mexicans with a positive view of the relationship between Mexico and foreign corporations. As school director Félix Martínez Decuir said, "Evidently, Benemerito is a great seedbed for missionaries and for leaders in the Church, the community and the business world."[43] Like the Mexican Revolution itself, Mormonism transitioned from a radical re-envisioning of economics and the social order into a paragon of classical liberal capitalism.

From 1920 to the present, the history of the LDS Church has been intertwined with the history of modern Mexico. From the Mormons of the colonies in Chihuahua who have played on the Olympic national basketball team over the years to the myriad Mormon politicians in parties such as the PRI, PAN, PVEM, and PRD, Mormons have taken an active interest in the modernization of Mexico after the revolution. And with reportedly 1.3 million members in Mexico, the Latter-day Saints represent the third-largest single church of non-Catholics in that country, just after the Luz del Mundo Church of Guadalajara and the Jehovah's Witnesses with a reported 1.5 million each. Nevertheless, while Mormonism represents a significant group compared to other individual church entities, the overall total number of Protestants in Mexico dwarfs Mormonism with a possible population of over 8 million (including Luz del Mundo and excluding Jehovah's Witnesses). Similarly, those professing no religion in Mexico amount to just over 5 million. While some US Mormons might see such small numbers and consider Mexican Mormons as insignificant third-world partners, they have a long history together—and a complex future ahead.[44]

In the United States, illegal immigration divides not only Mexican and Anglo Mormons but also some Mormons from the leadership in Salt Lake City. While conservative Mormon Republicans in states like Arizona (such as former state representative Russell Pearce or US senator Jeff Flake) advocated for laws to regulate and expel Mexicans, the LDS Church itself took a softer line, probably owing to the growth of the LDS Church due to Latino converts. Indeed, while baptism into the Church of Jesus Christ of Latter-day Saints is not permissible for those currently breaking civil laws, undocumented immigrants are still permitted baptism. In addition, for Latinos pre-baptismal instruction occurs entirely in Spanish, and converts become members of Spanish-language congregations—a far cry from the "English only" position of many anti-immigrant activists. For example, in Mesa, Arizona, site of much of the resistance to Mexican immigration, the number of Spanish-language LDS congregations has grown from five to thirteen between 2002 and 2007. And Arizona is not alone. From 2000 to 2006 the number of Spanish-language LDS congregations in the United States rose from 389 to 639, and by 2011 it was 765—nearly doubling in a decade. And while Mexican Mormons waited decades for the creation of stakes run by Mexicans in Mexico, states like California and Florida have all-Spanish-language stakes with leadership drawn from migrants from Mexico and other areas in Latin America.[45] In 1876 the LDS leadership assumed that US colonization of Mexico meant successful growth, but in the twenty-first century, it appears that the growth of Mormonism in the United States is drawing heavily on Mexican and other Latin American settlements in the United States.

Such a position, however, causes conflict for conservative Mormons and their perception of the LDS Church. In Utah, where 80 percent of legislators are Mormon, the LDS Church backed a deal in 2011 known as the Utah Compact, which directed law officers away from enforcing federal civil immigration codes. In effect, with the backing of the LDS Church, Utah avoided creating the kind of laws found in states like Arizona and Alabama. One LDS opponent of that compact stated, "I am shocked that the church would support a bill that literally sacrifices 50,000 Utah children, who are the victims of identity theft, for the benefit of illegal aliens."[46]

In Mexico, Mormons and the growth of Mormonism seem to raise less controversy. Sociologists and Mormons Gary Shepherd and Gordon Shepherd have noted that while the LDS Church has avoided conflicts with the state, Mormons have not always been able to avoid clashes with other religions.[47] As in other Latin American nations, the competition for sheep to swell the flocks is sharp between evangelicals, Mormons, Jehovah's Witnesses, Seventh-day Adventists, and charismatic Catholics. Such divisions, however, tend to center on theology and not nationalism, and Mormonism is not, as it was at the start of the twentieth century, at the heart of any significant debates over the future of Mexico.

As for leadership, Mexican Mormons see to their own leadership needs at the local level, as was first envisioned by the Third Convention participants of the 1930s. And while many of Mexico's missions are headed by US citizens, most missionaries who serve in Mexico do not come from the United States, but from Mexico and other places in Latin America.[48] In addition, Mexican Mormons practice the LDS Church's highest form of worship, which is attendance at the LDS temple. This is considered a sign of the maturity of a congregation, singling out its ability to provide not only enough paid maintenance employees and volunteer lay clergy to staff the building but also congregants to worship there. As of 2014, Mexico had thirteen LDS temples: two in Chihuahua, and one each in Mexico City, Tamaulipas, Sonora, Nuevo Leon, Jalisco, Veracruz, Oaxaca, Tabasco, Chiapas, Yucatan, and Baja California Norte.

Such numbers, however, can be deceptive. The so-called leaky bucket or revolving door of disaffiliation after conversion so prevalent among Protestants in Latin America is no stranger to the LDS in Mexico. Although no official number of inactive members publicly exists, there are some indications that the number of baptized Mormons who are active in their congregations is far lower than the reported total number of baptized members. For men active in the lay pastorate of the LDS Church (there is only a lay pastorate at the local level), the activity rate appears to be at 19 percent.[49] In addition, Mormon Mexicans are overwhelmingly urban (two-thirds are in cities with a population of over 100,000) and young (60 percent are under the age of twenty-nine), which indicates either a foundation for expansion or a population that drifts from the movement as they grow older.

As scholar Henri Gooren discovered in his research of "conversion careers" of Latin American Pentecostals, Catholics, and Mormons, disaffiliation from Mormonism might happen for many reasons. At conversion, there is often insufficient support from the congregation, and new converts find it easy to return to old lifestyles.[50] Considering that of the million members added to the LDS Church between 1987 and 1989, 60 percent were located in Latin America (and with membership in Mexico alone doubling

between 1980 and 1989) it is doubtful that the new converts serving in the lay
pastorate provided adequate support or training for subsequent converts.[51]
Gooren also states that because the LDS Church is a demanding religion, his
informants felt too much was expected too early and they withdrew.[52] And
while some Mormons might be leaving for other Protestant groups or the
Catholic Church, in a survey of disaffiliation from the LDS Church in Utah,
sociologists Stan Albrecht and Howard Bahr show that nearly 42 of those
who disaffiliated from Mormonism simply remained unaffiliated. A firm
grasp of LDS numbers in Mexico and the history of schism there is difficult,
and long-term studies of disaffiliation could prove informative.[53]

Growth also entered a period of decline at the start of the twenty-first
century, from 22 percent growth in 1990 to just over 3 percent in 2006.[54] In
addition, the number of "units" or congregations in Mexico is reported by
the LDS Church (as of 2014) as 1,980. If one generously (and erroneously)
assumed all those units are wards (large congregations) with maximum
active membership of 500 each, the Mexican membership would still be shy
of a million members, at 990,000.[55]

OVERVIEW OF THE CHAPTERS

The history of Mormonism in Mexico runs parallel to the relationship
between the United States and Mexico, alongside the battle between liberals
and the Catholic Church, through the 1910 Revolution, and, finally, through
the efforts of Mexico to modernize in the post-Revolutionary era. The following chapters chart many of those key relationships through a variety of time
periods and geographic locations. Nevertheless, this collection is divided
into three distinct thematic areas. Chapters 1 and 2 reflect the foundations of
Mormonism in Mexico in the Anglo polygamist (and at times communitarian) north. Chapters 3 to 6 examine the mission field experience of
Mormonism in central Mexico and the mostly (but not exclusively) mestizo/
indigenous conflict with Anglo-Mormon missionaries and LDS Church officials. Finally, chapters 7 and 8 explore the borderlands experience of
Mormons, bringing New Mexico and Arizona into the picture. This collection represents not only a sampling of the cumulative history of Mormons in
Mexico, but because of the extensive record keeping of church organizations,
it also brings forward the voices of the indigenous, the rural poor, and
women, who all too often disappear from the written records of the

nineteenth and early twentieth century. Through the story of the lives of these Mormon Mexicans, we see how they used a particular religion as a community-building strategy during the Porfiriato (1876–1911), through the Mexican Revolution (1910–1920), and into the Golden Age of Mexican economic and cultural growth (1940–1968).

In chapter 1, Barbara Jones Brown explores the key reason Mormons entered Mexico after 1876: to continue their practice of polygyny, or plural marriage. While Jones Brown is keenly aware of the contradictions in Mexican law and Mormon marriage practice, she points out that only the 1910 Mexican Revolution finally stifled the LDS practice of plural marriages—something that nearly half a century of legal proceedings and extralegal violence had not been able to accomplish in the United States. In chapter 2, George Ryskamp explores the complex formation of a transmigrant identity for Mormons in the colonies of Chihuahua. While many resisted Mexicanization in the early years of colonization, a complex identity formation allowed them to feel at home both in Mexico and the United States while practicing a religion considered dissident in both. Ryskamp provides a fascinating example of the creation of a "border people" who simultaneously maintain dual identities and even "strengthen their identification with and loyalty to their parent societies."[56] This approach is reinforced by Brandon Morgan's research in chapter 8, which demonstrates that part of that complex cross-border identity formation came as a result of participating in business ventures in the trade corridor from Deming, New Mexico, to the Mormon colonies in Chihuahua. Nevertheless, as Daniel Herman argues in chapter 7, the formation of this cross-border identity did not always prove peaceful, as Mormons exported their own brand of violence and justice and later expressed it in the form of anti-immigrant legislation in the twenty-first century.

Chapters 3 and 4 by Bill Smith and Jared M. Tamez, on the other hand, explore the growth of conflict deep in central Mexico between not only US and Mexican identities but also over the very definition of Mormonism. From the socialist and anarchist desires of Rhodakanaty to the expectations of female power in worship, Anglo missionaries found themselves in a state of continual defense against attempts to define Mormon practice and culture in Mexican terms. In contrast, Elisa Pulido's discussion in chapter 5 of the Third Convention movement is one of reconciliation, but one predicated on the ability and willingness of the LDS church leadership to back away from its "wise patriarchy" approach and instead rely on conciliatory overtures such as the ability of female missionaries to build alliances in music and women's auxiliaries.

All the authors situate the actions of Mormons within the context of Mexican and US history, though perhaps none as explicitly as Stuart Parker, whose chapter 6 contribution explores the writings of the so-called apostate Mormon Margarito Bautista. As Parker demonstrates, the Mexican Revolution created a fertile arena of intellectual creation, and men like Bautista formed their own response in the same vein as thinkers and reformers like José Vasconcelos. And, as our afterword by Matthew Butler argues, Mormonism in Mexico has been particularly malleable and flexible in response to the political, economic, and social winds that have swept Mexico. As such, this collection marks only a starting point for scholarship on Mormons in Mexico, not a culmination.

With this volume, the first collection of essays and research on Mormons in Mexico—by scholars whose primary focus is not Mormon history, per se, but rather Mexico and the borderlands—the editors hope to spark a conversation between those who study Mormon history and those who study Mexican history and prompt them to recognize the intertwined nature of those two areas of scholarship. We also hope to encourage scholars of modern Mexico to recognize that including Mormons in the discussion of areas such as US relations with Mexico, gender, colonization, business, revolution, conversion and apostasy, identity, and education will add richness and depth to their sources and variety to their cases studies, particularly as a wealth of well-organized archival and published journals and documents have been preserved in both Spanish and English by Mormons. As for scholars of Mormonism, we hope that this collection will prompt some to find a place for research outside of collections and conferences on confessional histories or religious studies. We hope that they will venture into the context of Mexican and borderlands history and seek out more research on Mormons in Mexican collections, such as the National Archive in Mexico City or regional and municipal collections. And finally, perhaps we can encourage both sides of this fascinating area of research to consider the myriad possibilities that exist. In Mormon theology the term *Zion* means "of one heart and one mind," and the title of this collection, *Just South of Zion*, reflects not only the tension between US and Mexican Mormons—as well as regional divides between Chihuahua and central Mexico—but also the fact that Mormons in Mexico have always been just shy of their religious goal of unity. This situation exists in great part because of the diverse practices and beliefs of those who profess the religion. More can be done on class, education, politics, the experience of Mormons outside of core LDS areas like Chihuahua or central Mexico, and groups who do not participate in the rites of the LDS Church but still confess Mormon beliefs.

Certainly there is much to learn by looking at one of the most active groups of transborder migrants in US-Mexican history—the Mormons.

NOTES

1. For a look at the variety of sources and ways in which Mormons learned about the Rocky Mountains and the Great Basin, see Lewis Clark Christian, "Mormon Foreknowledge of the West," *BYU Studies* 21, no. 4 (1981): 403–15.
2. In this collection we use "Mormon" for any group that uses the Book of Mormon as a book of scripture. Thus, while the majority of this collection does focus on the Church of Jesus Christ of Latter-day Saints (LDS), not all the Mormons in the collection are LDS.
3. Val D. Rust, *Radical Origins: Early Mormon Converts and Their Colonial Ancestors* (Urbana: University of Illinois Press, 2004), 6, 96, 101.
4. *History of the Church of Jesus Christ of Latter-day Saints* (Salt Lake City, UT: Deseret Book Company, 1950), 7:66–67, 102–7.
5. Executive Document No. 60, Secretary of War to General Kearny, 1846, as quoted in Brigham Henry Roberts, *The Mormon Battalion: Its History and Achievements* (Salt Lake City, UT: Deseret News, 1919), 11–12. While a ship of Mormon settlers was headed for California and the port of Yerba Buena (modern-day San Francisco) under the command of Sam Brannan, it is most likely that the emigrants cited in this letter are those traveling overland to the Great Basin and erroneously thought to be headed to California by the US military.
6. F. LaMond Tullis, *The Mormons in Mexico: The Dynamics of Faith and Culture* (Logan: Utah State University Press, 1987), 203–4.
7. *Deseret News*, May 29, 2011. This is the position of independent scholar and former president of the Mormon History Association, William P. MacKinnon, delivered at the closing session of the 2011 Mormon History Association conference in St. George, Utah.
8. What was practiced by Mormons after their arrival in Utah is probably more properly described as polygyny. However, because no distinction was made between polygamy and polygyny in the nineteenth-century critiques of Mormonism, the term "polygamy" (the idea that men and women can have multiple spouses) has become synonymous with the Mormon practice of polygyny (the practice of only men having multiple spouses).
9. Daniel Webster Jones, *Forty Years Among the Indians* (Salt Lake City, UT: Juvenile Instructor Office, 1890), 220.

10. Book of Mormon, 1 Nephi 13:34.

11. Joseph Fielding Smith, *Teachings of the Prophet Joseph Smith* (Salt Lake City, UT: Deseret Book Company, 1993), 85.

12. Jones, *Forty Years*, 259.

13. Ibid., 277, 290.

14. Ibid., 283.

15. Ibid., 274.

16. Ibid., 279.

17. Carlos Illades, *Rhodakanaty y la formación del pensamiento socialista en México* (Barcelona: Anthropos, 2002), 101–3.

18. F. LaMond Tullis, "Early Mormon Exploration and Missionary Activities in Mexico," *BYU Studies* 22, no. 3 (1982): 10.

19. Tullis, "Early Mormon Exploration," 7.

20. Moisés González Navarro, *Los Extranjeros en México* (Mexico City: El Colegio de México, 1994), 243–44.

21. For more on the use of Mormons in Canadian colonialism and the clash with Mormon polygyny, see Sarah Carter, *The Importance of Being Monogamous: Marriage and Nation Building in Western Canada to 1915* (Edmonton: University of Alberta, 2008).

22. Tullis, *Mormons in Mexico*, 57.

23. Ibid.

24. Ibid., 82.

25. John Mason Hart, *Empire and Revolution: The Americans in Mexico since the Civil War* (Berkeley: University of California Press, 2002), 242.

26. Friedrich Katz, *The Life and Times of Pancho Villa* (Stanford, CA: Stanford University Press, 1998), 90–91.

27. Ibid., 48.

28. Kurt Bowen, *Evangelism and Apostasy: The Evolution and Impact of Evangelicals in Modern Mexico* (Montreal: McGill-Queen's University Press, 1996), 31.

29. Mark L. Grover, "Execution in Mexico: The Deaths of Rafael Monroy and Vicente Morales," *BYU Studies* 35, no. 3 (1995–1996): 6–28. Monroy and Morales are portrayed in confessional histories as martyrs for their faith, while BYU scholar Grover argues that the two men were simply victims of the factionalism that plagued Mexico during the 1910 Revolution.

30. For more on Hall, see John Womack, *Zapata and the Mexican Revolution* (New York: Vintage Books, 1970), 236–39, 298–99.

31. For more on Protestant organizations in Mexico and the influence the 1910 Revolution had on their growing independence, see Deborah Baldwin, *Protestants and the Mexican Revolution: Missionaries, Ministers, and Social Change* (Chicago: University of Illinois Press, 1990).

32. Tullis, *Mormons in Mexico*, 123. Tullis cites Pratt's journal as the source.

33. According to early LDS organization, an area with minimal membership fell

under the supervision of a mission president, under which existed districts headed by presidents of their own. Within those districts existed wards (large congregations headed by bishops) and branches (small congregations headed by branch presidents). In central Mexico, the district president was Isaías Juárez, a Mexican of "raza y sangre" and a leader of the National Campesino's Confederation (CNC) who had recently returned from exile during the Calles administration. All bishops and branch presidents outside of the Mormon colonies in Chihuahua were Mexicans of raza y sangre.

34. Tullis, *Mormons in Mexico*, 139. Author and independent historian Fernando Gomez argues that the Third Convention was not a nationalist move, but an attempt to stabilize the LDS church in Mexico after the disruptions of the revolution. See Fernando Gómez, *From Darkness to Light: The Church of Jesus Christ of Latter-day Saints and the Lamanite Conventions* (Mexico City: El Museo de Mormonismo en Mexico, A.C., 2004), 42–47.

35. Tullis, *Mormons in Mexico*, 142–43.

36. *Deseret News*, May 27, 1946.

37. For more on Bautista, see Jason Dormady, *Primitive Revolution: Restorationist Religion and the Idea of the Mexican Revolution, 1940–1968* (Albuquerque: University of New Mexico Press, 2011).

38. *New York Times*, July 25, 2009.

39. *Church News*, July 10, 2004.

40. Tullis, *Mormons in Mexico*, 191–92.

41. "Se clausura oficialmente el Centro Escolar Benemérito de las Américas," Sala de Prensa, México, La Iglesia de Jesucristo de los Santos de los Últimos Días. http://www.saladeprensamormona.org.mx.

42. *Church News*, November 27, 1999.

43. Ibid.

44. Luz del Mundo and LDS Church numbers of 1.3 and 1.5 million are self-reported numbers. On the Mexican census, the numbers appear much smaller (188,000 and 315,000 respectively), but probably due to low counts on the Mexican census as well as differentials in reporting. For example, the Mexican census reports approximately 188,000 total members of the Luz del Mundo organization. But more than that attend religious festivals in Guadalajara each August. Because of their view of themselves as Israelites, they might report on the census as Jewish or Israelite or simply as Cristiano. The Mexican census provides the number of 8.36 million Protestants of various denominations, though the accuracy of that number is, once more, debatable. *Panorama de las religiones en México 2010* (Aguascalientes, Mexico: Instituto Nacional de Estadística y Geografía, 2010), 3–10.

45. *East Valley Tribune*, May 30, 2007. LDS Online Almanac. http://www.ldschurchnewsarchive.com/almanac/1/Almanac.html.

46. *Salt Lake Tribune*, March 17, 2011.

47. Gary Shepherd and Gordon Shepherd, "Mormon Missionaries and Mormon

Scholars in Mexico," in *Religion in Latin America: A Documentary History*, ed. Lee M. Penyak and Walter J. Petry (Maryknoll, NY: Orbis Books, 2006), 235.

48. Ibid., 236.

49. Lowell C. Bennion and Lawrence A. Young, "The Uncertain Dynamics of LDS Expansion, 1950–2020," *Dialogue: A Journal of Mormon Thought* (Spring 1996): 19.

50. Henri Gooren, "Conversion Careers in Latin America: Entering and Leaving Church among Pentecostals, Catholics, and Mormons," in *Conversion of a Continent: Contemporary Religious Change in Latin America*, ed. Timothy J. Steigenga and Edward L. Cleary (New Brunswick, NJ: Rutgers University Press, 2007), 62, 64–65.

51. Tim Heaton, "Vital Statistics," *The Encyclopedia of Mormonism* (New York: Macmillan, 1992), 1520.

52. Gooren, "Conversion Careers," 62, 64–65.

53. Stan L. Albrecht and Howard Bahr, "Patterns of Religious Disaffiliation: A Study of Lifelong Mormons, Mormon Converts, and Former Mormons," *Journal for the Scientific Study of Religion* 22, no. 4 (1983).

54. *Times and Seasons*, May 6, 2009. http://timesandseasons.org.

55. Facts and Statistics: Mexico. The Church of Jesus Christ of Latter-day Saints, Newsroom, The Official Source for News Media, Opinion Leaders, and the Public. http://www.mormonnewsroom.org/facts-and-statistics/country/mexico.

56. Oscar J. Martínez, *Border People: Life and Society in the U.S.-Mexico Borderlands* (Tucson: University of Arizona Press, 1994), 307.

CHAPTER ONE

The 1910 Mexican Revolution and the Rise and Demise of Mormon Polygamy in Mexico

BARBARA JONES BROWN

ON JANUARY 21, 1903, seventeen-year-old Julia Abegg proudly donned her wedding gown, the first dress she had ever made entirely on her own. She and her betrothed, both American emigrants to Mexico, traveled to Colonia Juárez, Chihuahua, to be married, or "sealed" as the Mormons called it. The marriage was peculiar by both American and Mexican standards, not so much because Julia's husband, Anson Bowen Call (referred to by his family as Bowen), was twenty-two years her senior, but because he already had two wives.[1]

Polygamy, or "celestial marriage," had been part of the Mormon faith for some sixty years. Early members of the Church of Jesus Christ of Latter-day Saints believed that living the principle in this life prepared them to receive God's highest celestial blessings in the next. "He that abideth not this law can in nowise enter into my glory, but shall be damned, saith the Lord," proclaimed part of a revelation on celestial marriage, recorded in 1843 and received by the church's founding prophet, Joseph Smith.[2]

Polygamy did not sit well with many Americans, who viewed it and slavery as "the twin relics of barbarism."[3] In 1882, Congress passed the Edmunds Act, making bigamous cohabitation a misdemeanor and forcing many polygamous men into hiding or prison. Latter-day Saints believed the act violated their First Amendment guarantee of freedom of religion. Because federal efforts at prosecution focused on Utah, many Mormons who wanted to live in polygamy simply scattered to other locations, including Wyoming's Star Valley; Cardston, Alberta, Canada; and northern Chihuahua, Mexico.[4]

After a small number of Latter-day Saint colonizers established camps in Chihuahua's Casas Grandes Valley in the mid-1880s, local officials, aware of the Mormon practice of polygamy, ordered the colonists' expulsion. Mormon apostles Moses Thatcher and Erastus Snow hurried to Mexico City to talk with federal officials, hoping to have the order rescinded. There, with Helaman Pratt of the LDS Mexican Mission interpreting, they met with the new president of the Mexican Republic, Porfirio Díaz, and officers of his cabinet. In their meeting with secretary of public works Carlos Pacheco, the Mormon leaders brought up the issue of polygamous families who wanted to settle in Chihuahua. Although polygamy was illegal in Mexico, Díaz's plans for developing his country's economy included the establishment of foreign colonists, particularly on the arid lands of Mexico's northern states. Pacheco knew the Mormons' reputation as good farmers fit the requirements that Mexican leaders had built into their nation's colonization laws. The Mexican leaders' desire to enrich the nation through colonization transcended their motivation to enforce anti-polygamy laws. Pacheco rescinded the expulsion order and, according to Pratt's diary, told the Mormon leaders that if they would colonize in peace and practice their marriage customs quietly, Latter-day Saints were welcome. The Mormon immigrants later named one of their colonies after Pacheco. In December 1885, Latter-day Saint settlers, many of them polygamous families from Arizona, began moving in earnest into Chihuahua.[5]

That same year, Bowen Call married his first wife, Theresa Thompson, in the Mormon temple in Logan, Utah. In spite of the passage of the Edmunds Act, before Theresa consented to marry Call, she made certain that he intended to live the principle of celestial marriage so they could be worthy of God's highest blessings. If Bowen did not intend to marry plural wives, Theresa said, she did not intend to marry him.[6] Like many Latter-day Saints of their day, Theresa and Bowen's desire to live what they believed to be God's higher law of plural marriage transcended their motivation to abide by the federal government's laws requiring monogamous marriage.

In 1887, Congress passed the Edmunds-Tucker Act, which strengthened the government's ability to enforce the new anti-polygamy law. Among the act's myriad effects, Edmunds-Tucker dissolved the church corporation and enabled the government to take possession of church property valued at more than $50,000—including three temples in Utah. It decreed that individuals who practiced polygamy be fined up to $800 and imprisoned for up to five years for each instance of plural marriage.[7] Shortly after the act passed, Bowen and Theresa Call moved from Bountiful, Utah, to Star Valley, Wyoming.

In Star Valley, the young couple began talking about fulfilling their main purpose for moving there. "I think Mother was even more concerned than Father was about the necessity of practicing the principle [of plural marriage]," their son Anson B. Call Jr. later said. "They both settled on one young lady they thought would be compatible" with their family—eighteen-year-old Harriet ("Hattie") Cazier. When Bowen asked Charles Cazier "if he objected to his daughter being courted with the idea of her becoming his plural wife," Cazier responded, "Don't ask me! I'm not the one who's going to marry you. Go ask her!" Bowen did, and he and Hattie became engaged in 1888.[8]

When Bowen and Hattie traveled to the Logan temple in June 1889 to be married, temple officials told the surprised couple that they could not perform their marriage sealing. Bowing to the Edmunds-Tucker Act, church leaders had directed that no plural marriages be performed in Latter-day Saint temples, under threat of the federal government closing them. Bowen soon went to Salt Lake City to ask Wilford Woodruff, the fourth president of the church, what to do. "He advised me to go to Mexico," Bowen said, "and also advised me to sell all of my property." Because Mormon polygamy was not being prosecuted in Mexico, thousands of Latter-day Saints were moving there to practice polygamy in peace. Bowen, Theresa, and Hattie soon followed Woodruff's advice.[9]

On October 6, 1890, during the church's semiannual general conference in Salt Lake City, Woodruff issued a carefully worded "Official Declaration" or "Manifesto" on plural marriage, stating that "we are not teaching polygamy or plural marriage, nor permitting any person to enter into its practice ... in our Temples or in any other place in the [Utah] Territory." Because the Supreme Court had ruled that anti-polygamy laws were constitutional, Woodruff said, "I now publicly declare that my advice to the Latter-day Saints is to refrain from contracting any marriage forbidden by the law of the land."[10] But in Canada and Mexico, where Latter-day Saint polygamous unions were not being prosecuted, Mormon communities were flourishing. The church's First Presidency, comprised of Woodruff and his two counselors, authorized Mormon apostles to perform plural marriages in Mexico and Canada and encouraged Latter-day Saints who wished to live the celestial law to move to these areas.[11]

On November 27, 1890—less than two months after Woodruff's Manifesto—Bowen and Theresa, their three little daughters, and Hattie Cazier boarded a train in downtown Salt Lake City and headed south for

their new life in a land completely foreign to them. "The challenges of sub-
sistence on the frontier, added to complications arising from life in plural
households, confronted the faithful with severe trials," writes the historian
B. Carmon Hardy. "Some marriages did not survive. Those that did provide
remarkable examples of nobility and self-denial." Hardy's words aptly
describe the Calls and their life in Mexico.[12]

By the time the Calls arrived in Chihuahua in late 1890, three Mormon
settlements or colonies had sprung up—Colonia Díaz on the Casas Grandes
River near the Mexico–New Mexico border, and Colonias Juárez and Dublán,
some fifty miles south of Colonia Díaz and two hundred miles southwest of
El Paso, near the Mexican town of Casas Grandes. Díaz was named for the
nation's president; Juárez for Mexico's former jurist and president, Benito
Juárez; and Dublán for Manuel Dublán, treasury secretary of Mexico, who
helped the Mormons purchase land for colonization.[13]

On December 4 the family reached Díaz. Bowen and Hattie immediately
caught a wagon ride with a local resident to Colonia Juárez to be married.
Though Theresa later told Bowen she felt "thankful that we had the privilege
to enter into the higher laws of the Gospel . . . it was like taking the very heart-
strings out at the time." Now a plural family, the Calls made their home in
Colonia Dublán, about seventeen miles northeast of Colonia Juárez.[14]

A few years later, Hattie died of pneumonia. With Theresa's encouragement, Bowen married a third wife, nineteen-year-old Dora "Dottie" Pratt, in
1898. He married his fourth and final wife, Julia Abegg, in 1903. Soon after
their marriage, Julia traveled to Utah, visiting relatives there for several
months, though she kept her recent marriage a secret until years later. In fact,
though Bowen and his other plural wives, Hattie and Dottie, spoke openly
about who had performed their 1890 and 1898 plural marriages, Julia and
Bowen did not even divulge to their own children the name of the person
who performed their marriage. They were asked not to.[15]

Their silence was tied to a national uproar in the United States over the
Latter-day Saints' continued practice of polygamy. On January 26, 1903, five
days after Julia and Bowen's marriage, Utah elected Mormon apostle Reed
Smoot to the United States Senate. Following his election, a group of non-
Mormon attorneys, businessmen, and ministers from Utah sent a protest
letter to Washington, charging that Latter-day Saints were still practicing
polygamy, encouraged by church leaders, including Smoot. The Senate
allowed Smoot to be seated but appointed a committee to investigate the

accusations. The ensuing Senate hearings began in early 1904 and lasted more than three years. Though Smoot epitomized the majority of monogamous Latter-day Saints, he faced accusations regarding the "peculiarities of Mormonism," including some Mormons' ongoing practice of polygamy, particularly in Mexico, in spite of Woodruff's 1890 Manifesto.

The hearings caused an American tumult. "In the Capitol, spectators lined the halls, waiting for limited seats in the committee room, and filled the galleries to hear floor debates. For those who could not see for themselves, journalists and cartoonists depicted each day's admission and outrage," writes the historian Kathleen Flake. "At the height of the hearing, some senators were receiving a thousand letters a day from angry constituents."[16]

At the proceedings' end in 1907, Smoot retained his seat and remained in office for twenty-six more years. But the hearings had a profound effect on the already shrinking minority of Latter-day Saints who continued to practice polygamy. Shortly after the onset of the proceedings in early 1904, Senator Smoot and the church's legal counsel, Franklin S. Richards, urged LDS president Joseph F. Smith to do something at the next general conference to redress the church's damaged reputation. On April 6, 1904, President Smith issued what became known as the Second Manifesto, which reaffirmed the first. "If any officer or member of the Church shall assume to solemnize or enter into any such marriage," Smith added, "he will be deemed in transgression against the Church, and will be liable to be dealt with according to the rules and regulations thereof and excommunicated."[17]

The 1904 Manifesto marked a genuine dividing line that resulted in a definite reduction, if not cessation, of approved polygamous marriages. But while the performance of new plural marriages essentially ceased, those who married into polygamy before 1904 continued to practice the principle, still living together as plural families.[18] It was not the Smoot hearings or Smith's 1904 Manifesto, but the Mexican Revolution of 1910–1920 that brought on the beginning of the end of LDS polygamous families living together in family units. Just as the revolution brought radical change to Mexico, the conflict dramatically disrupted the Mormon colonists' way of life.

The violence of the Mexican Revolution drove the Anglo colonists from Mexico three times, in 1912, 1914, and 1917, in what the Mormon colonists called "the exoduses." Opposed to imperialism in their country, some revolutionaries hoped to permanently drive the Mormon colonists and other foreigners out of Mexico and redistribute their lands to local Mexicans.[19]

Needing food, clothing, arms, ammunition, and horses to carry out their warfare, rivaling Revolutionary factions in northern Mexico eyed the resource-rich Mormon colonies and other foreign interests that Porfirio Díaz's administration had encouraged. "Look at the homes these gringos live in; look at the huts that you Mexicans live in," one faction leader said in a speech in Pearson, a British sawmill settlement near the Mormon colonies. "Look at the fine clothes that these gringos wear; look at the rags you Mexicans wear. All of this property belongs to you. These gringos must be run out of the country, and the property divided among Mexicans. Mexico is for Mexicans, and the United States is for the gringos. . . . Under Díaz they flourished, but now there is a change in the Government and we will drive them out."[20]

During the decade of the revolution, rebel soldiers demanded thousands of dollars in merchandise from the Mormon colonists and other Americans, took produce from their fields and barns, slaughtered their animals for food, and confiscated horses, mules, and wagons for transportation. Hoping to remain neutral and avoid violence, the Latter-day Saints accommodated the soldiers. But when the US government implemented an arms embargo in March 1912 to stop the flow of weapons to Mexican Revolutionaries, the rebels began to demand the colonists' guns and ammunition. Unwilling to turn over their means of protection—and after President William Howard Taft urged all 75,000 Americans in Mexico to leave—on July 27, 1912, local Mormon leadership decided that women, children, and elderly men should evacuate to the United States.[21]

By sundown of July 28, "wagon after wagon load of women and children gathered . . . at the depot, leaving all their earthly possessions behind them. What a sight!" Bowen Call said, invoking collective Mormon memory of expulsion from Missouri and Illinois more than six decades before. "About seven or eight hundred women and children were being driven from their homes." Among them was five-year-old George Romney, who later became governor of Michigan, 1968 presidential candidate, US secretary of housing and urban development, and father of 2012 GOP presidential nominee, Mitt Romney. By 1:30 a.m. on July 29, about one thousand colonists were waiting at the Dublán train stop, saying farewells in the moonlight, "not knowing if they would ever be together again," said Anson Bowen Call Jr. "This was a very sad occasion."[22]

Bowen and two other local leaders called the people to order and, after a "very solemn prayer," addressed the assembly, "offering them all the

Anglo Mormons returning to the United States, circa 1912. Photographer unknown. Courtesy of the Museum of Mormon Mexican History.

encouragement we could, to face a cold winter, homeless and without means of support, and many of them without the loving protection of their husbands and fathers, who remained behind to protect their interests at home," Bowen said. For many in that crowd, the cold winter of living apart from their husbands and fathers would last the rest of their lives. That day marked not only the end of the thriving community in Colonia Dublán, but also the beginning of the final chapter of the Latter-day Saints' polygamous way of life.[23]

In the mass exodus of 1912, some 4,500 Mormon colonists fled their Mexican homes. Though they did not know it then, about 90 percent of them would never return. Responding to requests for help, El Paso railroad officials quickly sent into Chihuahua every railroad car they could round up. Unfortunately, many of them were cattle and freight cars. By the time the northbound train reached Dublán, daylight had come and all of the passenger cars were full of American refugees. For the Mormon men who temporarily stayed behind to protect their homes, the image of their "loved ones loaded into boxcars . . . under a scorching semi-tropical sun," said Bowen, "was a very pitiable sight." Dottie had died from appendicitis several years before. Theresa, Julia, and twelve Call children bid Bowen good-bye and rolled into the unknown with nothing but a few trunks, a little bread, and, literally, some sour grapes.[24]

Less than two weeks later, the men of the colonies began their long journey on horseback to the United States after receiving death threats. The column of some 235 riders and one wagon, headed by a horseman carrying a white flag, stretched out over a mile and a half. On August 12 they reached Hachita, New Mexico, where many of them, including Bowen, took a train on to El Paso.[25] Bowen's reunion with his family was short-lived. Three days later, Theresa, Julia, and the children boarded a train for Utah, accepting the federal government's offer to American refugees for free railway transportation to any location in the United States. The free ride out of the refugee camps of El Paso scattered the polygamous families. Bowen and a few other Mormon men stayed behind at the border, waiting to return to Chihuahua to reclaim their homes and farms.[26]

Twenty-seven-year-old Julia, traveling with her three children, may have welcomed the long time it took to reach her former home of Utah. She feared prosecution for her polygamous marriage. When the train finally pulled into the Salt Lake train station at midnight on August 22, she was so worried that federal marshals might be there looking for polygamous families that she was glad "it was dark so if necessary I could slip to one side."[27]

Several months later, in the spring of 1913, Bowen felt the situation in Colonia Dublán was secure enough for his wives and children to return. Theresa, wary of the dangers of Revolutionary Mexico, urged Bowen to consider making a new start somewhere in the United States, but in the end he convinced her to return to their home in Dublán. I "still have my face turned towards Mexico and cannot think but we will all go back and enjoy the fruit of the labors of twenty-two years," he wrote her. "We have too much there to pull out and leave and get nothing for it. . . . O, what could we do to start over again without a dollar and as you know I cannot work as I once did."[28]

Beyond financial concerns, Bowen also feared that living in the United States would mean the Calls could no longer live together as a polygamous family unit. "I do not know whether we could live in the U.S. or not," he hinted to Theresa in a letter. "I continue to look towards our home in Dublán." Theresa, Julia, and the children returned to Revolutionary Mexico in 1913, willing to face enormous risks so they could continue to live together as a plural family. They were the exception.[29]

From 1913 to 1914, only about two hundred Latter-day Saints returned to Colonia Juárez and sixty to Colonia Dublán. "Our colony was pretty much deserted," thirteen-year-old Anson Jr. would remember. "Only a few Americans were there, and Mexicans were living in many of the [abandoned] homes. Some of the houses had been ransacked and looted."[30]

The return of the few hundred Mormon colonists to Mexico did not last long. In April 1914, the US intervention and occupation of Veracruz again brought anti-American sentiment in Mexico to a fever pitch. Protests against Americans broke out across the country.[31] "Mexicans who until this morning have been very friendly are now outspoken in their threats towards Americans," one Latter-day Saint leader wrote in a telegram to Salt Lake City's church headquarters on April 23. "Under the present conditions our colonists are in grave danger, threats having been made that certain families would be exterminated." On the same day, LDS Church president Joseph F. Smith telegraphed back, "Our advice is . . . to warn our people to get out of Mexico as soon as possible." Smith's counsel was reinforced the following day, when the American consul in Chihuahua City urged all Americans to leave Chihuahua at once.[32]

Less than twenty months from their last frantic departure, the Calls and the other colonists in Dublán and Juárez hurriedly packed a few things and left again by railroad, most of them arriving in El Paso by April 27. Because many of the colonists who fled Mexico in 1912 were still living near the Mexican border in Texas, New Mexico, and Arizona, the newly exiled colonists were able to go to family or friends in these areas. Others went to Utah or Idaho. Bowen and Theresa and their younger children stayed with their eldest daughter and son-in-law, Ethel and Eugene Romney, in Hachita, New Mexico. Julia, seven months pregnant, stayed with her children at her mother's home in Binghampton, Arizona.[33]

While Julia Call's marriage provides an example of a polygamous family that remained intact through the Mexican Revolution, the marriage of her mother, Louisa Abegg Done, is an example of one that did not. In 1899, after the untimely death of her first husband, Louisa had moved from Utah to Colonia Dublán with young Julia and her other three children. There Louisa became the plural wife of Abraham Done, also from Utah. They had five children together. Abraham left Dublán with his three wives and children during the mass exodus of 1912. Like most of the former colonists, the Dones never returned to live in Mexico. The financial losses caused by the exodus left Abraham unable to provide for two of his three wives and all their children. Like other polygamous exiles, Abraham was also no longer able to live with Louisa and their five children because of the United States' prosecution of polygamy. Abraham and his first wife, Lizzie, moved to Provo, Utah, while Louisa and her five youngest children searched for work and a home in Utah. After an unsuccessful month, Louisa's sons from her first marriage, twenty-one-year-old Moroni and nineteen-year-old Eli, paid for her return trip to El Paso.

Louisa and her five Done children eventually moved into a new frame home that Eli built in Binghampton, where Abraham Done visited them occasionally. Binghampton was a small farming community five miles northeast of Tucson. Although only a handful of Mormon families, led by Nephi Bingham, inhabited the area in the early 1900s, the 1912 and 1914 exoduses brought in many Latter-day Saint exiles, increasing Binghampton's population to some 350 residents by the time Julia and her children arrived at the end of April 1914. Many of the newer residents were still "living in a rather primitive condition, in tents and adobe buildings, not having had time for finished improvements," wrote one exile.[34]

During her stay in Binghampton, Julia had a disturbing conversation with Effie Young, a friend from Dublán, regarding one of the places in the United States where the Calls briefly considered relocating. "I don't think you would like it there because even the Bishop thinks it was awful for plural marriage to be practiced in Mexico," Effie told Julia. Effie then repeated disparaging remarks the bishop had made about polygamy. The Mormon bishop's remarks reflected the growing divide between monogamous and polygamous Latter-day Saints, with pro-monogamous Mormons now representing the vast majority. Julia recorded Effie's comments in a letter to Bowen, along with other rumors she heard that plural marriages performed even in Mexico after the 1890 Manifesto were not recognized by the church.[35]

Julia's experience was typical for many polygamous colonists pushed into the United States by the violence of the Mexican Revolution. As Mexico underwent its own wrenching transition, the twentieth-century LDS Church was painfully separating from its polygamous past of the nineteenth century. According to the historian B. Carmon Hardy, the Mormon exoduses from Mexico

> left the displaced colonists in confusing circumstances. They were accustomed to view themselves as [having] lived a higher principle and had sacrificed dearly to keep it alive. But now they found it necessary to sit quietly while bishops and stake authorities in the United States, faithful to instructions, sermonized on the error of those who failed to observe the Manifesto. Unaware of the special permission given, local leaders sometimes brought action against former colonists living in their wards. Refugees were routinely passed over for

ecclesiastical advancement. . . . Polygamous men and women found themselves drifting toward obscurity among their own people. Some encountered hostility from relatives who now considered plural marriage adulterous. One pluralist, after taking his wives into New Mexico from Texas, was accused of white slavery.

Most trying was the sense of abandonment by the leaders. As a younger colonist recalled, whereas in Mexico the [church] authorities had praised them, saying that a higher reward awaited them for living as they did, after the exodus to the United States this no longer was true.[36]

Bowen realized that if the Calls stayed in the United States like most Mormon colonists had chosen to do, their polygamous family would be subject not only to prosecution, but also to some ostracism among their own Mormon people. In Mexico they could live free of both, and Bowen chose to risk even Revolutionary violence and continued financial loss in order to protect his family from prosecution, prejudice, and possible breakup. This time, Theresa agreed, telling Bowen, "We are all one family and we want to remain that way. Mexico is the place we can live as we should." Thus Bowen replied to Julia's letter, "I know we cannot live [in the United States] with the same degree of peace that we can [in Mexico]—so far as our families are concerned. I can put up with anything for their sake."[37]

But after they returned to Mexico for the second time, the rumors Julia heard in Arizona continued to haunt her, and she shared her concerns with Bowen. "We had heard that it had been said from the stand [pulpit] in Salt Lake City, that no plural marriages performed since the [1890] Manifesto were approved by the Church," Bowen later said. "And though it was several years later and Julia had given birth to several children, we decided that if these rumors were true, we would not live together any longer, as we did not desire to do wrong."[38]

Julia was out by the family's milk house when she took her oldest child, Lorna, about nine years old, into her confidence. "It may be," she told Lorna, "that we are not going to live with Papa anymore and we may have to go somewhere. I don't know where we are going, but I want you to be prepared and ready for it." Little Lorna was dumbfounded. "I thought that Papa and Mama [we]re getting a divorce," she said. "Mama and Papa hadn't quarreled. Papa hadn't beat her. I didn't know any reason why they should get a divorce." Julia tried to comfort her daughter, saying, "I want you to know that he is your father and always will be your father and he loves you and you love him, but we may not be living where he lives anymore." The incident "bothered me a great, great deal," Lorna said. "For nights I would wake up in the night and couldn't sleep."[39]

When he heard that Mormon apostle Anthony W. Ivins was coming to El Paso, Bowen soon traveled there to see him. "I asked him about this matter," Bowen said, "and told him who had performed my marriages and when and where." Ivins replied, "I don't know why this rumor was said, but don't you worry about that one minute, because all of your marriages are all right, and they have all been done with the knowledge and approval of the president of the Church. You go ahead and keep your covenants and take care of your wives and families and support them, and don't worry about it." Ivins's counsel must have come as a relief, but Lorna didn't remember Julia ever informing her that the issue had been resolved, leaving her with a lingering sense of disquietude for some time.[40]

Although their losses from the revolution left the Calls practically penniless, Lorna eventually felt happy and secure in her family life, and she did not want that to change. "We lived humbly and simply, mostly from the things we raised," she said. "We were really poor people, but we as children didn't know or feel it. We were rich indeed for we lived in a home where there was love, a home where we learned the sweet concern of our parents."[41]

After a third and final exodus in 1917, fewer than two hundred remaining Mormon colonists, the Calls among them, again returned to Dublán, never to flee Mexico again. On March 11, 1917, Venustiano Carranza (1917–1920) was officially elected president of Mexico. On May 1, 1917, a new constitution went into effect in Mexico, federalizing nearly all the reformatory demands made by regional Revolutionaries since 1910.[42]

As for the Mormon colonists who hoped to realize their own ideals, most of them gave up their homes and their polygamous way of life in Mexico, "taking with them a bitterness that lasted many decades," Lorna later said. Only a few hundred Mormon colonists remained in Mexico after 1917. Though polygamous men and women there lived out their lives as plural families, with few exceptions their sons and daughters married monogamously. Those who chose to continue the principle of celestial marriage by marrying into polygamy eventually left or were excommunicated from the Church of Jesus Christ of Latter-day Saints, some forming their own dissenting groups.[43]

Thus Mexico, which provided a refuge for Mormon polygamy to thrive under the Díaz regime, also saw the final breath of the polygamous way of life for mainstream adherents to the Church of Jesus Christ of Latter-day Saints. The Mexican Revolution essentially ended what US federal prosecution, Senate hearings, and Mormon manifestos did not. Forced back into the United States by the revolution's anti-American violence, more than 90 percent of Mormon polygamous families never returned to Mexico. The polygamous families who stayed in the United States faced federal prosecution, financial challenges, and ostracism from their monogamous Latter-day Saint counterparts. Many did not continue to live together as cohesive plural-family units. The Revolution's "significance," Lorna Call later remembered, "was far greater than we understood when we were living through it," not only for Mexico, but also for the Latter-day Saint polygamous way of life.[44]

NOTES

1. William G. Hartley and Lorna Call Alder, *Anson Bowen Call: Bishop of Colonia Dublán* (Provo, UT: Lorna Call Alder, 2007), 182.
2. Doctrine and Covenants 132:27.
3. Republican Platform of 1856. http://www.ushistory.org/gop/convention_1856republicanplatform.html.
4. "Anti-polygamy Legislation," in *Encyclopedia of Mormonism*, ed. Daniel H. Ludlow (New York: Macmillan, 1992), 1:52; "Dispersion of Plural Marriage," in *Historical Atlas of Mormonism*, ed. S. Kent Brown, Donald Q. Cannon, and Richard H. Jackson (New York: Simon & Schuster, 1994), 117.
5. B. Carmon Hardy, *Solemn Covenant: The Mormon Polygamous Passage* (Urbana: University of Illinois Press, 1992), 175–76; Anthony W. Ivins, "History of Mexican Mission," *Deseret Evening News*, January 15, 1900.
6. Hartley and Alder, *Anson Bowen Call*, 70.
7. United States Code Title 48 and 1461, *United States Statutes at Large* 24:635.
8. Anson Bowen Call, "Life Story of Anson Bowen Call," in *A Collection of Short Stories and Events in the Life of Anson Bowen Call*, ed. Lorna Call Alder (Provo, UT: Lorna Call Alder, 1998), 2–3; Carole Call King, ed., *A Good, Long Life: The Autobiography of Anson B. Call, Jr., 1900–1993* (n.p.: Anson B. Call Jr., 1994), 2; and "Afton, Star Valley, Wyoming," in *Encyclopedic History of The Church of Jesus Christ of Latter-day Saints*, ed. Andrew Jenson (Salt Lake City, UT: Deseret News Publishing Company, 1941), 6.
9. "Life Story of Anson Bowen Call," 3; Lorna Call Alder, "Life Sketch of Harriet Cazier Call," in Alder, *Collection of Stories*, 103; and Hardy, *Solemn Covenant*, 175–76.

10. Doctrine and Covenants, Official Declaration 1, 291–92.

11. "Life Story of Anson Bowen Call," 4, 10–11; Hardy, *Solemn Covenant*, 168, 171, 175–76.

12. Hartley and Alder, *Anson Bowen Call*, 81; Hardy, *Solemn Covenant*, 8.

13. Hartley and Alder, *Anson Bowen Call*, 87; Jenson, *Encyclopedic History*, 199.

14. "Life Story of Anson Bowen Call"; Mary Theresa Thompson Call to Anson Bowen Call, November 27, 1896, Anson Bowen Call Correspondence, 1895–1925, LDS Church History Library, Salt Lake City, Utah.

15. Hartley and Alder, *Anson Bowen Call*, 100, 173–74; Lorna Call Alder, "Life Sketch of Julia Sarah Abegg Call," 112; and Barbara Jones Brown, oral history interview with Lorna Call Alder, February 10, 2005, transcript in author's possession.

16. Thomas G. Alexander, *Mormonism in Transition: A History of the Latter-day Saints, 1890–1930* (Urbana: University of Illinois Press, 1986), 19–20; Kathleen Flake, *The Politics of American Religious Identity: The Seating of Senator Reed Smoot, Mormon Apostle* (Chapel Hill: University of North Carolina Press, 2004), 5; and Hardy, *Solemn Covenant*, 251.

17. Hardy, *Solemn Covenant*, 259–60; Reed Smoot to Joseph F. Smith, March 23, 1904, First Presidency Correspondence, and Joseph F. Smith, *Conference Report*, April 1904, 97, both in LDS Church History Library, Salt Lake City, UT.

18. Hardy, *Solemn Covenant*, 261.

19. See Bill L. Smith, "Impacts of the Mexican Revolution: The Mormon Experience, 1910–1946" (PhD diss., Washington State University, 2000), and Joseph Franklin Moffett, "General Pershing, Pancho Villa, and the Mormons in Mexico," 4 (unpublished TS compiled from 1932–1982, LDS Church History Library, Salt Lake City, UT); "Colonists are Threatened by Bandit Leader," *Salt Lake Tribune*, January 27, 1914, 1.

20. Hartley and Alder, *Anson Bowen Call*, 222; Joseph B. Romney, "The Exodus of Mormon Colonists from Mexico, 1912" (master's thesis, University of Utah, 1967), 19.

21. "Life Story of Anson Bowen Call," 12, 16–18; Hartley and Alder, *Anson Bowen Call*, 239–40.

22. "Life Story of Anson Bowen Call," 13; Tom Mahoney, *The Story of George Romney: Builder, Salesman, Crusader* (New York: Harper & Brothers, 1960), 59–62; and King, *Good, Long Life*, 24. For more on how collective memory of 1830s and 1840s violence in Missouri and Illinois shaped Mormon identity, see David W. Grua, "Memoirs of the Persecuted: Persecution, Memory, and the West as a Mormon Refuge" (master's thesis, Brigham Young University, 2008).

23. "Life Story of Anson Bowen Call," 13; Mildred Call Hurst, "Life History of Mildred Theresa Call Hurst," December 1977, 3 (unpublished TS, photocopy in Alder family possession).

24. "Bishop Bentley's Detailed Report on Mexican Colonies," *Deseret Evening News*, February 17, 1914, 10; Romney, "Exodus of Mormon Colonists," 18; King, *Good,*

Long Life, 33; Hurst, "Life History of Mildred Theresa Call Hurst," 3; "Life Story of Anson Bowen Call," 13; and Cleo Afton Call Clark, biographical sketch in Hartley and Alder, *Anson Bowen Call*, 633. For more on the 1912 Mormon exodus from Chihuahua to El Paso, see Fred F. Woods, *Finding Refuge in El Paso* (Springville, UT: Cedar Fort, 2012).

25. "Life Story of Anson Bowen Call," 15–16; Hartley and Alder, *Anson Bowen Call*, 254–55.

26. "Life Story of Anson Bowen Call," 16; Papa (Anson Bowen Call) to Family, August 28–29, 1912, and A. B. Call to Theresa, September 3, 1912, Anson Bowen Call Correspondence; and King, *Good, Long Life*, 25.

27. Hartley and Alder, *Anson Bowen Call*, 268–69, 626.

28. A. B. Call to Theresa, Nov. 27, 1912, and Bowen to Theresa, January 26, 1913, Anson Bowen Call Correspondence.

29. A. B. Call to Theresa and Family, November 13, 1912, and Bowen to Theresa, January 29, 1913, Anson Bowen Call Correspondence.

30. Hartley and Alder, *Anson Bowen Call*, 302–3, 348; "Bishop Bentley's Detailed Report on Mexican Colonies," *Deseret Evening News*, February 17, 1914, 10; Romney, "Exodus of Mormon Colonists," 18; and King, *Good, Long Life*, 33.

31. Hartley and Alder, *Anson Bowen Call*, 343, 345–46

32. "Minutes of Meeting of First Presidency and Council of the Twelve Apostles," April 23, 1914, Journal of the History of the Church of Jesus Christ of Latter-day Saints, LDS Church History Library, Salt Lake City, UT; "Mormon Colonists Hasten to Border," *Salt Lake Tribune*, April 25, 1914, 5.

33. "Mormon Refugees Arrive at El Paso," *Salt Lake Herald-Republican*, April 28, 1914; "Life Story of Anson Bowen Call," in Alder, *Collection of Stories*, 17; "Ivins Returns from Border," *Deseret Evening News*, May 25, 1914, 1; and Hartley and Alder, *Anson Bowen Call*, 352–53.

34. Lorna Call Alder, "From Dublan, Mexico to Binghampton in 1914," 12–13; "Louisa Matilda Wilhemine Haag Abegg Done," life history compiled from Louisa's writings by her granddaughter, Ione J. Simonson, June 1988 (photocopy in Alder family possession); Hartley and Alder, *Anson Bowen Call*, 352–53; Julia to Bowen, July 17, 1914, original in Alder family possession; and Julia to Bowen, June 1, 1914, in Alder family possession.

35. Hartley and Alder, *Anson Bowen Call*, 368–69; Julia to Bowen, August 14, 1914, in Alder family possession.

36. Hardy, *Solemn Covenant*, 295–96.

37. Frank Alder, oral history interview with Anson Bowen Call, August 1945, in Alder, *Collection of Stories*, 119; Bowen to Julia, September 9, 1914, Anson Bowen Call Correspondence, LDS Church History Library, Salt Lake City, UT.

38. Francis Call Alder, oral history interview with Lorna Call Alder, April 5, 2003; "Life Story of Anson Bowen Call," 10.

39. Alder, oral history interview with Lorna Call Alder, April 5, 2003.

40. Ibid.; "Life Story of Anson Bowen Call," 10–11.

41. Personal writings of Lorna Call Alder (n.d.), in Alder family possession, 3.

42. Hartley, and Alder, *Anson Bowen Call*, 475–76.

43. Personal writings of Lorna Call Alder (n.d.), in Alder family possession, 3. For more on dissenting groups' continued practice of polygamy, see B. Carmon Hardy, "The Persistence of Mormon Plural Marriage," *Dialogue: A Journal of Mormon Thought* 44, no. 4 (Winter 2001): 43–105.

44. Hartley and Alder, *Anson Bowen Call*, 530, 532; personal writings of Lorna Call Alder (n.d.), in Alder family possession, 3.

CHAPTER TWO

Mormon Colonists in the Mexican Civil Registration

A Case Study in Transnational Immigrant Identity

GEORGE RYSKAMP

ON THE MORNING of September 14, 1889, in compliance with the Mexican law requiring registration of all births, marriages, and deaths, Henry Eyring rode with his infant son the nine miles from his home in the Mormon colony of Colonia Juárez to the Civil Register Office in the municipal seat of Casas Grandes, Chihuahua. When they arrived at nine that morning, Henry presented the baby to Heradio Rivera, judge of the Civil Register, as required by Mexican civil law. Judge Rivera dutifully recorded in his large register book the birth of Carlos Fernando Eyring, born twenty-four days earlier in Colonia Juárez, that Henry was the boy's father, and that the boy was an *hijo natural*, that is, illegitimate, all as declared by Henry. Henry further requested that his son be considered a Mexican citizen. Unlike in nearly all such birth records, there was no mention of the child's mother or of Henry's marital status. There was no interpreter, as there was for many of the Mormon colonists, which indicated that Henry made his declaration in Spanish (which he was working hard to learn). Francisco Iturraldi and Atanacio Flores served as witnesses and joined the judge in signing the document. Henry finalized the act by signing his name in a large bold script: Enrique Eyring.[1]

This practice of civil registration was not the first or only way Eyring demonstrated his participation in the Mexican liberal nation-building project underway, and his act marked just one more step toward the integration of US Mormons into Mexico in the late nineteenth century. The Mormons entered a country controlled and shaped by the politics of Mexican president Porfirio Díaz. While striving for political stability, modernization, and economic growth, Díaz welcomed foreigners into all aspects of Mexican life. In their grand effort to remake Mexico on the European model, Díaz and his supporters, even those who professed Catholicism, encouraged participation and even colonization by non-Catholics in Mexico. As a result, Mormons set up colonies in northern Mexico.[2] On several occasions Díaz himself actually extolled the Mormons for their example of energetic and effective farming and light industry, which turned the deserts where they lived into productive orchards and farms. He even personally signed the naturalization papers granting Henry Eyring and others Mexican citizenship.[3]

The simple step of registering births, as done by Henry Eyring and other Mormon colonists from Colonia Juárez and Colonia Dublán over 1,600 times between 1885 and 1912, demonstrates much about the colonists' efforts to create a Mexican identity. A detailed study of these civil registration records sheds light on the extent of those efforts, as well as the inherent conflicts for the colonists as they struggled to build and maintain three distinct identities. The identity that the Mormons created in the Great Basin of the Rocky Mountains emphasized religion as the first consideration in all aspects of life. Therefore, the original identity for the Mormon colonists was as Saints in the Kingdom of God and devout members of the LDS Church. This allegiance was particularly strong because they and their leaders had founded the colonies in response to persecution by the United States government, and many, if not most, practiced polygamy, believing that in so doing they were responding to a higher order of God's law.[4]

They also saw themselves as Anglo-American. At first blush an Anglo-American identity seems contradictory to the Mormon experience—the Mormon colonists had fled from persecution in the United States. Civil registration birth records show that at least 18 percent of the colonists who appear as parents in the birth records came from countries other than the United States. The particularly peculiar institutions of theocracy and polygamy had set nineteenth-century Mormons apart from the dominant American identity of the period. Nevertheless, in terms of other cultural elements such as building styles, language, literature, and food, they remained culturally Anglo-American.[5]

Lastly, Mormon colonists saw themselves as Mexican citizens. The Mexico with which the Mormons initially identified was not the same as that of the average Mexican citizen in Chihuahua in 1910, but was an idealized progressive, European-oriented society expounded by the central government of the Porfiriato. Beginning with the colonists' first negotiations with the Díaz government, through the naming of their colonies, and then their obtaining citizenship and participating in national affairs, the colonists were welcomed and praised by Díaz and his lieutenants as examples of industry to the Mexican people.[6] Nevertheless, with time that identity would come to be based on more than national political connections and eventually incorporate elements of Mexican daily life, language, history, and culture.

The success of the colonists' efforts to add a Mexican identity to their other two identities should not be evaluated in terms of traditional assimilation immigration theory, but in terms of alternate theories of transnational migrant identity advanced in the last two decades among migration scholars.[7] The colonists never did try to totally assimilate into Mexican society, but instead attempted to achieve a triangular identity as Mormon Anglo-American Mexicans. Those efforts to create this transmigrant identity were severely challenged during the first decade of the twentieth century by dramatic shifts in the definitions of what it meant to be Mormon, with the 1904 Manifesto ending the practice of plural marriage outside the United States; and their alliance with Mexico after the overthrow of Porfirio Díaz in 1910 and the Mexican Revolution that followed. For most colonists who fled from Revolutionary Mexico in 1912 and never returned, those efforts appear to have failed. But for colonists and their descendants who returned after the 1910 Revolution—and even for many who never returned—a transmigrant identity had been created.

MEXICAN CIVIL REGISTRATION

As part of the liberal changes made under the reform administration of Benito Juárez, Mexico adopted legislation in 1857 creating a system of mandatory registration of births, marriages, and deaths.[8] As was true in Spain and other Latin American countries, conservatives viewed the legislation as an attack on the Catholic Church.[9] Initial compliance was mixed. Beginning with the adoption of the federal civil code in 1870, further legislation increased compliance, mostly of the recording of births and required that copies of the records be sent to state civil register offices.[10] With the advent of the administration of Porfirio Díaz in 1876, civil registration was no longer viewed as a tool of reform but, as in many countries, a part of the state-making modernization process of the nineteenth century.[11] By the time the first Mormon colonists arrived in 1885, the system had been in place for nearly a generation and had become for many Mexicans a part of what it meant to be a citizen.

In contrast, most of the Mormon colonists likely viewed vital registration as a foreign concept, having been born in Utah or having left the Midwest or England before the vital registration movement gained momentum in the decades from 1845 to 1885. In Utah, even marriages were not registered until after statehood in 1896.[12] Only those who came from New England or from European countries such as France or Italy might have had exposure to the practice of civil registration of births, marriages, and deaths. Thus, for the Mormon colonists the very act of registering a birth represented conforming to a new requirement associated with Mexican identity. That concept of identity would certainly have been heightened by the formality of the registration procedure, and especially by the question asking if each parent wanted the child to be considered as a Mexican citizen.

The Mexican Civil Registration law required that the father (or other person if the father was not available) appear before the local judge and present the child for verification that he/she was living, declaring under oath the child's date, time, and place of birth; legitimacy or illegitimacy; names given to the child; name, age, marital status, occupation, place of residence, and place of birth of the father and of the mother; and the grandparents' names and places of origin. The entire proceeding was recorded by the judge and the document was signed by him, the declarant, and two male witnesses from the community.

Initially, registration was done at municipal offices. In geographically large municipalities, registration offices were opened in one or more of the other villages that made up the municipality. In the case of Casas Grandes, although the presence of marriage records from 1868 and deaths from 1867 would indicate that birth registration likely began in that same period as well, the existing birth registrations begin in 1885—the registers from 1867 to 1885 have been lost. Separate birth registers for Colonia Juárez begin in 1893, and for Nuevo Casas Grandes in 1897.[13] Anglos, the vast majority of whom were Mormons, appear in the birth registrations of all three localities.

DATABASE OF BIRTHS REGISTERED AT CASAS GRANDES

Data drawn from birth records always provides demographic perspectives with limitations.[14] Those appearing as parents are women in their

Anglo Mormons in camp settling Northern Mexico. Date and photographer unknown. Courtesy of the Museum of Mormon Mexican History.

childbearing years and their husbands, residing in the colonies when the children were born. Many of the entries in the colonies often even omit information suggested by the civil registration law, including the names of mothers or fathers. Factors beyond the existence of the records themselves are important, particularly in analyzing issues related to polygamous families. For example, a man may appear in the database as the father of only one family but be a practicing polygamist whose first wife is no longer bearing children or has remained in the United States.

This study encompasses all Anglos appearing in the civil registration records of these three Mexican municipalities because no statement of religious affiliation is made in the records. Thus, while there were definitely Anglos who were not Mormons residing in some of the mining districts lying within these municipalities, the actual number of non-Mormons in the database (extracted by comparing known Mormons against registration records) is so small as to be statistically insignificant. In spite of these reservations, the records do provide a sufficient demographic overview of the Mormon colonists to analyze their developing concepts of identity.

In the civil registration records, 693 different men and 677 different women appear as parents, having produced 1,643 children between the years 1886 and 1912. Of those 693 men, 459 appear with only one wife giving birth,

80 appear with two wives, 37 have three wives named, and the remaining 117 did not on any occasion declare the name of a wife. Of those declaring wives, 121 did so in at least one declaration, while not doing so at the time of other births. The high number of men who appear without declaring a spouse accounts for the seeming anomaly that in a database with a significant percentage of practicing polygamists, more men are identified than women.

It is impossible from these birth records alone to calculate what percentage of the families were polygamous, but internal evidence in the database indicates that at least 37 percent of the women mentioned as mothers practiced polygamy.[15]

Even without completely accurate figures, the registers of births show that a sufficiently high percentage of the colonists practiced polygamy to raise issues relating to identity. The statistic of 37 percent of the women practicing polygamy is a higher rate than reported in any area in Utah practically at any time, and especially in the years after 1880 that Kathryn Daynes defines as the late period of Mormon polygamy when the number of polygamous marriages was declining.[16] These statistics evidence the sense of identity that many colonists had as persons called to live a "higher order of the gospel" by practicing polygamy.[17]

The marital status of parents and the legitimacy of children in the civil register raise several issues. Out of 1,643 reported births, only 894 children are declared legitimate. In only slightly fewer cases (729) the children were declared illegitimate. In the few remaining entries no declaration was made. The parents are identified as *casados* (married) in 510 entries of the 1,643 entries. One hundred eight fathers declared themselves to be *solteros* (single or not married), but nine of those declared they were *solteros con habitación* (single with habitation).[18] The majority (885) gave no indication as to marital status, although this standard information appears in nearly all of the entries for those who were not Anglo Mormons.

The database reveals another anomaly: 487 men and 138 women who registered their children without declaring the other parent. All the men and most women who did not name a spouse declared the registered child as illegitimate. Further analysis indicates that the vast majority of these women are not unwed single mothers who do not know the father's name or wish to identify him, but women living in a daily relationship they consider a valid marriage and for whom there is no doubt as to the father of the child.

Why do these women and all the men who do not identify the mothers of their children take this approach? Why did over half of the men make no declaration as to their marital status? Clearly the majority of the declarants were unwilling to make a legally binding declaration under oath as to their marital status. Apparently the Mormons were willing to conform to Mexican law but did not want to create a legal declaration of their polygamous status, which might later be used against them if Mexican officials should decide to prosecute polygamists. Some had already been imprisoned in the United States or spent years in hiding because of their practice of polygamy. All had friends and family who had done so. At this critical juncture their desire to create a Mexican identity conflicted with a deep-rooted fear inherent in their Mormon identity. To avoid that conflict they created birth records as required by Mexican law, but avoided any declaration as to marital status, or records showing children born to different mothers but fathered by the same man that might later be used to prove cohabitation.

In a few entries the men are identified as *casados con habitación* (married with habitation) or *casados según costumbres* (or *ritos*) *mormones* (married according to Mormon customs or rites), indicating at least recognition if not tacit acceptance of Mormon polygamous practices by Mexican officials. In a strongly Catholic country, the adoption of the Mexican Civil Marriage Law in 1859 created a situation of extreme disjunction relative to Mexican attitudes toward marriage. The legislature attempted to replace the religious morality of Catholic marriage with a secular morality of marriage performed by the civil registrar. As was the case in every Catholic country where civil registration was proposed, the Catholic Church opposed this policy and fought to maintain the traditional religious order. The unintended result, particularly among the rural, the poor, and the indigenous populations, was a rejection of both alternatives in favor of informal unions that—while often lifelong—were solemnized neither in the church nor the civil registry.[19] Such a transitional society has been described by scholars as anomic, and one in which "the relaxed restraints provided the social space in which non-conformers could flourish."[20] Mexico in the period from 1860 to 1910 was an anomic society. Having relaxed the old order of moral restraints relating to marriage, Mexican society had not yet effectively replaced them with new legislation. This is not to say that in actual practice the informal union was the norm in Chihuahua in those years because, while statistics for those years for Chihuahua are not readily available, those for Jalisco, which has many population parallels with Chihuahua, show an illegitimacy rate that only runs between 10 and 20 percent.[21] What is suggested, however, is that the inherent conflict over what defined a marriage at the time made both

Mexican officials and citizens generally more likely to be tolerant of noncon-
formity such as that exhibited by the Mormons.

GEORGE MARTIN HAWS AND HIS
PLURAL WIVES: A CASE STUDY

The story of George Martin Haws is typical of many of the Mormon colonists. After volunteering to settle Arizona in 1877, by 1880 he was living with
his wife, Josephine, and a small daughter in Smithville (later named Pima),
Arizona. From Pima they moved to Central, Graham County, Arizona,
where in 1886 they decided to enter into plural marriage. Later that year he
married his second wife, Susan Ann Cluff, younger sister of Josephine, in the
Mormon temple in Saint George, Utah.

Following the issuance by LDS president Wilford Woodruff (1887–1898)
of the 1890 Manifesto ending the practice of polygamy by Mormons in the
United States, George and his two wives and six small children moved to the
Mormon Mexican colonies in Chihuahua, settling in Colonia Juárez around
October 1891. By 1900, they had moved even further south to Colonia
Chuichupa and then to nearby Guadalupe. George served as the first bishop
of the Chuichupa ward created in 1900. After the 1912 exodus, like so many
other colonists, the Haws family took refuge first in El Paso, Texas, and then
in southern Arizona. After 1920 George returned to Colonia Juárez, where
he died in 1936.

George Haws married three times: to Josephine in 1877, to Susan in 1886,
and to Martha in 1900. Josephine had her last child in 1900 at age forty-two,
after three years of bearing no children, perhaps explaining the decision to
declare Susan's child born in 1899 as legitimate. Three of the children for
whom Josephine is the named mother are designated as legitimate (born
1892, 1894, and 1897), but her last daughter, Theresa, born in 1900 but not
registered until 1909, was listed as illegitimate. Martha, although never mentioned in the birth records, is the mother of three of the eight children born
after 1900.[22]

George Martin Haws appears in the civil registers as a father on eighteen
occasions (twice as George Martin, twelve times as George, once as G. M.,
and three times as Jorge M.). Only five out of the eighteen entries give a wife's
name. On two occasions George identified himself and his wife as casados
with the wife named Josefina or Josefa. On another occasion he identifies

Josephine as the mother but makes no statement as to their marital status. On three occasions he is identified as soltero with no wife mentioned, and twice he gives the mother's name as Susan Ann without any indication as to marital relationship. He registers fourteen of his eighteen Mexican-born children without stating the mother's name.

The pattern of the timeliness of the declarations made by George Haws is equally complicated. He declared the births of children born in 1891, 1892, 1893, 1894, 1897, 1899, and 1906 within sixty days of their births. Then on January 21, 1909, he declared the births of two children, one born in September 1903 and the other in May 1908. On February 8, 1909, he declared the births of nine children born in years ranging from 1892 to 1909, including four sons who had previously been declared. A final child born in May 1909 was declared within sixty days of the birth. Two children were not declared: a son who died the same day he was born and a daughter who was born in 1910 when George resided far from Colonia Juárez and times were difficult for polygamists. This erratic registration of births suggests George may have been hiding proximate polygamous births by registering them randomly, which likewise supports the idea the he and the other polygamists were reluctant to leave declarations or other facts providing legally binding evidence of polygamy. Nevertheless, he slowly conforms to Mexican legal requirements and indicates a growing sense of Mexican identity, including becoming a federal employee about 1908, giving some of his children Spanish names (including Porfirio), and ultimately returning after the 1912 exodus.

SPANISH-LANGUAGE USE AS AN INDICATOR OF DEVELOPING MEXICAN IDENTITY

Developing a Mexican identity must of necessity go beyond relations with the government and the registration of births. Achieving at least minimal fluency in Spanish was not only a factor in creating a Mexican identity but was also essential for the adult Mormon colonists to effectively relate to the larger Mexican society. In the earliest entries for Mormon colonists, a note explained that the Mormons registered using a translator. Subsequent volumes show that in later years many of the Mormons spoke at least some Spanish and also served as witnesses. In the 1890s Henry Eyring taught night classes on the fundamentals of the Spanish language and the basics of Mexican law.[23] Spanish was a part of the curriculum at the Academia Juárez in Colonia Juárez and became mandatory after the revolution. Marion G. Romney, who left the colonies at age fifteen in 1912 and eventually served as a member of the Quorum of the Twelve Apostles, reported fifty years later that while he remembered little Spanish, he was left with a keen sense of connection with the Mexican people.[24]

The use of Spanish given names by Anglo Mormons is a further indication of cultural efforts to create a Mexican identity. In the early years of colonization before 1900, only about 10 percent of Mormons listed children with clearly Spanish names in the civil registration births analyzed in this study. After 1900 that number approached 50 percent. The exact number is impossible to ascertain because of names that are the same in both languages such as Saul, David, Samuel, and Aaron, as well as the use of uniquely Mormon names such as Mahonri and Helaman.

Some of the adult Mormons consistently appear in the records with the Spanish versions of their given names and even used them when signing. Probably three of the most significant were three members of the Colonia Juárez Stake Presidency, key LDS Church community leaders Alexander F. MacDonald, Henry Eyring, and Joseph Bentley. Others included Henry's son Edward, Eugene Romney, Edward Turley, Mariano Naegle, and Edward Taylor. Even a few surnames were translated into Spanish—for example, George Lake's name appears several times as George "Laguna." George Martin Haws not only appears three times as Jorge M., but he also gave some of his children Mexican names: Porfirio Díaz, David Moises, Ernesto, and Ana. In addition, he calls his first wife Josefa or Josefina.

MEXICAN CITIZENSHIP AS AN INDICATOR OF DEVELOPING MEXICAN IDENTITY

When asked for his place of birth by the registrar, Joseph Bentley emphatically declared at the registration of the births of five of his sixteen children (by three wives) that he was a naturalized Mexican citizen, the only such declaration in the 1,643 birth record of Mormon colonists.[25] Bentley, who served for many years as a counselor in the Juárez Stake Presidency, was one of a small group of colonists who became naturalized Mexican citizens. He and other Mormon leaders encouraged other colonists to become citizens; Bentley even went so far as to obtain citizenship for his business partner, Anson Bowen Call, while Call was on a church mission to England.[26]

Although only a small group of Mormons applied for Mexican citizenship, many more took the simple step of giving that citizenship to their Mexican-born children. Significant numbers of civil register birth entries state that the father requested that the children be registered as Mexican citizens. Those parental requests indicate that the Mormons did not view themselves as mere sojourners but intended for their children to put down roots in Mexico.

The colonists also participated in civic activities. Those who were citizens voted.[27] In the vast majority of civil register birth entries at least one and often both of the witnesses were Mormons. Whether originally prompted by translation difficulties or not, such participation is still evidence of Mormon involvement in official acts and acceptance of such by the civil authorities.

CONCLUSIONS: MORMON COLONISTS AS TRANSMIGRANTS AND THEIR IMPACT

The concept of a transnationalist identity is not limited to the modern US-Mexico border, nor is it one that would be foreign to the Anglo-Mormon colonists of the nineteenth century. Certainly they would have seen themselves as "immigrants whose daily lives depend on multiple and constant interconnections across international borders whose public identities are configured in relationship to more than one nation-state."[28] Hartley's descriptions of Anson Bowen Call and his family accurately reflect the lives of transmigrants. One in particular captures Call well in that light:

> For the rest of his life Bowen voted and participated as a Mexican citizen, joined with fervor in signing the national anthem of Mexico and shouted *gritos* with the best of them. . . . Nevertheless, in his heart he was still very much an American and felt loyal to the United States. He still loved "The Star-Spangled Banner" and the freedoms it stood for, and he followed American politics and elections avidly, reading the daily newspapers.

There is little doubt that Bowen sang with equal or greater fervor the Mormon anthem, "Come, Come Ye Saints," either in English or in the Spanish translation by Bowen's fellow colonist Rey Lucero Pratt, who, while serving later as president of the Mormon mission in Mexico, was a strong proponent of acquiring elements of a Mexican identity.[29]

The birth registrations of the colonists from 1885 to 1912 show their efforts to create a Mexican identity. Those efforts become understandable when viewed in the broader context of transmigrant identities, which for the Mormon colonists were triangular: saints in the Kingdom of God living in the Republic of Mexico while remaining culturally Anglo-American. To weave these strands into a coherent quotidian identity, even one that we would today call transnational, was difficult. That difficulty was enhanced to the breaking point by the changes that at least two of those identities underwent during the years between 1900 and 1912.

Although the official end of the Mormon practice of polygamy in the LDS church started with the Manifesto of 1890, for the Mexican Mormons the identity as polygamists did not initially change but was heightened after 1890 as they continued to live and even entered into new polygamous marriages. Colonists viewed themselves as still being privileged to live the higher order of plural marriage. In 1904 Joseph F. Smith, church president, issued what has been called the Second Manifesto, prohibiting all polygamous marriages, specifically in Mexico. Recognizing the challenge for the identity of the Mexican colonists, President Smith went immediately to Mexico to explain the change. Those who were unable to accept this change were ultimately excommunicated from the Church of Jesus Christ of Latter-day Saints.[30]

With a Mexican identity tied to the vision for Mexico outlined by Porfirio Díaz, the colonists showed little awareness of the seeds of revolution being sown by the failure of Díaz and his followers to deal with the social and economic needs of the majority of Mexican people.[31] In 1904 Anthony W. Ivins, then Juárez stake president, declared in General Conference in Salt Lake City that "the few Saints who are there (they now number thirty-seven hundred souls) have accomplished a great work. . . . We keep entirely out of politics; we mind our own business, and are left in peace—thank heaven for that!"[32]

Even if the colonists had been more aware, they could have done little to change the events sweeping across Mexico beginning in 1910. The forces behind the revolution were so complex and involved with so many competing and often violent forces, that over one million Mexicans from all over the nation fled to the United States in the decade from 1910 to 1920, often filling the roofs of trains in their urgency to cross the border.[33] Even in the United States, without the racial distinctions of the very large mestizo and indigenous populations and the extreme poverty found in Mexico, the American

Progressives fought similar battles in those same years, which redefined the identity to which most Americans belonged. The Mormon exodus of 1912 resulted from the failure of Diaz's government to deal with the socioeconomic needs of Mexico's people rather than from any actions taken or not taken by the colonists. In the end, the shifting fortunes of armies led by competing factions forced the Mormons' exodus from Mexico—not their failure to create an adequate Mexican identity.

After 1915 fewer than half the colonists who fled in 1912 returned to their homes in Mexico. As the Mexican nation stabilized in the beginning of the 1920s, those who returned were able to effectively build on the Mexican identity developed in those early years.[34] Transmigrant theory provides an understanding of why the three identities persist in an equilibrium that has now lasted a century since the exodus of 1912. Today their descendants are excellent examples of successful transmigrants, stable like a three-legged stool in their triangular identity, moving comfortably back and forth across the border with strong economic, social, and religious roots on both sides.[35]

NOTES

1. Casas Grandes, Chihuahua, Mexico Civil Register, Births vol. 1889, act 141.
2. Janet Bennion, *Desert Patriarchy: Mormon and Mennonite Communities in the Chihuahua Valley* (Tucson: University of Arizona Press, 2004), 80–98, 143–69.
3. William G. Hartley and Lorna Call Alder, *Anson Bowen Call: Bishop of Colonia Dublán* (Provo, UT: Alder, 2007), 170–71; Nelle Spilsbury Hatch, *Colonia Juárez: An Intimate Account of a Mormon Village* (Salt Lake City, UT, Deseret Book Company, 1954), 106–10.
4. Hartley and Alder, *Anson Bowen Call*, 203.
5. F. LaMond Tullis, *Mormons in Mexico: The Dynamics of Faith and Culture* (Logan: Utah State University Press, 1987), 57–60. For a discussion of Mormon efforts to enter the mainstream Anglo-American culture after the 1890 Manifesto, see Konden Rich Smith, "Appropriating the Secular: Mormonism and the World Columbia Exposition of 1893," *Journal of Mormon History* 34, no. 4 (Fall 2008): 153.
6. Hatch, *Colonia Juárez*, 105–10; Tullis, *Mormons in Mexico*, 59.
7. For decades, immigration studies generally followed the single analytical theory of Oscar Handlin and the University of Chicago school of immigration history—that successful immigrants were those who totally assimilated. Over the last two decades anthropologists and historians looking at migrating groups have proposed different theories, recognizing that not all groups have total assimilation as their goal. Rather than "melting in the pot," these groups maintained clear strands of identity with the country of origin over many years and even for

generations after migrating to the recipient country. From this recognition has come a new perspective on those migrating, referred to as transnational migration. A transnational migrant, or transmigrant, is an immigrant who develops and maintains multiple relationships—familial, economic, social, organizational, religious, and political—that span borders. The transmigrant operates within processes that "forge and sustain multi-stranded social relations that link together their societies of origin and settlement with a multiplicity of involvements in both home and host societies. . . . [They] take actions, make decisions and develop subjectivities and identities embedded in networks of relationships that connect them simultaneously to two or more nation-states." Linda Green Basch and Nina Glick Schiller, *Nations Unbound: Transnational Projects, Postcolonial Predicaments* (London: Routledge, 1994), 7.

8. Julia Tuñón Pablos, *Women in Mexico: A Past Unveiled*, trans. Alan Hynd (Austin: University of Texas Press, 1999), 43–47.

9. Juan Baro Pazos, *La codificación del derecho civil en España (1808–1889)* (Santander: Servicio de Publicaciones de la Universidad de Cantabria, 1992), 11; Robert J. Knowlton, "Clerical Response to the Mexican Reform, 1855–1875," *Catholic Historical Review* 50, no. 4 (January, 1965): 509–28.

10. Sherburne F. Cook and Woodrow Borah, *Essays in Population History: Mexico and the Caribbean* (Berkeley: University of California Press, 1971), 1:62–64; A. Sanchez-Cordero, "Cohabitation without Marriage in Mexico," *American Journal of Comparative Law* 29 (1981): 279.

11. For a general discussion of this process, see James C. Scott, John Tehranian, and Jeremy Mathias, "The Production of Legal Identities Proper to States: The Case of the Permanent Family Surname," *Comparative Studies in Society and History* 44, no. 1 (January 2002): 4–44.

12. Kathryn Daynes, *More Wives Than One: Transformation of the Mormon Marriage System, 1840–1910* (Urbana: University of Illinois Press, 2008), 65–66.

13. Catalog entries for civil registration records for Casas Grandes, Nuevo Casas Grandes and Colonia Juárez, all in Chihuahua, Mexico, in the *Family History Library Catalog* at https://www.familysearch.org.

14. The numbers set forth below have been manually compiled from six years of research by students at Brigham Young University of marriage records from Casas Grandes, Nuevo Casa Grandes, and Colonia Juárez for the years 1885 through 1912. Certainly, the specific numbers will change as the work on the database is completed and the material is transferred to an Access database program format for analysis. Nevertheless, the general trends and concepts derived from them for those issues surrounding identity considered here will undoubtedly remain constant as further demographic work and subsequent analysis is completed.

15. This calculation of the percentage of the population that practiced polygamy does not take into account those polygamous families in which children were not born to more than one wife while the family resided in the colonies of Dublán or

Colonia Juárez between 1885 and 1912. Several of the men in the list of those for whom only one wife appears in the register are recognizable from other sources as practicing polygamists. Many of the men not declaring the name of any wife were also likely to have been polygamists. Also not included in these figures are the 132 women who declared the birth of children and made no mention of any husband. An initial sampling from these entries was compared with other database entries and the *Ancestral File*, and most appear to have been married polygamously. *Ancestral File* is a computerized body of 40 million people from around the world collected by LDS and non-LDS volunteers. It can be accessed at https://familysearch.org/family-trees.

16. Daynes, *More Wives Than One*, 91–127.

17. Hartley and Alder, *Anson Bowen Call*, 77–81. Anson Bowen Call related exactly this motivation that as late as 1902 brought him and his first wife to reside in the Mexican Colonies.

18. The phrase "*con habitación,*" not often seen in Mexican records, apparently refers to a man who is living with a woman without the benefit of a legal marriage ceremony.

19. Woodrow Borah and Sherburne F. Cook, "Marriage and Legitimacy in Mexican Culture: Mexico and California," *California Law Review* 54, no. 2 (May 1966): 965–79, 996–1002; Sanchez-Cordero, "Cohabitation without Marriage in Mexico," 279.

20. Daynes, *More Wives Than One*, 189–90.

21. Borah and Cook, "Marriage and Legitimacy in Mexican Culture," 996, table 2B.

22. For George Martin Haws entry and accompanying family groups, see http://www.new.familysearch.org.

23. Hatch, *Colonia Juárez*, 34–35.

24. F. Burton Howard, *Marion G. Romney: His Life and Faith* (Salt Lake City, UT: Bookcraft, 1988), 207–11.

25. Family History Library (FHL), microfilm 773939, 565.

26. Hartley and Alder, *Anson Bowen Call*, 170.

27. Ibid., 172.

28. Nina Glick Schiller, Linda Basch, and Cristina Szanton Blanc, "From Immigrant to Transmigrant: Theorizing Transnational Migration," *Anthropological Quarterly* 68, no. 1 (January 1995): 48–63.

29. W. Clayton, "¡Oh Está Todo Bién!" in *Himnos de Sión*, trans. Rey L. Pratt (Salt Lake City, UT: Church of Jesus Christ of Latter-day Saints, 1986), 214; Kenneth Rey Call, "Rey L. Pratt," in *Encyclopedia of Latter-day Saint History*, ed. Arnold Garr et al. (Salt Lake City, UT: Deseret Book Company, 2000), 942–43.

30. Daynes, *More Wives Than One*, 13–14, 208–9; James B. Allen and Glen M. Leonard, *The Story of the Latter-day Saints* (Salt Lake City, UT: Deseret Book Company, 1976), 440–44; Hartley and Alder, *Anson Bowen Call*, 186–87; Kenneth Cannon II, "After the Manifesto: Mormon Polygamy, 1890–1906," *Sunstone*

(January–April 1983): 27; D. Michael Quinn, "LDS Church Authority and New Plural Marriages, 1890–1904," *Dialogue: A Journal of Mormon Thought* (Spring 1985): 9–105; and B. Carmon Hardy, *Solemn Covenant: The Mormon Polygamous Passage* (Urbana: University of Illinois Press, 1992).

31. Michael C. Meyer and William L. Sherman, *The Course of Mexican History* (New York: Oxford University Press, 1995), 465–97.

32. David Dryden, *Biographical Essays on Three General Authorities of the Early Twentieth Century: Anthony W. Ivins, George F. Richards, and Stephen L Richards* (Salt Lake City, UT: History Division, Historical Department, The Church of Jesus Christ of Latter-day Saints, 1976), 42.

33. Meyer and Sherman, *Course of Mexican History*, 552–65.

34. Hartley and Alder, *Anson Bowen Call*, 528–39.

35. For discussion concerning the transmigrant activities of the colonists since 1915, see Jeffrey S. Smith and Benjamin N. White, "Detached from Their Homeland: The Latter-day Saints of Chihuahua, Mexico," *Journal of Cultural Geography* 21, no. 2 (Spring/Summer 2004): 57–76; Bennion, *Desert Patriarchy*, 31–98; and Tullis, *Mormons in Mexico*, 70–71.

CHAPTER THREE

Plotino C. Rhodakanaty

Mormonism's Greek Austrian Mexican Socialist

BILL SMITH AND JARED M. TAMEZ

BEYOND THE STANDARD account of LDS Church history in nineteenth-century Mexico, which focuses on the colonies in the north, is the history of the early stages of church activity in central Mexico. Although missionary work is key in this telling, Mexican nationals who actively sought out LDS missionaries and joined the church did so with an expectation of equality with members from the established center in Utah. The converts' perspectives are often missing from Mormon histories of the era, whether written by Mexican or American authors, as those authors tend to presume purely religious motivations for the converts. Indeed, the opening of the Mexican Mission involved one of late nineteenth-century Mexico's most fascinating individuals, Plotino Constantino Rhodakanaty. The Greek-born immigrant was both one of Mexico's first socialist thinkers and agitators, and one of Mexico's first converts to the Mormon faith. A more nuanced perspective of Rhodakanaty and other early converts must consider their conversion to and proselytizing for the LDS Church in the context of other writings on workers, the poor, and Mexican society. Doing so highlights the vast chasm of understanding that existed between Mormon elders such as Moses Thatcher (primarily expecting a tractable convert) and Rhodakanaty (expecting, among other things, an activist church).

Plotino Constantino Rhodakanaty was the first baptized member of the Mormon Church in central Mexico. Born in Greece around 1828 to an aristocratic Greek doctor and an Austrian mother, his father died in the Greek War of Independence. He returned with his mother to Austria and trained as a medical doctor in both Vienna and Berlin, developing an interest in philosophy and the political complications of the Austro-Hungarian Empire.

Rhodakanaty further developed his political outlook in Paris, where he moved in 1850 and turned first to liberalism and then to socialism. He later spent time in Spain learning Spanish in preparation for his move to Mexico to take advantage of laws that promoted agricultural colonization. By the time he arrived in Mexico City in 1861 he was an avowed socialist. Rhodakanaty's appearance in Mexico coincided with the end of the War of the Reform, which saw the victory of Benito Juárez and the liberals over the forces of Mexico's conservatives. Unlike the flood of Europeans who were about to enter Mexico to impose an Austrian monarch there, this Greco-Austrian socialist arrived seeking to abolish government altogether, and he hoped that Mexican liberalism would allow him the room to experiment with his own goals for society.

Rhodakanaty hoped to establish a utopian community, and Mexico's colonization laws seemed to promise easy access to land on which to develop his settlement.[1] By the time he arrived in Mexico, such laws had been repealed by a new president, yet Rhodakanaty stayed in Mexico. Although a few Mexicans promoted socialism before Rhodakanaty's arrival, the Greek was "the first individual in the country who knew exactly what socialism was" and who possessed the writing ability to publish socialist doctrine widely.[2] Whether other dogmatic socialists preceded Rhodakanaty in Mexico or not, he soon organized what he called an Escuela Libre (Free School) where people could learn their rights without religious instruction, and he achieved limited success.[3] One historian of the Mexican Revolution, Adolfo Gilly, credits Rhodakanaty's teaching and influence to the earliest socialist uprising in Mexico. In 1868, a student of Rhodakanaty and of the anarchist Francisco Zalacosta, Julio Chávez López (enrolled at their agrarian school in Chalco), led a group of nearly a thousand peasants to occupy haciendas in Mexico State and Morelos. As Gilly argues, "Although the peasant leader was influenced by Rhodakanaty's Fourierist ideology, his methods combined Zalacosta's anarchist doctrine of direct action with the older peasant tradition of armed uprising."[4] Despite the Greek's pacifism, echoes of Rhodakanaty are certainly present in the Chávez López manifesto in which he declares,

> We seek to destroy at root the present evil of exploitation, which condemns some to be poor and others to enjoy riches and well-being; which turns some into wretches even though they work with all their might, and provides others with a life of bliss and leisure.

We want land to sow in peace and reap in tranquility, so that everyone is free to sow where it suits them best without having to pay any
kind of tribute; so that everyone is free to united as they think most
fit, forming larger or small agrarian societies that will jointly defend
themselves without any need for a group of men to command and
punish them.[5]

The Benito Juárez regime executed Julio Chávez López for his rebellion in
1869—in the courtyard of the Chalco school founded by Rhodakanaty.

Although he might have served as inspiration and teacher to Chávez
López, the pacifist distanced himself from the revolutionary even before the
uprising at the school. The historian John Mason Hart writes of Rhodakanaty,
"[He] feared the violence and turmoil of a revolution. . . . He favored the
peaceful transition of capitalism into a society based upon the Proudhonist-
Bakuninist idea of voluntary organizations grouped into loosely knit feder-
ations."[6] While the Greek activist might have wanted to abolish political
parties, wage systems, and class division, he was not willing to engage in
violent action to see it done.

Such ideas and Rhodakanaty's lengthy experience with European
socialism bolstered his standing among other Mexican leftists. This credibility enabled him to participate in founding the Gran Círculo de Obreros
(Great Circle of Workers) in 1872. The Círculo fought for better working
conditions for Mexican workers and sought to expand its influence
throughout the republic. Although this organization and its founder, José
de Mata Rivera, have been much discussed in working-class histories,
Rhodakanaty remains something of an enigma. He did not sit on the
Círculo's board of directors, was not much of a self-promoter, and often
signed pamphlets with an alias, making him easy to overlook. But he
"dreamed of a great Mexican workers' movement in the European style,"
and frequently contributed to the Círculo's main publishing organ, *El
Socialista*, in his zeal to promote such a movement.[7] He worked tirelessly
for the promotion of both agrarian (rural labor and small holders) and
(urban) workers' rights, yet never strayed far from his dream of establishing a utopian community. Unlike other Mexican promoters of mutual societies who feared that political or religious involvement would lead to
disagreement and discontent among their adherents, Rhodakanaty pushed
the workers movement to political action and was willing to look to religion for inspiration.[8]

To accomplish his aims, Rhodakanaty founded a second organization called La Social in 1876 (though Hart argues La Social was formed in 1865 as an extension of a socialist student group).[9] Through seminars and conferences organized by La Social, Rhodakanaty promoted three main goals: diffusion of socialist doctrine, promotion of revolutionary social change, and "the rehabilitating emancipation of women." The development of options beyond the "home, kitchen, and sewing" constituted this emancipation, and to this end Rhodakanaty included two women among the first coterie of directors of La Social. Despite La Social's efforts, no women were named to the governing board of the Worker's Congress.[10]

Sometime in 1876, Rhodakanaty was exposed to Mormonism. A few years previously, Melitón Gonzáles Trejo, a Mormon convert from an aristocratic Spanish family, arrived in Salt Lake City with the goal of translating the Book of Mormon into Spanish. He translated approximately one hundred pages, largely at his own expense, and helped in the ensuing publication of *Trozos Selectos del Libro de Mormon*, or, *Select Passages of the Book of Mormon*.[11] Trejo subsequently participated in the first LDS expedition from central Mexico to northern Mexico in 1875 to 1876. While in Chihuahua City, expedition leader Daniel W. Jones oversaw the selection of five hundred "prominent men" in nearly one hundred Mexican cities in April 1876, and sent them each a copy of the *Trozos Selectos*. Each recipient received a letter that instructed them where to turn for further information on the LDS Church.[12]

Although it is unknown whether or not the Mormons targeted Rhodakanaty specifically with the mailing, a copy of *Trozos Selectos* apparently reached the activist. In June 1876, Rhodakanaty wrote a short poem for *El Socialista* that chided those who doubted his Greek origin, and signed it the Águila Mormón, or Mormon Eagle. The poem read, in part:

He was born in beautiful Greece, they say
and it can be proven with documents;
and a rush, a hurricane of thoughts
stir in him, perhaps they will immortalize him!

He is a doctor, but only an "agnostic-doctor,"
for he cures with medicine-thoughts,
and to pay him, no more compensation than
saying: "Sir, you made me happy."

Today his forehead is crowned with *Confhusia*,
and he is the man behind La Social;
but he doesn't know how he'll survive.
          — E. G. Águila Mormón[13]

It thus follows that Rhodakanaty already knew of the sect and felt some affinity for the Book of Mormon. Although he had not previously identified with any ecclesiastical organization, he liked the Mormons' view of Christ's humanitarian and philanthropic teachings and saw in them "the origins of socialism."[14] The opening sentences to one of his most important works and one of the first socialist tracts printed in Mexico, *Cartilla Socialista* (Socialist Primer, Or Rather, The Elemental Catechism of the Socialist School of Charles Fourier), bears this out. He wrote, "It has been eighteen centuries since humanity was moved to listen to the eloquent and sublime voice of twelve inspired fishermen who preached the doctrine of Jesus Christ. This doctrine was that of socialism."[15] As he went on to say of his hope, "I believe evil has no absolute or immutable control of the nature of man, only the imperfection of social institutions which can all be changed and are susceptible to improvement, perfection, and transformation by the intelligence and will of man."[16] There was room, therefore, in Rhodakanaty's philosophical universe for an organized religion that promised real social change.

Rhodakanaty first wrote not to the church hierarchy, but to Trejo in early 1878. Somehow he had learned of Trejo, who was then residing in the Mormon settlement of Tres Alamos in southeastern Arizona, and the two exchanged letters.[17] Unfortunately, these letters have been lost and the topics discussed are unknown. Eventually, Rhodakanaty corresponded with President John Taylor, who succeeded Brigham Young as the LDS Church's third prophet. Taylor sent Rhodakanaty several publications.[18] In the course of these contacts, Rhodakanaty became acquainted with Mormon concepts of communitarianism, which were more popularly known among Mormons as the United Order.

The United Order was a Mormon concept initiated by Joseph Smith wherein heads of families deeded all real and personal property to a church bishop, who gave them an allotment in return to cover family necessities. The main goals of these communities (several existed briefly in the Midwest in the 1830s) included relative income equality, group self-sufficiency, and the elimination of poverty. In the 1870s, in response to the increasing incorporation of LDS communities into a non-Mormon economy, Brigham Young reintroduced the practice. Between 1874 and 1894, over two hundred Mormon communities attempted to form utopian societies. Nearly all operated as voluntary producer cooperatives where no one received wages, but all families shared in the net profit turned by the community as a whole. Only a handful were truly communal, where people donated everything to the local leadership and shared "more or less equally in the common product, and functioned, ate, and worked as a well-regulated family." The most famous of these, the appropriately named Orderville, Utah, attained almost complete self-sufficiency and even exported goods to surrounding communities between 1875 and 1885.[19] Indeed, most Mormon communities that attempted to live as United Orders ceased rather quickly as "the rhetoric of cooperation" and "having all things in common" gave way to joint-stock ventures and, eventually, to a "reality of extensive competition" that rivaled non-Mormon towns.[20] Tres Alamos, where Melitón Trejo lived with his family, also operated as a utopian community for a time.

Rhodakanaty was struck with this aspect of Mormon thought and practice. Here, it seemed, was an organized religion that provided the framework for the kind of society he envisioned. He reported that between fifteen and twenty of his adepts also believed in the veracity of Mormonism, and "at first requested, then virtually demanded, that he and his friends be included in the kingdom."[21] Since this necessitated baptism at the hands of men authorized to perform the ordinance, the LDS Church decided to send the first proselyting missionaries to Mexico City. Thus, the opening of the Mexican Mission in 1879 owed everything to the unexpected emergence of Plotino Rhodakanaty as an enthusiastic potential convert.

The letter written by Rhodakanaty to Taylor and other leaders dated December 15, 1878, has never been analyzed properly.[22] Generally looked upon as an impassioned request for membership, the letter contains statements that reveal the expectations Rhodakanaty held upon his conversion. Applying his own brand of "Christian Socialism" to what he knew of the Mormon Church, Rhodakanaty expressed his belief that Mormonism would lead to a "humanitarian transformation not just of a religious order, but also in moral, social, and political" spheres. In referencing their "humble social position," Rhodakanaty and his six cosignatories requested the Mormon priesthood *as* "honrados y laboriosos obreros" (honest and laborious workers) and not to *become* so after baptism, as the common English translation of the letter states. As part of the workers' movement they had little need to become workers or be validated as such through baptism into the new faith.

Even the phrase "honrado obrero" may have carried more significance with Rhodakanaty, who held workers in the highest esteem and may have intended "honrado" as "honored" instead of "honest," though both definitions are correct.

A subsequent section of the letter is usually taken as an expression of intent to proselyte in Mexico. This seems obvious from the letter, but in light of his attraction to leftist thought, certain questions arise: What exactly was to be taught? What did Rhodakanaty have in mind by this letter? It states, in part, that the men were "vehemently desirous to perform our mission as providential instruments of divine will for the salvation of so many poor souls as there are today in this country." In the English translation, an additional phrase describing other Christian churches is added to the sentence, yet in the original Spanish, Rhodakanaty inserted a comma between the two ideas—implying a separation of thought. In this case, "poor souls" ("pobres almas") signifies not just the poor in spirit, but the literal poor, the masses in Mexico for whom Rhodakanaty fought before and after his association with the Mormons. The possibilities for the poor in Mormon-style United Orders would have been appealing. A subsequent diatribe against other faiths "that swarm amongst us, leading consciences astray, tearing apart social unity and lacerating sensitive hearts," fits well in the context of Christian Socialism. A final phrase, in which Rhodakanaty proposes preaching Mormonism in Mexico "in order to accomplish radical reformation and the salvation not just of our country, but the world" echoes the aims of La Social. Rhodakanaty and Taylor were engaged in a good-faith dialogue while in reality neither fully understood the other. This would bode ill for future collaboration.

The nascent movement continued, however, with the church authorities in Salt Lake City readying a missionary expedition and Rhodakanaty continuing to organize. On September 1, 1889, Rhodakanaty and his group launched the newspaper *La Voz del Desierto*.[23] The first issue billed the paper as a monthly "Periodico Mormonico"[24] intended to be the official organ of the Mexican branch of the "Christian Church of the Latter-day Saints." The paper positioned itself as a forerunner for a fuller establishment of the church in Mexico, as John the Baptist (the voice that cried in the wilderness) prepared the way for Jesus Christ.

> The Christian Church of the Latter-day Saints is the only true church and the only one able or capable of leading the nation through the true ways of positive progress. . . . We are firmly

persuaded that it will triumph always over its iniquitous adversaries because, submissive and faithful to the governments of the country where it is established, it is the most powerful support for justice to the people and the most firm support of both temporal and eternal happiness.[25]

In this manner, Rhodakanaty and his group conceived of Mormonism as the one true hope for justice and for social and spiritual reform. The writers also attempted to appeal to elements of Mexican nationalism (linking Aztec blood to the blood of Israel) and to profess loyalty to the Mexican government, effectively downplaying the LDS Church's American identity in favor of appeals to Mexican institutions and culture—a tactic used by future Mexican Mormons in their dealings with the LDS Church. Rhodakanaty and his group continued to construct a vision of Mormonism that would enact radical social, moral, and political reform. Rhodakanaty and his group had clear expectations about what Mormonism was and did—expectations that were at variance with what the Utah missionaries considered fundamental aspects of their gospel message.

Against this backdrop, a small group of missionaries including Trejo ("our respected and beloved brother" according to Rhodakanaty's letter) and Mormon apostle Moses Thatcher entered Mexico City in November 1879, to meet with Rhodakanaty and his group. Within a week of their arrival, Thatcher baptized Rhodakanaty and an associate of his, Silviano Arteaga.[26] Just three days later Thatcher organized the Mexico City branch of the church with Rhodakanaty as its presiding authority or branch president in Mormon parlance. A month later, having baptized no fewer than twelve people in Mexico City, Thatcher was disappointed to note in his journal that only four of those twelve attended the weekly worship services. Thatcher had his suspicions about the cause. "I fear that some of them had other than pure motives in attaching themselves to the Church—A desire for earthly rather than eternal gain."[27]

The disparate expectations held by the two sides persisted. The elders from Utah arrived with no set financial support from church headquarters and, though having some personal funds available, had expected some amount of material support from church members. This roughly paralleled the way contemporary US-based Protestant groups conducted their efforts in Mexico at the time, with Methodists, Presbyterians, and Baptists all hoping local congregants would supplant initial American investment in

Tom. I.   México, Setiembre 1 º. de 1879.   Núm. 1.

LA VOZ DEL DESIERTO

PERIODICO MORMONICO.

ORGANO DE LA RAMA MEXICANA DE
"LA IGLESIA CRISTIANA DE LOS SANTOS DE LOS ULTIMOS DIAS."

SE PUBLICA POR AHORA CADA MES.—VALE TRES CENTAVOS.

Voz del que clama en el desierto: aparejad el camino del Señor: enderezad sus vías:—Arrepentios y bautizaos porque el reino de los cielos se acerca. EVANGELIO.	Y ví una multitud innumerable, que se habia juntado de todas las naciones, de todas las tribus, de todos los pueblos y de todas las lenguas, que estaban en pié delante del Trono. APOCALIPSIS.

EL ESPIRITU DE LA IGLESIA DESIERTA A LA NACION MEXICANA.

SALVACION ETERNA.

Lució por fin para México el venturoso dia en que se iniciara en su rico suelo la creadora de su felicidad temporal y eterna, la providencia social de todos los pobres y desheredados de riquezas espirituales y materiales, la elaboratriz, en fin, de sus destinos inmortales, que es "la Iglesia Cristiana de los Santos de los Ultimos dias."—El sol fulgente de este dia es el augurio mas felíz; es el presagio de una dicha sin límites; es el anuncio de próspera bonanza para los buenos hijos de México y cuya raza es la simiente escogida por el Eterno para sus altos fines providenciales en el órden de la humanidad. Sí, Mexicanos magnánimos y generosos, vosotros sois descendientes de los antiguos Israelitas y la sangre azteca que circula en vuestras venas es la de aquel Joséf que mandó en Egipto, porque el origen de vuestros padres viene de Jerusalem, y el dia de vuestra redencion emanciparia ha llegado y glorioso es vuestro porvenír. Se rasgó ya el crespon fúnebre que por tantos siglos os tenía encubierta la *verdad religiosa*, desfigurada é infamada por los sectarios del error y de la impostura. Esa divinidad tutelar de los pueblos santos, se atavía hoy con el ropage de soberana y deja los arapos de la abyeccion para presentarse magnífica y explendente, como la erguida palma que cobijará con su benéfica sombra á todos los mártires de su justa causa: el Espíritu indómito de nuestra *Santa Iglesia* hoy saluda desde el desierto de Utah con su angélica sonrisa tan pura y perfumada como la de sus hermosas hijas á los valientes campeones que se agrupan á su alrededor para combatir denodadamente por su divina fé que desciende de lo alto para la salvacion eterna de todos los pueblos creyentes que se preparan digna y santamente á esperar la segunda venida del Mesías en gloria y magestad; porque el tiempo se acerca. Romped, pues ¡oh pueblos todos de la tierra! las duras cadenas con que os tienen atados los tiranos y opresores de vuestra conciencia; sacudid su nefando é ignominioso yugo; emancipáos de su horrible tutela y venid á respirar con ahinco las auras límpidas y trasparentes con que os brinda amorosa "la *Iglesia Cristiana de los Santos de los Ultimos dias*.»

Y tú, México querido, despierta al alto destino que te aguarda y recibe los escritos de vuestros profetas y el Dios de vuestros padres cumplirá todas sus predicciones respecto á tus hijos, porque tú eres la tierra prometida por el Eterno para la construccion de su santo templo que será el núcleo de la predicacion del Evangelio eterno que en toda su plenitud, será llevado primero á los Gentiles y despues á los Judios para que se implante en seguida esa ciudad santa y morada celestial de los justos de todas las naciones, que es *la Nueva Jerusalem.*

Copy of Plotino C. Rhodakanaty's publication *La Voz del Desierto*, 1879. Photo courtesy of Jared M. Tamez.

mission efforts with Mexican funds. Also similar to the Mormon case, these hopes were not realized for many decades.[28]

Complicating the situation, Rhodakanaty and those in his circle expected the church to make large scale expenditures, as did the contemporary Protestant churches, which set up schools and clinics to help alleviate temporal needs and nourish spiritual leanings. Thatcher misread these expectations as a scheme to buy converts, ones who would be insincere and uncommitted to the Gospel.[29] In the Mexican cities of the time, the majority of social services were provided by the Catholic Church and/or one of the many monastic orders, and these groups pushed back against nascent Protestant congregations by denying access to such services to non-Catholics. This led to the establishment of Protestant institutions including, for example, day and boarding schools by 1882.[30] Thatcher's misunderstanding of the Protestant approach, his own expectations of Mexican converts, and Rhodakanaty's misunderstanding of the Mormon approach to proselytizing all set the stage for conflict.[31]

Though several others stopped attending church meetings and disassociated themselves from Mormonism within a few months of joining, Rhodakanaty continued to labor in the branch. In December, he began translating deceased Apostle Parley P. Pratt's tract *A Voice of Warning*, the first portion of which Rhodakanaty had already translated and published in *La Voz del Desierto*.[32] The Elders held meetings of the Mexico City branch in Rhodakanaty's home throughout 1880 and Rhodakanaty's wife asked to be baptized in May, 1880.[33] Also in May, as missionary James Z. Stewart argued with convert Domingo Mejia about the way to pursue missionary work in Mexico (as it became clearer later, Stewart advocated the Protestant system of setting up schools and clinics), Rhodakanaty gifted Stewart a copy of the New Testament.

Despite his zeal, Rhodakanaty became increasingly frustrated with Thatcher over the issue of communalism. Rhodakanaty pressed for the formation of a United Order community for the members in central Mexico, while Thatcher believed that the obstacles in the way of such a settlement in the Mexico City region were too great. Instead of conceiving of utopian communities existing as an extension of the LDS Church, Rhodakanaty "acted as if he thought the Mormon gospel existed to serve the ideal of communitarianism."[34]

No records indicate Rhodakanaty's activities between May 1880 and January 1881, but Rhodakanaty's disposition seems to have changed. By

January 1881, about a year after Rhodakanaty's baptism, Thatcher bemoaned what he felt was Rhodakanaty's spiritual (as well as temporal) poverty. Thatcher reiterated to Rhodakanaty that "if he still held the erroneous idea that we would ever propogate [*sic*] the gospel by employing with salaried hireling preachers, starting schools and buying converts as do the Protestant here he just as well dismiss it at once fore we never would." He also told Rhodakanaty that he had thus far failed in his responsibilities to himself and to the branch and urged him to repent of his "slackness" and rededicate himself to the branch and to preaching the gospel. Rhodakanaty responded that the elders would make little progress in Mexico unless willing to establish public institutions such as schools and clinics. [35]

Just a few months later, not having heard from Rhodakanaty after their last exchange, Elder Thatcher called on Rhodakanaty to resign as branch president. Thatcher called a special meeting in which he planned to read the resignation notice, should it be submitted. The morning of the meeting, Domingo Mejia,[36] who had formed part of Rhodakanaty's study group and who was baptized three days after Rhodakanaty and Arteaga, came in to the mission headquarters. Angrily, he charged that the elders were hypocrites, teaching one thing and practicing another. He said, according to Thatcher, "we [the elders] were not charitable and did not assist the members with means—and that we should divide our substance with the poor, etc." Thatcher invited him to attend the meeting and give due cause why he should not be excommunicated. Mejia proclaimed that Thatcher had no authority to excommunicate him and said that Rhodakanaty felt as he did.[37]

At the meeting, Rhodakanaty's resignation notice was read to those present. Mejia was present and reiterated his former position. He quoted Paul's curse on those who would preach "any other gospel" but the Lord's and affirmed that the elders taught a different gospel and would thus be cursed. He angrily left the meeting. By unanimous vote, the small congregation accepted Rhodakanaty's resignation and Mejia was excommunicated from the church for apostasy. Silviano Arteaga, who had been baptized right after Rhodakanaty, was sustained as the new president of the Mexico City branch.[38]

It is difficult to determine why some who had been close to Rhodakanaty (such as Arteaga) chose to stay in the church while others left. Perhaps they were not as committed to the issues of communitarianism as Rhodakanaty and Mejia were. Perhaps they felt a spiritual meaning in their Mormonism that superseded other concerns. Whatever the root cause, previous confessional treatments of this episode have alternately depicted Rhodakanaty as either unconverted, weak in faith (and failing to keep his baptismal commitments), or as trying to change Mormonism to suit his own socialistic agenda (or perhaps a combination of the these). These approaches fail to capture the complexity of the events that unfolded. Rhodakanaty had not tried to co-opt Mormonism, he had not simply "dropped out" when unable to get what he wanted from the Mormon Elders, nor had he simply failed to keep his commitments.[39]

Rhodakanaty and those who left the LDS Church with him indeed became disillusioned, and the records show that both their interest in Mormonism and their disillusionment were sincere. Mormonism, as they understood it, at least in part from the church literature they read, could be a powerful force for social change. But facing the reality of what Thatcher and the other missionaries taught, they realized that Mormonism could not have the power to enact social change (as they conceived of it) if it was unwilling to aggressively attack the temporal as well as the spiritual ills besetting society. As rational actors, sincerely committed to the ideals they had perceived in Mormonism, they left the church when they realized it was not what they had expected. It is important to note that Thatcher's hard-line stance against what he perceived as Rhodakanaty's desire to set up a Protestant system in the mission was also influenced by Thatcher's own personal interpretations of Mormonism and his mischaracterization of Protestant efforts. Subsequent mission leaders, such as Anthony Ivins, would authorize small loans, establish schools in different areas of the mission, and even directly hand out money to those the missionaries determined to be in need.[40] Indeed, nearly a quarter century after Thatcher made his accusations against Rhodakanaty, LDS Church president Joseph F. Smith declared that "it has always been a cardinal teaching with the Latter-day Saints that a religion which has not the power to save people temporally and make them prosperous and happy here, cannot be depended upon to save them spiritually, to exalt them in the life to come."[41] Clearly, even among the established hierarchy, there existed some difference of interpretation in how to accomplish the goals of Mormonism.

Moses Thatcher may not have been Rhodakanaty's only concern, however. The regime of President Porfirio Díaz (1876–1880, 1884–1911) grew increasingly authoritarian and intolerant of the communist, socialist, anarchist, and eventually even the liberal political clubs, newspapers, and discussion groups that existed in Mexican political life at the end of the nineteenth century. The Díaz regime dissolved the National Congress of Mexican Workers affiliated with and supported by Rhodakanaty and forced either the closure of or staff turnover at every socialist and anarchist press for which Rhodakanaty wrote. Indeed, many of his associates fled Mexico or were arrested, probably prompting him to leave the country in 1886.[42] While the Díaz regime seemed more kindly disposed to the law-and-order Anglo-Mormon colonists of Chihuahua (despite concerns about polygamy), the regime had little tolerance for the "Aguila Mormón" and father of the Mexican Left.

The Rhodakanaty episode was the first but not the last instance of conflict between a Mexican branch president and American mission leaders. Significantly, individuals like Arteaga, who had witnessed this conflict and its denouement, would participate in a subsequent conflict regarding the supremacy of local and Mexican authority over the authority of the Utah elders. By the time of the latter conflicts, the ground shifted away from perceptions that the Mormon missionaries failed to meet certain communitarian standards and toward notions of Mexican nationalism and anti-foreign sentiment. These tensions over authority serve as bookends that mark an inauspicious beginning for the mission and an equally difficult end.[43]

If Rhodakanaty's initial expectations regarding membership in the sect are understood properly in the context of his leftist ideals, then his split with Mormonism (and that of many followers) hardly comes as a surprise. If, however, one assumes a true religious conversion, then Rhodakanaty's disillusionment is more puzzling. He produced only one tract of note after his separation from the Mormon Church (1882's *Treatise on Elementary Logic*, designed for use by school teachers) but continued promoting workers' rights, before "disappearing" from the scene by 1886.[44] Still, despite his relatively brief association with Mormonism (even if dated from his 1876 poem), Mexican Mormons claim Rhodakanaty as one of their own, and point to him as evidence of their faith's contributions to the pre-Revolution era in the areas of leftist thought, workers' rights, and options for the poor. On the other hand, while the LDS Church has kept him in the periphery of their own official histories, always taking care to mention his letter to John Taylor, baptism request, and ordination (but not his apostasy), even that positive legacy might be slipping. In January 2014, the official magazine of the LDS Church, *The Ensign*, included a short history of the LDS in Mexico. While it mentioned Trejo's distribution of copies of the Book of Mormon, the arrival of missionaries in 1876, and the start of baptisms, no mention was made of the Austrian Greek Mexican so central to all of those moments.[45]

NOTES

1. Carlos M. Rama, *Utopismo Socialista (1830–1893)* (Caracas: Biblioteca Ayacucho, 1987), lix.
2. Rama credits José C. Valadés with this statement, taken from an appendix (titled "Los orígenes del socialismo en México") to *La Protesta*, which he described as an Argentine book published in 1924. Another author, Jorge Basurto, cites Valadéz (different spelling) as the first to discuss Rhodakanaty, but in an appendix titled "Sobre los orígenes del movimiento obrero en México" in an Argentine book entitled *La Protesta* published in 1927. Attempts to locate either version of *La Protesta* have proven unsuccessful, and whether this represents separate articles and/or books is unclear. Rama, *Utopismo*, lx; and Jorge Basurto, *El proletariado industrial en México (1850–1930)* (Mexico City: Instituto de Investigaciones Sociales de UNAM, 1975), 71.
3. Raymundo Gómez Gonzáles and Sergio Pagaza Castillo, *El Águila Mormón o el Anarquista Cristiano: Plotino Constantino Rhodakanaty, Primer miembro de la Iglesia de Jesucristo de los Santos de los Últimos Días en México* (Mexico City: Museo de Historia del Mormonismo en México, A.C., 1997), 102.
4. "Fourierist" makes reference to the ideas of communal living and organization of François Marie Charles Fourier. Adolfo Gilly, *The Mexican Revolution* (New York: The New Press, 2005), 8.
5. Ibid., 9.
6. John Mason Hart, *Anarchism and the Mexican Working Class, 1860–1931* (Austin: University of Texas Press, 1978), 24.
7. Basurto, *El proletariado*, 67.
8. Carlos Illades, *Estudios sobre el artesanado urbano en el siglo XIX* (Mexico City: El Atajo, 1997), 131. In 1998, UNAM published Illades's *Obras, Plotino Constantino Rhodakanaty, edición, prologo, y notas*. For more comprehensive treatments of Rhodakanaty's thought, see Carlos Illades, *Rhodakanaty y la formación del pensamiento socialista en México* (Rubí, Barcelona: Anthropos Editorial; México: Universidad Autónoma Metropolitana, 2002) and Carlos Illades, *Las otras ideas: estudio sobre el primer socialismo en México, 1850–1935* (Mexico City: Ediciones Era: Universidad Autónoma Metropolitana Cuajimalpa, 2008). Both books briefly review Rhodakanaty's interest with Mormonism, but neither attempts a sustained analysis of Rhodakanaty's engagement with the faith.
9. Hart, *Anarchism*, 23.
10. Gómez Gonzáles and Pagaza Castillo, *El Águila Mormón*, 103, 107, 115. The two women were Jesús Valadez and Soledad Sosa, and there were five total directors.

11. Trejo Family, "Oral History Interview with Gordon Irving, Salt Lake City, Utah, 1973," MS 200 12, LDS Church Archives, 20–21.

12. Tullis, *Mormons in Mexico*, 25.

13. *El Socialista* (Mexico City), 18 June 1876, 2. There is no such word as "confhusia" in Spanish or Greek, and it is unknown what Rhodakanaty meant by being "crowned with confhusia."

14. Gómez Gonzáles and Pagaza Castillo, *El Águila Mormón*, 22.

15. Plotino C. Rhodakanaty, *Cartilla Socialista; o sea Catecismo elemental de la Escuela Socialista de Carlos Fourier* (Mexico City: n.p., 1871), 1.

16. Ibid., 4.

17. Tullis, "Early Mormon Exploration," 296.

18. Tullis, *Mormons in Mexico*, 35.

19. Dwight L. Israelsen, "United Orders," *Encyclopedia of Mormonism: The History, Scripture, Doctrine, and Procedure of the Church of Jesus Christ of Latter-day Saints* (New York: Macmillan, 1992), 4:1493–94.

20. Alexander, *Mormonism in Transition*, 185.

21. Tullis, "Early Mormon Exploration," 296.

22. Plotino C. Rhodakanaty, "Letter, 15 December 1878, Mexico City, to the President and Apostles of 'The Christian Church of the Latter-day Saints,' Salt Lake City, Utah," LS, LDS Church Archives. A transcript of the original Spanish version of Rhodakanaty's letter and an English translation done by Eduardo Balderas of the Translation Division of the LDS Church are used for this section. Although the LDS Church Archive holds the original, it is quite difficult to read. Therefore, the Spanish transcript found on pages 178 and 179 of *El Águila Mormón* and the English translation on pages 309 and 310 of "Early Mormon Exploration" are the sources we consulted for the letter.

23. Translated as "the voice from the desert" (or wilderness), likely derived from the Biblical reference to John the Baptist. Jared Tamez discovered one copy each of the first two issues of the newspaper (and presumably the only two issues produced) while researching at the Brigham Young University Harold B. Lee Library Special Collections in 2010. These are the only known copies in existence.

24. Literally, "Mormonic Newspaper" (or simply, "Mormon Newspaper"), which was perhaps a play on words such as "Masonico" or Masonic. It is difficult to tell whether Rhodakanaty intended anything more profound than a simple wordplay.

25. *La Voz del Desierto*, no. 1 (September 1879). The second issue was published on October 1. Moses Thatcher's mission journal indicates that a third issue was contemplated, but does not confirm that it was published. It was likely not published, as the newspaper is not subsequently mentioned and there are no known copies of any issues beyond the first two.

26. Rey L. Pratt, "History of the Mexican Mission," *Improvement Era* 15, no. 1 (1911–1912), 486–87.

27. Thatcher, Journal, December 14, 1879.

28. Deborah J. Baldwin, *Protestants and the Mexican Revolution* (Chicago: University of Illinois Press, 1990), 14–26. Baldwin omits the Mormons entirely from her study.

29. Thatcher, Journal, January 29, 1880.

30. Baldwin, *Protestants and the Mexican Revolution*, 24–25.

31. See Jean Pierre Bastian, *Protestantes y Sociedad en Mexico* (Mexico City: Casa Unida de Publicaciones, S. A., 1983) for a description of the Protestant missionary system that included the establishment of schools and medical clinics.

32. Thatcher, Journal, December 15, 1879.

33. Stewart, Journal, May 9, 1880.

34. Tullis, *Mormons in Mexico*, 39.

35. Thatcher, Journal, January 29, 1881. It is worth noting that eventually, Mormons in the Chihuahuan colonies would go on to establish schools that served Mormons as well as non-Mormons, the most prominent of these being Academia Juárez.

36. Little is known about Mejia apart from what is found in Thatcher's journal. He was an associate of Rhodakanaty from before the arrival of the missionaries and was among the first to be baptized after Rhodakanaty. He merits further investigation.

37. Thatcher, Journal, August 27, 1881.

38. Ibid., August 28, 1881.

39. The phrase "dropped out" referring to Rhodakanaty and others is used in Gordon Irving, "Mormonism and Latin America: A Preliminary Historical Survey" and LaMond Tullis, *Mormons in Mexico*, 39. A 2001 master's thesis characterizes Rhodakanaty and like-minded early converts as apathetic and not holding to their commitments. See Elizabeth Mary Ann Bennion, "Relations Between Mormon Mexican Colonists and the Mexican People: From Founding Through the Exodus of 1912" (master's thesis, University of Utah, 2001). Furthermore, confessional Mormon historians have been perhaps too quick to accept Thatcher's perspective on Rhodakanaty and Protestantism at face value. The historian Kenneth W. Godfrey writes, "Elder Thatcher, only months into his apostolic ministry, to his credit believed the Church in Mexico should be established on the firm soil of true faith. Realizing that the expenditure of only a few dollars would probably result in numerous baptisms, he opted to withhold financial aid, hoping to find instead sincere truth seekers. He was willing to sacrifice spectacular numerical success on the altar of steady, sound, more secure patterns of conversion." Kenneth W. Godfrey, "Moses Thatcher and Mormon Beginnings in Mexico," *BYU Studies* 38, no. 4 (1999), 141–42. Tullis writes, "The elders concluded that this success [of the Protestant Churches] came because the Protestants gave their tracts away and "bought" their converts with perquisites and stipends, a

practice the Mormons would not or could not emulate." Tullis, *Mormons in Mexico*, 40.

40. Anthony W. Ivins, Diaries, Utah State Historical Society, Salt Lake City, UT.

41. Joseph F. Smith, "The Truth about Mormonism," *Out West* (September 1905), 242.

42. Hart, *Anarchism*, 27–28.

43. For a detailed discussion of the events surrounding the closing of the Mexican Mission in 1889, see Jared Tamez, "'Out of This Part of Babylon': Colonizing Mexican Mormons and the Decline of the Mexican Mission of the Church of Jesus Christ of Latter-day Saints, 1879–1889" (master's thesis, University of Utah, 2014).

44. Gómez Gonzáles and Pagaza Castillo, *El Águila Mormón*, 17. It is unknown whether Rhodakanaty died, retired to private life, or returned to Europe. Some Mexican Mormons believe he changed his identity to avoid incarceration by the Porfirians and rejoined the LDS Church.

45. Sally Johnson Odekirk, "Mexico Unfurled: From Struggle to Strength," in *The Ensign*, January 2014.

CHAPTER FOUR

"Our Faithful Sisters"

Mormon Worship and the Establishment of the Relief Society in the Mexican Mission, 1901–1903

JARED M. TAMEZ

IN HER 1995 book, *The Reformation of Machismo: Evangelical Conversion and Gender in Colombia*, Elizabeth E. Brusco notes "contradictions" that she encountered in her study based on what she calls "a discordance between my own commitment to a feminist perspective, which identified certain social forms as connected to women's subordination, and my anthropological training, which compelled me to take a culturally relativistic view."[1] Her wrestle with this discordance led her to reshape her approach to women and the Pentecostal movement in Colombia. Rather than asking how women became empowered through conversion to Pentecostalism, Brusco explores how Pentecostalism elevated notions of domesticity in a way that altered gender roles and encouraged greater regard for and participation by men within the domestic sphere.[2]

Speaking to some of the dynamics behind studies such as Brusco's, but in the context of the history of women in the Church of Jesus Christ of Latter-day Saints, Catherine A. Brekus, professor of American religious history, explains that the nineteenth-century struggle over Mormon polygamy saw opponents describe Mormon women as deluded and degraded slaves to an overbearing Mormon patriarchy.[3] Brekus argues that anti-polygamy literature proved influential in painting Mormon women as passive and uninteresting as subjects of religious or historical study. While lamenting the general lack of attention to women's experiences in the field of US religious history, Brekus further notes, "Neither women's historians nor American religious historians have seemed interested in including Mormon women in their narratives, implicitly suggesting that they should not be considered as serious historical actors."[4] Aside from lingering stereotypes about Mormon women and suspicion of Mormon patriarchy, for Brekus, one of the main roots of this disinterest is how historians conceptualize historical agency.

Brekus, incorporating insights from scholars such as Sharon Hays and Saba Mahmood, argues that many historians understand agency in terms of liberation from and struggle against prevailing structures and that this approach often overlooks those women who seem to accept or even support these structures. At the same time, Brekus calls for balance and the recognition that social structures do constrain the ability of women to act. "While previous generations of historians virtually ignored women, recent scholars have been so determined to portray women as historical agents that they have sometimes exaggerated their freedom to make choices about their lives."[5] Brekus proposes a model for approaching historical agency that attempts to bridge these divides by emphasizing that "agency is not limited to challenging social structures; it also includes reproducing them." Speaking specifically of Mormon women, Brekus observes that "women's historians outside of the LDS community have been fascinated by nineteenth-century women's religious organizations like the Woman's Christian Temperance Union and the Female Antislavery Society, but they have written little about the LDS Relief Society."[6]

The Relief Society is the LDS Church's women's organization, begun in the 1840s by LDS Church founder Joseph Smith, and which, it was proposed, would look after the poor and administer to the temporal and spiritual needs of Mormon women as well as the broader Mormon community. Smith's instructions to the Relief Society at its initial meeting set an expectation that women and men were acting within Mormonism in separate albeit related spheres: "The Society of Sisters might provoke the brethren to good works in looking to the wants of the poor, searching after objects of charity, and in administering to their wants, to assist by correcting the morals and strengthening the virtues of the female community and save the Elders the trouble of rebuking; that they [the elders] may give their time to other duties &c. in their public teaching."[7] While the formal public ministry and church governance remained firmly under the purview of the male priesthood, Mormon women sought, within the space of the Relief Society, to play active roles in shaping Mormon society and even acting to "provoke" or encourage men to attend to their duties in the priesthood.

Despite the fact that Mormon missionaries established a mission in Mexico City in 1879, it was not until 1903 that church leaders moved to organize a branch of the Relief Society among the Mexican Mormon women in central Mexico.[8] Brekus's model provides a useful lens to explore the experience of Mormon women in early twentieth-century Mexico and reveals broader possibilities for attention to gender dynamics in Mexican religious history. This essay discusses how the boundaries of ecclesiastical authority were negotiated and the role that gender played as American Mormon missionaries sought to reorganize branches of the LDS Church in central Mexico. These negotiations focused largely on the structure of public worship services, which decreased the public role that women worshipers had occupied early in the process of reorganization and served to place Mormon women's religious expression more formally under the guidance and review of male priesthood leaders. At the same time, emphasis on family and domesticity, which attended the creation of the Relief Society program in the Mexican Mission, provided opportunities for women to shape Mormonism from within as well as opportunities to critique the religious activity of men.

The first stage of the LDS Church's Mexican Mission lasted ten years. Upon arrival in Mexico City in 1879, missionaries began to proselytize in the states of Hidalgo, Morelos, and Mexico. These efforts yielded about 250 converts spread out over several small branches. The mission closed in 1889 and American missionaries were withdrawn. In effect, these branches were left to operate on their own for a period of about twelve years.[9] On June 1, 1901, LDS Church leaders reopened the mission by sending Ammon Tenney to Mexico City. Tenney's goal was to reestablish contact with church members baptized during the mission's first decade and reassert the authority of the mainstream LDS Church to govern the congregations that had been left to operate independently. In most cases, the branches ceased to meet after the missionaries left in 1889, and some branch leaders with their respective congregants joined the worship services of other religious groups. As Ammon Tenney sought out those who had been baptized in the 1880s and reorganized LDS Church branches, he found that the resulting meetings were tinted with what he identified as the "sectarian" mannerisms of Protestant worship.[10] The Simón Zuñiga family, members of one early congregation—at Atlautla, in Mexico State (south of Amecameca)—preserved the minute book that recorded when regular meetings resumed in Atlautla and the pattern of regular branch meetings and the way regular branch meetings were carried out. The record is now housed at the LDS Church History Library in Salt Lake City and it, along with the detailed journals of Tenney and other mission records recount the story of how Tenney worked to structure the

1903 Cuernavaca, Morelos, Mexico LDS conference. Photographer unknown.
Courtesy of the Museum of Mormon Mexican History.

worship services of these Mexican branches so as to more closely emulate the
pattern followed in Utah and other more established Mormon congregations. These records also demonstrate that ideas about gender and the role of
women in these services were central to Tenney's efforts.

The minutes for the December 31, 1901, meeting at Atlautla are typical of
the type of meeting that Tenney encountered. The meeting began with an
opening hymn, and then a prayer was said. After an additional hymn,
President Simón Páez spoke. Tomacita Lozada selected another hymn to
sing. After the hymn, Margarito Bautista, the branch secretary, prayed. Next,
Juana Bautista selected a hymn, after which Juanita Páez prayed. Juanita Páez
then selected yet another hymn to sing. After this hymn, President Páez
"exhorted all the congregation that all should give their testimony, select a
hymn, and say a prayer because it was so ordained in the Holy Law." Tomacita
Lozada proceeded to pray and Juan Rodriguez selected a hymn. Juanita
Bautista spoke on the Biblical passage Matthew 6:1–3, which discussed charitable giving.[11] She then prayed and a closing hymn was sung followed by the
closing prayer by President Páez. Among the seven participants, seven hymns

had been sung and four prayers made, with women participating in roughly half of those instances. Comparing this to a typical entry in an 1875 Methodist Meeting Guide (see note 10), one can readily see a similar pattern of alternating prayer with hymn singing and brief scriptural exhortations. The Atlautla minutes also reveal that women played a prominent role in worship services in the first few months after Tenney's arrival.[12]

It appears that Tenney first encountered this meeting structure in Cuernavaca, where he initially proselytized upon reaching the mission. With the assistance of American Mormon Hubert L. Hall, Tenney began holding meetings at Hall's Cuernavaca hotel with some prospective converts whom Hall recruited, as well as Mormons from Cuahuixtla and Cuautla, who had been baptized in the 1880s. In one of their earliest meetings, Tenney observed while Francisco Barco, president of the Cuautla branch, opened the meeting. Tenney recounted in his journal that several men spoke at the meeting (no women were mentioned) and he wrote: "Between each of the remarks the Presiding Elder would select a hymn and they would all raise to their feet & sing standing." Later that afternoon the group held another meeting with about thirty in attendance. Tenney took the opportunity to instruct the congregation on the Mormon pattern of prayer. He wrote, "My next effort was to teach them the rules governing meetings. How they should be conducted & that the President should not act as deacon but each in his sphere & calling thus giving to each their proper honor, that singing so much was not actually necessary but not a sin."[13] For Tenney, the branch leader should not simply act as a meeting coordinator, but have a stronger preeminence in presiding over and leading the meeting. He expected a more pronounced hierarchy and deference to priesthood authority. The following week, after a three-hour meeting, Tenney reported that the congregants requested him to speak further and he took the time to give additional guidance on meeting structure. "[I spoke] on the rules & bylaws that governs us as branches of the church for they had kept up some kind of organizations but had dropped into the rules of the Protestants who have branches in every direction. They do, however, manifest a willing spirit to learn & have in the short time of 10 days changed materially."[14] The significance of this expectation was deeper than mere administrative formality. Without a professional clergy, Mormonism provided for universal ordination for adult males who met basic thresholds of good moral character. Thus, ordination to the priesthood, observance of priesthood duties, and deference to priesthood leaders were all bound up in how masculinity was constructed in Mormonism. Tenney's mission to reform Mormon worship, then, was not only a question of how many hymns to sing, but had at its root a preoccupation with teaching recently ordained Mexican converts how to be Mormon men.

In the following weeks, Tenney followed up with further instructions about priesthood duties such as administering the sacrament (or communion), and collecting tithes and other offerings. In Cuernavaca and Cuautla, although Tenney spoke approvingly of the women present and their faith, their participation is conspicuously absent in Tenney's accounts of these meetings. Hence, Tenney focused his efforts in the first few months on building the branches at Cuernavaca and Cuautla where he found receptive congregants and felt comfortable being assertive in shaping church order. The dynamic was different in some of the branches of Mexico State.

Tenney began making sporadic visits to the villages of Atlautla, Chimal, and Tecalco in Mexico State and holding occasional meetings. The congregations in that region had been among those that asserted independent control of their branches from the Utah missionaries in the 1880s.[15] Tenney sought to proceed more carefully and gradually to shape their meeting patterns. In Atlautla, Tenney chose the aforementioned Simón Páez as branch president.[16] Simón and his wife, Juana, became friends and allies of Tenney's efforts in the region. Tenney spoke favorably of the family and was particularly struck with Juana and their daughter, Juanita.

> They are among the finest specimens of Lamanites I have met especially Sister Juana Paes [sic], the wife & mother of the family. This lady & sister is surely possessed of more than ordinary good principle. She invited me to visit a sick relative & by invitation I administered to him and he was much relieved. The daughter of this family, Sister Juana Paes [sic] is being educated & appears to be advancing rapidly & has some hopes of qualifying herself as a teacher & return as such to Colonia Juarez & enter the Juarez Academy.[17]

The Páez women were not the only ones who impressed Tenney. In his writings, Tenney often wrote about the women he encountered in Mexico in terms of the traditional notions of piety, purity, domesticity, and submission—four paramount virtues of femininity.[18] He also made reference to the Cult of True Womanhood.[19] Tenney took special pains throughout his mission journal to identify women who exhibited these traits and often painted vivid word pictures of poignant scenes involving women's tears, which he interpreted not only as signs of their earnestness and sincerity, but often also as signs of the Holy Spirit's affirmation of Tenney's divinely approved mission.[20] While Tenney's attitudes toward women, as a white American male in Mexico, reflect broader patronizing tropes of his era, they open a window into Tenney's notions of Mormon womanhood. If observation of priesthood order was an indication of promising adherence to ideals of Mormon maleness, the virtues Tenney observed in the women he encountered in these church branches indicated to him that they were well suited to life as Mormon women. But Tenney believed that the women, like the men, would need to be guided in proper participation in worship services. The next phase of Tenney's efforts would see these dynamics unfold in earnest.

In Tecalco, Tenney encountered some particularly pronounced resistance. So instead of asserting his authority to direct meetings outright, he acted more as an observer and counselor as the branch began meeting together again. About a month after meetings began Tenney wrote, "They continued their style of worship which was not according to the rules that govern the saints. After the first had prayed, two other ladies prayed in like manner and then three of the brethren prayed."[21] At one point in the meeting an unidentified woman "who had in all our public worship took a very active part" bowed down and prayed for Tenney. "I cannot even undertake to write the language that this good woman used in her appeal to the God of heaven. . . . She pled with the Lord to preserve my life that I might continue to carry the glorious light to her brethren & sisters who had wondered for ages in darkness." Feeling emboldened by this woman's public validation of his authority, Tenney took the opportunity to offer instruction. "I then arose and taught them how to dismiss, for as yet I had not dared to interfere lest I might offend them."[22] The next day Tenney reported a miraculous spiritual outpouring that saw those present "weep & pray & weap [*sic*] & preach while the tears flowed down their cheeks very freely."[23] Several weeks later, an exasperated Tenney watched as a man who had not been ordained to the priesthood directed the weekly meeting. Tenney lamented, "This brother does not hold the priesthood but I have been unable up to date to entirely turn them from their ways into which they have fallen."[24] While Tenney felt some measure of frustration with the male branch leaders, the women of Tecalco and the surrounding areas seemed increasingly helpful to him.

When Tenney came back in October, several women from Tecalco came to meet him at the train and accompany him to Atlautla. As was the custom, Tenney sought to hire someone to carry his bags, and the Tecalco sisters "defended me earnestly when a *cargador* (porter) tried to charge me too much to carry my bundles over to Atlautla." Tenney stayed with the Páez family and the group stayed up late into the evening while Juana took the lead in sharing the latest news about church members in the area. "Sister Juana is among the most interesting sisters we have," Tenney concluded.[25] Just a few days later, Tenney enlisted Juana's help in visiting Cirilo Flores, who had been the branch president at Tecalco during the 1880s. Flores had been one of the branch presidents who formerly rejected the authority of the Utah elders. Tenney hoped to bring Flores back to full participation with the branch, but found that the men he hoped to take with him were either busy or unwilling on account of ill feelings toward Flores. Juana volunteered to go with him and together they made the five-mile walk to Flores's house. "Sister Juana was so full of the spirit that she asked me to allow her to talk & she took the lead after he had told his grievance . . . and we were partially successful. . . . Sister Juana Páez is a noble & spirited woman & was the means of softening the heart of this stubborn & self-esteemed man."[26] For Tenney, Juana's deference to him and her faith provided the means for making progress toward reforming a backsliding priesthood holder. This episode illustrates the complex nature of Juana's role as a prominent woman in the emerging church organization and her influential role in shaping the development of Mormon branches in Mexico, including building priesthood leadership, despite her inability to hold the priesthood and officiate in public worship.

Finding increasing success in advancing his agenda, Tenney directed his attention to organizing a mission-wide conference in Cuernavaca in November 1901 at which LDS Church members could gather and be instructed together. Tenney must have given a great deal of thought to the place of women in worship services, because at the conference he gave instructions that served to channel the charismatic spirituality of Mexican Mormon women away from regular meetings and toward special testimony meetings.

> I arose and stated the nature of a testimony meeting explaining that
> it was intended especially for those that were not called to the stand
> to teach the people and that I desired that our sisters should take
> part in bearing their testimony or pray or sing as the spirit mite [*sic*]
> direct. The time was not sufficient to afford all that desired to speak
> notwithstanding we held [meeting for] 3½ hours & it was of the
> highest character. One of our sisters arose and bore an excellent

testimony and then called the attention of the conference to the fact that a . . . convert . . . had been badly cut with a butcher knife while defending our principles & the Elders that had been there & held worship in his house. This sister asked if it would not be proper to pray for this man & ask the Lord to heal him & thus by an exercise of our faith his life mite [sic] be spared. I arose & accorded what the good sister had said & called on Elder Barco to offer a prayer in behalf of the wounded. . . . Many of our sisters bowed down and with sobs and tears made good prayers. Others of both sexes testified and it was a time long to be remembered.[27]

Here, Tenney moved to place the religious devotion of the women into what he felt was its proper context in church worship. Instead of exhorting and praying as much in each meeting, a time that belonged more to priesthood leadership, the women could find a place for their devotion in testimony meeting. Significantly, although a woman initiated the suggestion to pray on behalf of the wounded church member, Tenney acted quickly to assert his prerogative as ecclesiastical leader and placed himself in a position to approve of the sister's suggestion and direct its fulfillment by calling on one of the local presiding officers, a male priesthood holder, to lead the suggested prayer. This served not only to solidify Tenney's authority over the various branch leaders, but also set an example of establishing male priesthood review of the religious expression of Latter-day Saint women in the Mexican Mission.

After over a year of labor, Tenney succeeded, in large measure, in fulfilling his desire to reorganize several branches of the LDS Church. The effort had seen men and the priesthood brought to greater prominence and women's devotion reduced in their participation in regular meetings and increasingly redirected to special testimony meetings. Up to this time, Tenney and other church leaders had not undertaken a formal organization of a Relief Society in the branches of the Mexican Mission, but on February 1, 1903, American women from the Mormon colonies in Chihuahua and Sonora addressed the Mexican Saints in preparation for its establishment. Hettie Tenney, wife of Ammon Tenney, and Nettie Taylor, wife of Apostle John W. Taylor, each spoke through interpreters to the gathered Latter-day Saints. The next speaker, Lexia Harris, made a few remarks "in the Spanish language, she being the first of our sisters from the north to address the native Saints in their own language since the re-opening of the mission."[28]

In the ensuing week, Tenney and other missionaries made preparations for a general conference at which Tenney would be released from his mission. Tenney recorded that "the good sisters who were appointed with Sister Juana Páez as chairman worked as if inspired by the Spirit . . . & all seemed to enjoy the many labors that were required to prepare for a conference where 250 to 300 would set down to one table & eat as one family."[29] Sunday morning "was beautiful and everything seemed to bespeak peace and good will to all and after, breakfast was served to about 250 persons." That afternoon, Nettie Taylor spoke to the women. She "gave some timely instructions to the mothers who have children to raise. There is a great responsibility resting upon all mothers, and their children will be either a blessing or a curse to them."[30]

In the days following that conference, Tenney and other missionaries traveled to the various branches to hold a final round of meetings. On February 22, Tenney, Lexia Harris, and others arrived in Atlautla and held a meeting. Tenney noted the event in his journal: "In this meeting, we having previously promised to give our faithful sisters an organization called the Relief Society. We had counseled over this situation and had arrived to a definite understanding we proceeded to sustain by unanimous vote Sister Lexia Harris as President of the Society in the Mexican Mission with Sister Juana Páez and Maxima Rios as councilors."[31] Juana Páez was then sustained also as the local president of the Atlautla Relief Society with Josephita Páez and Tomasita Lozada as counselors. For the branch at nearby Tecalco, Sister Petrita López was sustained as Relief Society president with María Regina and Concha Alarcón as counselors. Juanita Páez was sustained as the mission secretary. After the sustainings, each woman except for Lexia Harris and Máxima Ríos were set apart for their respective offices.[32] It appears that mission leaders wanted to set apart the women of the Mission Relief Society presidency for their respective offices before their local congregations. This is likely because aside from serving as general presidents, these women would also be presiding locally. And so, since Lexia and Máxima lived in Cuernavaca, their "setting apart" would take place on March 4. Harris was set apart as president of the Mission Relief Society by her husband Hyrum Harris (who was now mission president), and Máxima Ríos was set apart by Alonzo Taylor as second counselor.

Formally ordained to their respective duties, mission leaders considered that the organization was not yet complete as there had not been time to give the women formal instructions. Eleven days later, the Latter-day Saints held a meeting at Atlautla to complete the Relief Society organization. The meeting opened by singing a Spanish translation of the popular LDS hymn "O My Father," written by Eliza R. Snow, plural wife of founding prophet Joseph Smith and longtime president of the Relief Society in Utah.[33] Lexia Harris then addressed the women, and in doing so she taught them about the history of the Relief Society and its functions, echoing expressions that Joseph Smith had made at the society's inception. She said,

> The relief societies had two objects, both of which are calculated for the betterment of mankind. The first is the training of the women in the principles of the gospel and in their duties toward their families and also to work with their hands and thus obtain means for the benefit of the afflicted and poverty stricken. [She] spoke of the establishment of the Relief Society by the Prophet Joseph Smith.[34]

President Harris also stated that "anciently it was against the tradition then existing to educate the women but . . . now we have the revelation from God that the women are to work and qualify themselves for life's mission." After Harris, Juana Páez spoke and "made an earnest appeal to the husbands and fathers to not hinder the wives and daughters from coming to the associations and attending to their duties." Missionary Alonzo Taylor "spoke of the perfect organization that exists in the Church. Quoted from 1st Corinthians 12. It is necessary that all these officers and organizations exist in the Church in order that the body of Christ may be perfect." After Harris, Taylor, Jacobson, and Foster had also spoken, Zefremia Domínguez was set apart as local secretary. The sisters set Thursdays at 10:00 a.m. as their weekly meeting time.[35] The message that Harris and Taylor conveyed about the Relief Society was that it was the natural outlet for women's spiritual contributions in the church and as such, indispensable to the church's organization and divine mission. Harris's speech presented an expansive vision of the place of women within Mormonism, framing the Relief Society not only as an organization for the benefit of women, but for all mankind. Fewer of Páez's words were recorded, but they provide an important glimpse of the changes and continuities of women's influence in Mormonism. While on one hand, the Relief Society served to channel women's piety away from the general prominence manifested earlier in Mormonism's revival in central Mexico, it also created a space invested with significant cultural capital. Páez's injunction on men not to impede women in the exercise of their duties is one example of how the Relief Society allowed women to continue to shape Mormonism. That same afternoon the party held a meeting in Tecalco to complete the local organization there and give instructions. Harris counseled the sisters: "It is necessary for all to work in order to develop. Therefore the women as well as the men must take part in the work of the Church."[36] Harris expressed women's participation in the Relief Society as the means by which they achieved equality with men in their contributions to the growth of the church. This participation focused women's efforts on domesticity and charity, again, following widespread notions of genteel femininity. In this way, Mormon maleness and femaleness worked together to reinforce each other and their expected roles within Church culture.

In the short space of Ammon Tenney's two-year tenure as mission president, the role that women played in LDS worship services changed significantly, culminating in the establishment of the Relief Society in the branches of the Mexican Mission. A closer examination of this process reveals a much more complicated landscape of agency and power than meets the eye. Consistent with the work of Brekus and Brusco, this history describes how Mexican Mormon women, by their participation in the church structures available to them, and despite their ostensible lack of formal authority to preside in a highly patriarchal and hierarchical church structure, were instrumental in weaving the cultural fabric that bound together the small and somewhat disparate—but growing—branches of the Mexican Mission of the Church of Jesus Christ of Latter-day Saints in the early twentieth century.

NOTES

1. Elizabeth E. Brusco, *The Reformation of Machismo: Evangelical Conversion and Gender in Colombia* (Austin: University of Texas Press, 1995), 3.
2. Ibid., 3.
3. Catherine A. Brekus, "Mormon Women and the Problem of Historical Agency," *Journal of Mormon History* 37, no. 2 (Spring 2011): 58–87.
4. Ibid., 60.
5. Ibid., 77. See Sharon Hays, "Structure and Agency and the Sticky Problem of Culture," *Sociological Theory* 12, no. 1 (1994), 57–72. See also Saba Mahmood, *Politics of Piety: The Islamic Revival and the Feminist Subject* (Princeton, NJ: Princeton University Press, 2005).
6. Brekus, "Mormon Women," 79.
7. Nauvoo Relief Society Minute Book, LDS Church History Library, Salt Lake City, UT. Digital scans and transcripts available at http://josephsmithpapers.org/

paperSummary/nauvoo-relief-society-minute-book. For a broader history of the Relief Society, see Jill Mulvay Derr, Janath Russell Cannon, and Maureen Ursenbach Beecher, *Women of Covenant: The Story of Relief Society* (Salt Lake City, UT: Deseret Book Company, 1992).

8. Two earlier missionary expeditions entered Mexico, one from 1875 to 1876 to the US Southwest and Chihuahua and one in 1877 to Arizona and Sonora. However, these missions did not establish settlements or congregations, and only a few converts were baptized in the Arizona-Sonoran mission. For further information on these efforts, see LaMond Tullis, *Mormons in Mexico: The Dynamics of Faith and Culture* (Provo, UT: Museo de Historia del Mormonismo en México A.C., 1997). The more widely known Mormon colonies of Chihuahua and later Sonora were established in 1885 and acted as a permanent settlement for Euro-American Mormons seeking asylum from prosecution by the US federal government for polygamy. For more on the Mormon Colonies see Thomas C. Romney, *The Mormon Colonies in Mexico* (Salt Lake City: University of Utah Press, 2005); Blain Carmon Hardy, "The Mormon Colonies of Northern Mexico: A History, 1885–1912" (PhD dissertation, Wayne State, University, 1963); and LaVon Brown Whetten, *Colonia Juárez: Commemorating 125 Years of the Mormon Colonies in Mexico* (Bloomington, IN: Author House, 2010).

9. After the establishment of the Mormon colonies in northern Mexico in 1885, mission leaders planned to relocate some Mexican converts to the colonies in an attempt to provide them with a model for a good Mormon life and remove them from what they considered to be a deeply sinful environment in Mexico City and the surrounding areas. Disputes arose over work and other concerns and the majority of these Mexican converts left the colonies and returned to their homes in central Mexico. The converts' disenchantment with their experiences unsettled the members of their congregations and touched off nationalist sentiment against the American missionaries. These conflicts curtailed missionary work and LDS Church leaders decided to close the mission. See Jared Tamez, "'Out of this Part of Babylon': Colonizing Mexican Mormons and the Decline of the Mexican Mission of the Church of Jesus Christ of Latter-day Saints, 1879–1889" (master's thesis, University of Utah, 2014). Also see Tullis, *Mormons in Mexico.*

10. Most Mexican converts to Mormonism in the Mexican Mission's first decade came to Mormonism from a Protestant background. Notably, the Páez family of Atlautla, Mexico, and the Zuñiga family in Cuautla, Morelos, had strong family ties to Methodism. Whatever the extent of Protestant influence on Mormon religiosity in this context, an 1875 Mexican Meeting Manual for the Methodist Church gives guidelines for worship services that bear several similarities to the structure of early Mormon meetings in Mexico. See *Libro De culto de La Iglesia Metodista Eposcopal en Mexico: Juntamente con los himnos de las Iglesias Evangelicas* (Mexico: Imprenta de la Iglesia, 1875). For a broader discussion of

Protestantism in Mexico, see Jean Pierre Bastian, *Los Disidentes: Sociedades Protestantes y revolución en México, 1872–1911* (Mexico City: El Colegio de México, 1989).

11. Matthew 6:1–3 (King James Version): "Take heed that ye do not your alms before men, to be seen of them: otherwise ye have no reward of your Father which is in heaven. Therefore when thou doest thine alms, do not sound a trumpet before thee, as the hypocrites do in the synagogues and in the streets, that they may have glory of men. Verily I say unto you, they have their reward. But when thou doest alms, let not thy left hand know what thy right hand doeth."

12. Atlautla Branch Minutes, December 31, 1901, Church History Library, Salt Lake City, UT.

13. Ammon Tenney, Journal, July 7, 1901, Church History Library, Salt Lake City, UT.

14. Ibid., July 14, 1901.

15. The preface for the minutes of the Atlautla Branch noted that no regular meetings were held in Atlautla after the close of the mission in 1889 until Ammon Tenney made his appearance to reopen it.

16. Simón Páez and his wife, Juana, were baptized in the 1880s during the Mexican Mission's first ten years. When missionaries attempted to colonize Mexican converts into the Mormon colonies in the north in 1887, Simón, Juana, and their family were among those who relocated. While most of those who went to the colonies returned to their homes within a few months (see note 9), Simón, Juana, and their children remained. Two children were born to them in Colonia Juárez, one in 1887 and the other in 1891. They remained for a number of years and, for unknown reasons, returned to Atlautla by 1895. In the colonies, Juana would have been taught about and participated in the Relief Society which had been established among the American Mormons there. Their time in the Mormon colonies would have been the first substantial and sustained contact that any Mexican convert had with the Relief Society organization to that point.

17. Tenney, Journal, July 17, 1901. The "sick relative" was Margarito Bautista, later a key player in the Third Convention and founder of his own Mormon movement. See Stuart Parker, chapter 6 of this volume.

18. As an example, Tenney visited a church member, Brother Ray, with the intent of baptizing Brother Ray's wife Maria Casino. "She is rather above the average heights, well formed & of lite complexion, is the mother of one sweet little girl, 4 years old & is only 19 herself. . . . I baptized sister Maria Casino Ray in the presence of her husband Br. Milton S. Ray. . . . And thus ended the labor of love such an one has not often been my lot to perform for sister Ray was intuitively a Saint for from the first talk I had with this humble lady she said that she was willing & ready to be baptized. A few indeed that I have met seem so miled [sic] & even tempered, so pleasant & agreeable in all her actions as well as being feminine bearing the stamp of a lady." Tenney, Journal, September 17, 1901.

19. Also known as the "Cult of Domesticity," which refers to a belief system in the

nineteenth and early twentieth centuries of an idealized vision of women as middle-class; white; and steeped in religious piety, moral purity, mastery of homemaking, and submission to male authority. See Barbara Welter, "The Cult of True Womanhood: 1820–1860," *American Quarterly* 18, no. 2, part 1 (Summer 1966): 151–74.

20. On one occasion Tenney described the miraculous vision of a woman who had previously protested her husband's interest in Mormonism. "The evening before when her husband started to attend the meeting she railed out at him with bitter denunciations. This same night the Lord visited this sincere & chosen vessel & gave her a vision and she came to relate it to me and make right what she had said against me. . . . She began to also unfold to me the feelings of a converted heart & to relate to me the vision. Her tongue like one inspired as those on the day of Pentecost & her sweet & beautiful face glowed with the light of heaven. My heart was touched with her appearance and more so with the spirit that accompanied every word that fell from her lips." Tenney, Journal, October 2, 1901.

21. Ibid., September 22, 1901.

22. Ibid.

23. Ibid., September 23, 1901.

24. Ibid., October 12, 1901.

25. Ibid., October 10, 1901.

26. Ibid., October 14, 1901.

27. Ibid., November 11, 1901.

28. Lexia Harris was married to Hyrum S. Harris, who would take over for Ammon Tenney as president of the Mexican Mission. Hyrum and Lexia had lived previously in Mexico City while Hyrum studied law. Mexican Mission history, 1874–1977: Volume 2, 1874–1920, Part 2, 1888–1907, Church History Library, The Church of Jesus Christ of Latter-day Saints, Salt Lake City, UT: Image 68, February 1, 1903.

29. Tenney, Journal, February 5, 1903.

30. Mexican Mission history.

31. "Sustain" and "sustaining" in Mormon parlance refers to a congregation's acceptance of the subject to fulfill their "calling" or responsibility. This is usually expressed in open meeting by a show of raised right hands. Any congregants expressing opposition to the call are also given the opportunity to express it by show of hands, though such expressions are generally rare. Tenney, Journal, February 22, 1903.

32. "Setting apart" in Mormon parlance is the formal ceremony in which a presiding ecclesiastical authority lays hands on an individual's head, pronounces a blessing, and assigns that individual to a specific job (referred to as a calling) in the church's organization. Henceforth, the individual is tasked with faithfully fulfilling the duties connected with his or her calling.

33. Significantly, "O My Father" contains a reference to a "Heavenly Mother,"

understood in Mormon theology to be the divine wife of God or "Heavenly Father," and reflects the belief that all of humanity are the literal spirit offspring of heavenly parents. See Jill Mulvay Derr, "The Significance of 'O My Father' in the Personal Journey of Eliza R. Snow," *BYU Studies* 36, no. 1 (1996–1997): 85–126. For further discussion of the theology of a Heavenly Mother, see David L. Paulsen and Martin Pulido, "'A Mother There': A Survey of Historical Teachings about Mother in Heaven," *BYU Studies* 50, no. 1 (2011): 70–126.

34. Mexican Mission history, Images 69–70, March 15, 1903.

35. Ibid.

36. Ibid.

CHAPTER FIVE

Solving Schism in *Nepantla*

The Third Convention Returns to the LDS Fold

ELISA PULIDO

IN HIS BOOK *Evangelism and Apostasy: The Evolution and Impact of Evangelicals in Modern Mexico* Kurt Bowen admits that he has excluded Mormons from his analysis "because their inclusion in my fieldwork would have disturbed evangelicals."[1] Bowen's omission of the history of LDS Church's evangelizing efforts and schisms in Mexico is indeed unfortunate. With a century and a half of proselytizing in Mexico, thousands of missionaries currently working in twenty-four missions in Mexico, and the LDS Church's own dramatic chronology of apostasy, schism, and recidivism, the history of the LDS presence in Mexico has much to offer scholars examining indigenous church formation, transnational missiology, and apostasy studies.

From 1936 to 1946, the LDS Church in Mexico put its evangelism aside in order to focus on a sustained reconciliation effort, which resulted in the mass reunification of an apostate movement known as the Third Convention. Given the prevalence of religious schism among missionary sects in Latin America, particularly within the Pentecostal movement (currently the fastest growing religious movement in Latin America), the fact that nearly one-third of the membership of the LDS Church in Mexico left the mainstream church at this time is not surprising. The reunification of the vast majority of the dissidents to a hierarchical Anglo church, however, defies the historical trend.[2] According to sociologists of religion Roger Finke and Rodney Stark, statistics demonstrate that growing churches do not want to merge.[3] Yet Third Conventionists were sending out missionaries and baptizing converts—they were growing.[4] Thus, the prevalence of schism in Mexico and the growth of the Third Convention force the question: Why did the vast majority of the dissenters return to the main body of the Latter-day Saints?

Most studies on the Third Convention credit the diplomatic skills of mission president Arwell L. Pierce (1942–1950) as a major factor in the remarkable resolution of the rift.[5] While crediting Pierce's skills, this chapter will argue that a transcultural willingness to listen on both sides created a space in *nepantla*, or a space in the middle, where, through the sharing of resources and the rebuilding of community, the schism was eventually healed. My research has been influenced by the availability of interview subjects who were LDS missionaries in Mexico and witnessed reunification efforts between the LDS Church and dissenting groups from 1945 to 1948. These findings provide insight into the power struggles between LDS Church hierarchy and indigenous Latter-day Saints in Mexico, and into the motivators for reunification on the part of those who vied for authority and those who were excluded from positions of authority (i.e., women).

HISTORY OF INCREASING TENSION
WITH ANGLO HIERARCHY IN THE MEXICAN MISSION

In the early 1870s, the liberal Mexican government opened its doors to Protestant missionary agencies in the United States in order to create, as Mexican president Benito Juárez stated, "a viable alternative to the Catholic Church." Over the next fifty years, missionaries from various denominations in the United States came to Mexico in increasing numbers. The evangelizing efforts of these denominations were, however, interrupted by the violence of the Mexican Revolution and the expulsion of foreign clerics in Mexico beginning in 1926. In the case of Latter-day Saints, an interest in establishing colonies for polygamist members also diverted their focus from evangelizing.[6] As did converts of other Christian denominations, local Latter-day Saints continued to function as leaders and to proselytize in Mexico.[7]

When in Mexico, Protestant missionaries tended to assign the gathering of congregations and proselytizing activities to indigenous members, and reserve the performance of ceremonial functions and the making of policy decisions for themselves, a situation which heightened tensions between US and Mexican Protestants, who, in most cases, depended on the economic resources of their American counterparts.[8] In addition to receiving priesthood ordination and leadership training for both men and women, Mexican Latter-day Saints were anxious to have materials printed in Spanish, to have their young people called on missions, and to build chapels and schools—goals that they thought would be best supported by the appointment of an indigenous Mexican church president who could remain in Mexico despite political turmoil.[9]

To address these concerns, Isaías Juárez, district president of church units in Mexico, called two conventions in the early 1930s, where letters were drafted and sent to the First Presidency in Salt Lake City requesting a mission president of Mexican *raza y sangre*—or, in other words, they wanted the appointment of a mission president who was an ethnic Mexican of Indian, or at least mestizo, extraction.[10] The letter sent by the first convention received no answer. In 1932, Antoine Ivins, who had been directing the mission from the United States, answered and denied the request of the second convention.[11] The disillusionment felt by Mexicans Latter-day Saints found its roots in the religious history of Latin America. Nearly half a millennium of Catholic discipleship had produced few indigenous priests, with most of the ecclesiastical leadership coming from Spain and Portugal.[12] Like other post-Revolutionary Mexicans, Latter-day Saint Mexicans felt empowered by their new identity as citizens of a democracy.[13] Their continued survival in Mexico, despite the repeated departures of Anglo missionaries (Mormon or Protestant), further demonstrated that they were capable of leading themselves.

THE THIRD CONVENTION

Despite the Mexican members' repeated requests for a mission president *de raza Mexicana*, and despite the ongoing ban against foreign clerics, Harold W. Pratt was assigned to be president of the Mexican Mission in 1934.[14] The assignment of yet another Anglo mission president was a grave disappointment for many Mexican Latter-day Saints. After years of neglect and repeated periods of isolation from the main body of the church in Utah, Mexicans were certain that a mission president from among their own would help them acquire needed funds, call their sons and daughters on missions, and allow them to obey the Mexican law banning foreign clerics. Most importantly, they were certain a native mission president would hear them—and hear them in their own language.[15]

In response to Harold Pratt's appointment, some of the membership formed a Third Convention, once again petitioning the First Presidency of the LDS Church for an indigenous mission president and nominating Abel Páez for the position.[16] The First Presidency responded that church leaders were called only by the inspiration of God and were never selected by the congregation.[17] After the receipt of this response, some of the *convencionistas* returned to the main body of the church, but about eight hundred did not. In May 1937, the LDS Church excommunicated convention leaders Margarito Bautista, Abel Páez, Narciso Sandoval, Othón Espinosa Ysita, Pilar Páez, Felipe Barragán, Daniel Mejía, and Apolonio Arzate.[18] The excommunicated leaders selected Abel Páez as the president of their new ecclesiastical organization, The Church of Jesus Christ of Latter-day Saints, Third Convention. Along with about eight hundred members—one-third of the total membership of the LDS Mexican membership in central Mexico—they took some furniture to establish their own chapels.[19] This was not the end of the schism, as shortly after this initial break with the church, Margarito Bautista was ousted from the convention and joined by Daniel Mejía. Although they split from the main group of the dissenters, neither Bautista nor Mejía returned to the main body of the LDS Church.[20]

After their break from the LDS Church and all of its affiliated organizational entities, convencionistas continued to observe LDS Church practices and to teach its doctrines. For example, they continued to regard Joseph Smith, the founder of the LDS Church, as a prophet of God, to view the Book of Mormon as sacred scripture, to observe the LDS health code (no smoking and drinking) and to sing hymns promoting LDS tenets. Nevertheless, for more than six years, relationships between the Salt Lake–based leadership and dissenting convencionistas "were filled with suspicion and acrimony."[21] Arturo de Hoyos, a Mexican national and missionary in Mexico from 1945 to 1947, remembers the insults cast at his Anglo missionary companions by convencionistas, and said he often felt compelled to defend the Anglos verbally, and intimated that he would have been glad and able to do so physically as well, had the need arisen.[22]

WOMEN AND THE THIRD CONVENTION

Most of the records we have about heightened emotions, verbal and physical posturing, and arguments during the inception and life-span of the Third

Convention describe an altercation between males of differing ethnicities, and sometimes the same ethnicity, over a position (mission president) that could be held only by males. Though there is no public record of pro- or anti-convencionista outbursts on the part of women, women did have opinions on this subject. The tide of Mexican nationalism undoubtedly impacted indigenous women as well as men.

One of the original leaders of the conventionist movement, Margarito Bautista, is known to have had conversations with sympathetic full-time female missionaries of indigenous and Anglo extraction in the spring of 1936.[23] One of these missionaries, Ester Ontiveros, from Colonia Dublán, Chihuahua, corresponded with Bautista regarding the aims of the convencionistas, and mission records state that she was highly influenced by him and had been actively participating "in preparations for the convention."[24] As an indigenous resident of the Mormon Colonies, she may have felt it was time for the indigenous community to take their rightful place in church leadership. When approached about her activities with the convention, Sister Ontiveros stated that her father, Toribio Ontiveros, had just written to her from Colonia Dublán and "cautioned her to stand by the constituted authorities." The mission history reports that after "thinking things over" Ester Ontiveros decided "that she had been misguided."[25] The manuscript history of the Mexican Mission states,

> When explanations of church order and procedure, with the proper respect for authority[,] [were] explained to her, she humbled herself entirely and asked forgiveness promising to cooperate fully with authorities hereafter. She was transferred to Monterrey.[26]

Ester Ontiveros had to choose between conflicting loyalties—Mexican nationalism, Mormonism, and filial duty—to interests all headed by patriarchy. Whatever Ester Ontiveros's feelings about indigenous leadership may have been, she chose to obey her family patriarch, cease her involvement in the convention, and forward a letter to mission president Harold W. Pratt, which had been sent to her by Bautista.[27] The letter exposed Bautista as a leader in the convention, a role he had denied, and was certainly a factor in the decision to excommunicate him for rebellion, insubordination, and apostasy.

There is evidence that some indigenous women supported the convention privately, while publicly supporting their husbands' loyalty to the LDS

Church. For example, Jovita Parra, wife of Benjamin Parra (second counselor in the District Presidency), finally agreed with convention goals on April 11, 1936. Benjamin Parra withdrew his support for the convention shortly thereafter, and yet there is no indication that the Parras had a religiously split household thereafter.[28]

As seen above, family influence certainly played a role in the choices made by many women on both sides of the conflict. Those with dissenting husbands and fathers supported them, initially at least. Nevertheless, in at least two instances, the activities of male dissenters ultimately lead to the dissolution of their marriages. When schismatics in Cuautla returned to the LDS fold, Daniel Mejía left both Cuautla and his family. Theresa Bautista ultimately divorced her husband, Margarito, and renounced her Mexican citizenship as well.[29]

Last, if leadership opportunities for women were linked in the minds of indigenous females with marriage to a male leader, then the absence of an indigenous leader as a mission president might have also represented a lost leadership opportunity for married women. It would not have been missed that Anna H. Pratt, the wife of Harold W. Pratt, was placed in a position of leadership and confidence by virtue of her spousal relationship. At the time of the Third Convention, wives of mission presidents were set apart as presidents of the mission Relief Society (women's auxiliary).[30] In this role they traveled throughout the mission with their husbands and addressed conference attendees on such topics as the running of the Relief Society and its benefits, the importance of motherhood, and the raising of children.[31]

To date, no primary-source material suggests that indigenous women felt a loss in leadership opportunities for themselves. It is possible that these women recognized that the real locus of power lay with men and not with women, whether Anglo or indigenous, as local leadership responsibilities for women were decided upon by indigenous men acting as the leaders of local congregations. The Anglo women who came to visit were likely viewed as little more than itinerant speakers, who had no authority to implement or enforce instructions.

There is a suggestion in the mission records that indigenous female leaders were concerned about growing tensions among the members as early as 1934. In November of that year, about eighteen months before the Third Convention broke from the mainstream of the church, Tarcila M. de Páez, president of the Relief Society in the Central Mexico District, and wife of the first counselor in the District Presidency, Abel Páez, called for the "cooperation and union of all" at a conference in San Pedro Martir. She spoke in the same session of the conference as Anna Pratt, who did not appeal for unity, and Tarcila's remarks appear to have been made at a meeting attended by all members, both male and female.[32] Interestingly, Tarcila's husband became the recognized leader of the Third Convention, a position he maintained for ten years, from 1936 to 1946. It was not until the appointment of Arwell L. Pierce as the president of the Mexican Mission that dialogue between the two factions slowly resumed.

ARWELL L. PIERCE'S FIGHT TO SAVE THE UNION

In 1942, when Arwell L. Pierce was appointed president of the Mexican Mission, there were over 1,200 members of the LDS church, 15 branches, 6 chapels, and a small group of missionaries.[33] Pierce had been given the task to reunite convencionistas with the main body of the church. Pierce said that LDS apostle David O. McKay had told him he was "the Abraham Lincoln who must save this union."[34] From 1942 through 1946 Pierce persistently attended Third Convention meetings and conferences. Though the initial response to his presence was antagonism—just as it was for Anglo missionaries—Pierce was still very much admired by the young missionaries who served with him and indigenous members as well. Charles Eastwood remembers Pierce as a highly ethical and kind mission president, who was extremely generous with the convencionistas. According to Eastwood, who served his mission from 1946 to 1948, Pierce treated indigenous members as equals and asked all missionaries to do the same. Instead of saying "you" they were to say "we," and Eastwood, who was a district leader, passed this instruction on to other missionaries who reported to him. Apparently, tensions between the two sides had cooled considerably by 1946; Eastwood, who served his mission a year or two after Arturo de Hoyos completed his mission, said that he never heard any indigenous member complain about Pierce, and that missionaries were treated kindly by indigenous convencionistas and LDS members alike.[35] Andres Hinojosa, an indigenous member at that time, stated in an oral history that Pierce was "a very intelligent man, very refined and very prepared."[36]

Pierce patiently built friendships and listened to the convencionistas, and came to the conclusion that at least some of their complaints were legitimate. Mexican Latter-day Saints did need to build more chapels, and though convencionistas continued to teach LDS doctrine, there were few printed materials in Spanish for the use of either dissenters or LDS members.[37]

In an effort to befriend convencionistas, Pierce also shared his resources with them and used theirs in return. He even gave them rides in his automobile.[38] When new publications in Spanish were sent to the mission home, he shared them with the convencionistas. Missionary Daniel Taylor, who was editor of the *Liahona*, a periodical published by the Mexican Mission, stated that Pierce used the services of conventionist printer Apolonio Arzate to meet the mission's own publishing needs.[39] Conversely, when convencionistas came to the mission home to purchase Books of Mormon and hymnals (for which the convencionistas had no copyright) they were welcomed.[40]

By 1945, Pierce was comfortable enough with Abel Páez to point out other resources convencionistas were denying themselves by remaining separate from the community of the main church, such as temple worship and the counsel of living prophets. The dissenters had not lost their reverence for Mormonism's holiest sites. A surviving copy of the *Sendera Lamanita* (in the possession of Taylor), a monthly periodical published by convencionistas, includes a photograph of the LDS temple in Salt Lake on the back page, flanked by those of convencionista chapels in Ermita and Amecameca.[41] Up until 1945, no LDS temple services were conducted in Spanish. In that year, Spanish-speaking services were first held in the Mesa, Arizona, temple. When they began, Pierce journeyed by automobile with several missionaries and a few members to Mesa to attend.[42]

According to de Hoyos, when word reached convencionistas that temple services were available in Spanish, and that Pierce and others had made a trip to attend, they also wished to go.[43] A 1936 article in a church periodical printed in Utah describes LDS temples as places where, since 1833, members received revelation through covenant making, received the strength to avoid temptation, and learned to put jealousies aside. It defined an LDS temple as "a haven of peace, and a place where the hush of reverence casts its holy spell upon the visitor."[44] In his dedicatory prayer for an LDS temple in Idaho in 1945, Mormon president George Albert Smith thanked God for the privilege LDS couples have of marrying in temples not only for the duration of this life but also for the next, and he prayed that members would come to the temple to perform salvific rituals (called ordinances) on behalf of deceased ancestors.[45] Though these articles would not have been available in Spanish, these attitudes and teachings would have been extant between 1936 and 1946 and certainly reflect the attraction temple worship held for most members of the LDS Church.

Daniel Taylor agrees that the lure of participating in LDS temple rituals had an effect on convencionistas, who did not have the resources to build temples. He remembers chauffeuring Pierce and Páez in Pierce's car one day, when Pierce asked Páez if he wanted to be responsible for the inability of convencionistas to participate in LDS temple rituals. Páez responded that they would have to go to Mesa, a trip not easily afforded by most of the members. Pierce told Páez there would be temples in Mexico one day, and also asked if Páez wanted to be responsible for teaching his people to disobey the prophet.[46] According to Taylor, Pierce's "carrot"—the notion of temple worship within the reach of Mexicans—made an impression on Páez.

Pierce promoted the benefits of secure leadership that Mexican dissenters could rely on if united with the mainstream LDS community. When convencionistas began insisting on a mission president of Mexican extraction, Pierce told them that what they really needed was a stake president, as the Hawaiians had, but they would have to be united.[47] Taylor also reports that Pierce pointed out to Páez, who was diabetic, that if Páez's health failed, the conventionist community would be at a loss for leadership, a concern that would be addressed by uniting with the LDS members.[48]

THE LDS PROPHET COMES TO MEXICO

Though convencionistas contested Anglo leadership of the Mexican Mission, they still reverenced LDS prophets and apostles. Visits to Mexico made by LDS apostle David O. McKay and by LDS prophet George Albert Smith supported the church's cause. David O. McKay, an LDS apostle and member of the LDS Church's First Presidency, toured church operations in Mexico in 1943. McKay looked for potential building sites for chapels, listened to the concerns of Mexican members, and visited the home of Othón Espinosa, one of the original organizers of the Third Convention, to give a health blessing to Espinosa's infant granddaughter.[49] Because McKay visited homes of members and convencionistas alike, blessed them, and shared food at their tables, he fostered a joint community based on goodwill.[50] McKay, who would become the LDS prophet in 1951, was committed to church growth outside the United States; he believed the church had a worldwide destiny, universal appeal, and that it was "preeminently a social religion."[51]

In May of 1946, George Albert Smith came to Mexico to meet with members and dissidents and to visit with government officials, including Mexican president Manual Ávila Camacho. Smith was the first LDS president to visit Mexico.[52] For Mexican Latter-day Saints and convencionistas, his audience with Camacho surely signaled the importance that an association with the LDS Church in Salt Lake could have.[53] Smith spoke at a reunification conference with both mainline Latter-day Saints and convencionistas in attendance. The conference was held in Tecalco, the locale of the Third Convention. The conference was attended by 1,000 to 1,200 people, who sang, "Te damos, Señor, nuestras gracias que mandas de nuevo venir profetas con tu Evangelio."[54] Attendees reached out to touch Smith on his way into the chapel. Smith delivered a conciliatory speech and asked Abel Páez to speak. Páez stood up, confessed he was in error, and acknowledged George Albert Smith as God's prophet. Agricol Lozano was in attendance and remembers the reconciliation having a physical, charismatic effect upon the attendees: "It was a very significant moment, our bodies trembled from the emotion and the reconciliation took effect."[55] Several hundred convencionistas returned to the LDS fold the day of the conference.[56]

In order to ease the transition for both sides, Pierce chose several assistants from among the indigenous male leaders from both the LDS Church and the convention.[57] This committee was named the Comité de Consejo y Bienestar (Committee of Counsel and Well-Being). Former convencionista president, Abel Páez, was among those asked to assist, as well as Apolonio Arzate and Narciso Sandoval. LDS leaders included Guadalupe Zárraga, Bernabé Parra, and Isaías Juárez. These men were to counsel and advise Pierce, assist in local and regional conferences, and help prepare Mexico for the formation of an LDS stake.[58]

There were, of course, loose ends to resolve. For example, convencionistas had baptized around three hundred people while outside the LDS Church. Since the church hierarchy recognized none of those baptisms, these so-called members had to be baptized again. Small congregations loaded buses and came to Mexico City for the event. In order to soften their return to the LDS Church, Pierce requested that Third Convention leaders not have to be baptized again, as is normally the case in an LDS excommunication. Church leaders agreed to alter the nomenclature: should the convention leaders rejoin the main body of the LDS Church, their new baptisms would be termed ratifications.[59]

1946 reunification meeting between the Third Convention and the LDS Church.
Photographer unknown. Courtesy of the Museum of Mormon Mexican History.

Pierce personally performed all the re-baptisms for conventionist converts and ratifications by immersion for conventionist leaders—around one
thousand all told.[60] Busloads of members came to Mexico City to be re-
baptized. Pierce did not contact dissident congregations, but waited for them
to contact him. Some of these congregations, such as the congregation in San
Pablo, had been proselytized by convencionistas and had not been part of the
original schism. The convencionista missionaries had apparently left a good
impression of religious proselytizers in general in San Pablo. Eastwood
recalls that as he walked into the town of San Pablo, five- and six-year-old
children he did not know would run up and kiss his hands. He also recalls
that the convencionistas' converts in San Pablo had been well schooled in
their scriptures and were well acquainted with the tenets of Mormonism.

After the reunification conference, the local leader in San Pablo tele-
phoned Pierce and asked for permission to bring all his members the twelve
to fifteen miles by bus to Mexico City for re-baptism. The local leader specifically requested that Pierce personally re-baptize them all into the LDS
Church. The baptisms were performed by Pierce in a pool in Mexico City.[61]

It would be difficult to ascertain exactly how convencionistas felt about
the need for re-baptism. Was it a confirmation of Anglo power? Perhaps. The
fact that Pierce performed all the baptisms himself might have been seen as
an assertion of Pierce's authority as an Anglo mission president or as a

symbolic binding of himself to all of the newly baptized—a logical interpretation since the original schism had resulted over Salt Lake's refusal to appoint a mission president of Mexican race. It is possible that those who requested that Pierce re-baptize them did so in order to underscore their willingness to leave an old argument behind. It is also not difficult to imagine, that, after convencionista proselytes had boarded market buses bound for Mexico City and finally found places for themselves amid farmers with their crated chickens and baskets of papayas, they would have anxiously contemplated their upcoming baptism by an Anglo evangelizer and hoped that it would be an interesting, perhaps exotic, experience, or at least a charismatic one.

CONTINUING MISSIONARY EFFORTS

Most accounts of reunification efforts focus on Pierce's diplomatic skills up to the moment of Páez's confession of error. But interviews with missionaries who met with dissenters who did not reunify with the church at the visit of George Albert Smith provide interesting information on continuing grassroots reunification efforts. Missionaries did very little evangelizing as long as the schism lasted and for some time afterward. Their job was to fellowship with convencionistas and those who had split off from the convencionistas, and to strengthen the community in existing wards against further schism.[62] Many missionaries continued to attend both LDS and dissenter worship services after the Third Convention's reunification with the main body of the LSD Church.[63]

The possibility of further schism was very real, and in some instances, had already begun. Margarito Bautista, who had been asked to leave the Third Convention in 1936, founded his polygamous utopia a decade later in Ozumba, Mexico, which lies between Amecameca and Cuautla, an area with a long history of LDS Church evangelizing and conversion. At the time Bautista founded his colony, Anglo polygamist groups from the United States were actively recruiting members in Mexico as well.[64] In 1947, former missionary Eastwood remembers delivering a Sunday sermon in Tlalpan about false preachers who were visiting LDS congregations and teaching erroneous doctrines, including polygamy. As he spoke, an angry visitor stormed out of the building. After the service, members of the congregation informed him that the visitor was the head of a LeBaron polygamist clan, and that he had been trying to recruit new members for his colony in that area on more than one occasion. On another occasion, members in Ozumba told him Margarito Bautista had visited them the Sunday prior.[65] Two LeBarons, Joel and Vernon, were LDS missionaries in the Mexican Mission. Taylor reports that one evening, when Pierce was away from Mexico City, he received a call from a female missionary in Puebla, who asked him to come quickly, as the two LeBarons missionaries were preaching polygamy.[66] Additional opportunities to leave the LDS Church abounded. Between 1940 and 1950 Protestantism grew by 86 percent in Mexico; some of this growth belonged to innovative indigenous denominations such as La Luz del Mundo, whose leader referred to himself as the Apostle.[67]

On at least one occasion, the efforts of indigenous female congregants and white Anglo female missionaries affected the reunification of dissenters to the mainstream of the church. Laurie Teichert Eastwood recorded the following incident in a journal she kept as a young missionary. In the spring of 1946, Teichert, a missionary from Cokeville, Wyoming, was assigned to work with Irene Salmon, a female missionary from Salt Lake City, in a small LDS congregation in the city of Cuautla. Daniel Mejía, one of the original leaders of the Third Convention, had split off from the convention and was leading another group of dissenters in Cuautla. In her diary, Teichert refers to this group of dissenters as "convencionistas," though they had not been affiliated with the group led by Abel Páez for approximately ten years.[68] On June 7, 1946, Teichert wrote,

> We went walking out to find Daniel Mejía, the leader of the
> Convention in Cuautla. He worked at a sugar refinery. We went to
> his home and his family was very cordial to us and he was charming
> as he accompanied us back to town. The following day he took us on
> a guided tour through the refinery and gave us gifts of sugar, syrup,
> etc. From this time on we began attending meetings in our branch
> as well as the Convention branch but could not convince them to
> join with us.[69]

Since Cuautla was a farming community, there were many irrigation ditches in the area that bred mosquitoes. The male missionaries assigned to the area contracted malaria and were unable to help in reunification efforts. Teichert and Salmon continued to make contact with Mejía's congregation, mostly with women. On July fourteenth, a week after their visit to Daniel Mejía,

Teichert reports that a missionary conference was held in Cuautla at the dissenters' chapel."[70] Two months later, on September 10, Teichert wrote, "While
we were visiting the Convention Relief Society the women said they would
like a combined chorus of both branches for Relief Society conference. What
a thrill! The next day we held a practice at our branch and all their men came
to see that all went well."[71] This practice was attended by women from the
LDS congregation (branch) and all of the women from the dissenting branch,
including the wife of Daniel Mejía. Daniel Mejía was, in fact, one of the dissenting men who came to observe the practice.[72]

Ruth Torres, another missionary in Mexico at the time, cites the benefits
of shared resources and increased community as motivators in overcoming
schism. Torres is the descendent of one of the founders of the first Mexican
branch of the LDS Church in Salt Lake City, and her parents, natives of
Mexico, were well acquainted with members on all sides of the varying dis-
sents. According to Torres, women who had been formerly been friends, and
who had been separated by religious dissent, decided they wanted to enjoy
each other's company once again.[73] Torres also states that singing in choirs
was a favorite group activity for Mexican Latter-day Saints. She remembers
the enthusiasm with which they sang, performing with untrained zeal. These
performances "weren't exactly melodic," she recalls, but notes that they certainly had "volume."[74]

According to Teichert, the women of the dissenting congregation wanted
not only the combined vocal prowess of the women of both branches but also
the use of the LDS members' piano, as well.[75] A piano was not a resource the
non-LDS branch could afford, and they did not have any members who could
play the piano. Piano accompaniment at the LDS branch was generally provided by Anglo missionaries, as in this case, by Teichert herself. As the piano
could not be moved, it was necessary to hold the joint Relief Society conference in the LDS chapel. On September 24, a Relief Society Conference was
held with women from both congregations. Most of the attendees were from
the dissenting faction.[76] According to Teichert, the singing was indeed volu-
minous and the conference was a rousing success.[77] Three weeks later, on
October 16, Teichert and Salmon "received word that the [dissenting faction]
had broken away from Daniel Mejía and were ready to join our group."[78]
Four days later, on October 20, she wrote, "We held a reorganization meeting
in which both branches [of the church] were joined."[79] This reunification was
achieved five months after Teichert and Salmon began to attend meetings of
the women's auxiliary in the dissenting congregation.

In Cuautla, the reunification of the branches was largely engineered by women hoping to sing together, enjoy each other's company, and share in the use of a piano. As no women in the LDS congregation or the dissenting congregation were ordained to offices in the priesthood, reunification for them was not an issue of who wielded authority and who did not. In Cuautla, female members of both branches realized that together they could have greater voice and more community together than they could apart.

Interestingly, while the female members in Cuautla were interested in increasing their community through reunification, Torres is of the opinion that the disunity of the original male leaders of the Third Convention was a factor in the movement's decline.[80] After being excommunicated from the convention by Páez, Bautista built a polygamous communal society in central Mexico, which still survives to this day. [81] Abel Páez, Narciso Sandoval, Othón Espinosa and Pilar Páez, on the other hand, reunited with the LDS Church.[82] Daniel Mejía remained isolated with his congregation in Cuautla until all the members of his congregation, including his family, chose to return to the mainline church. Charles Eastwood reports that a lonely Mejía then moved to Chalco where he convinced a young LDS girl to move in with him. As the leader of the local LDS congregation, Eastwood visited Mejía and asked him to quit living with this congregant. Mejía refused.[83]

CONCLUSION

I have suggested that at a time of increasing Mexican nationalism, despite all historical predictors to the contrary, a transnational schism within the LDS Church known as the Third Convention was healed, at least in part, through the mutually perceived benefits of shared spiritual and material resources and increased associations. I have also argued that in at least one instance this rebuilding was a transcultural endeavor, largely engineered by an indigenous female community through outreach and joint celebration with each other and with women from the United States.

Two scholars of Latin American religion, Gaston Espinosa and Miguel A. De La Torre, use the Aztec word *nepantla* to describe a location in the middle.[84] *Nepantla* was coined "in the wake of the Spanish conquest of Mexico."[85] In the crucible of conflict, indigenous Mexicans learned to maintain their heritage and to survive the winds of change in this nepantla location. The meetings of dissenters became places in the middle the minute LDS members chose to join them in worship. The chapel in Mexico City where LDS president George Albert Smith spoke to indigenous members became a nepantla when convencionistas honored an LDS prophet and the LDS prophet shared the pulpit with a conventionist leader. Finally, the Cuautla Relief Society conference imagined by dissenting women, executed by indigenous dissenters and LDS women, and aided by white women from the United States was a mestizo solution in a nepantla, one that created a bridge for a communal future. One of the most fascinating aspects of this study is, in fact, that in the wake of a schism created over claims and counterclaims to patriarchal authority, the rift was healed in Cuautla by a transcultural feminine solution, in a female-generated nepantla outside patriarchal claims.

In his book *Boundless Faith: The Global Outreach of American Churches* Robert Wuthnow writes, "The future of American Christianity's engagement with globalization depends on coming to a clearer understanding of its past. . . . There are remarkable continuities between present efforts and earlier ones. . . . The challenge is to incorporate the historical legacy more fully into current discussions about international programs and to learn from this legacy."[86] Though Wuthnow's statement is directed toward mainline Protestant evangelists, the LDS evangelizing legacy in Mexico, though largely unknown, has much to offer the fields of missiology and apostasy studies. As demonstrated, the history of the Third Convention's reunification defies the historical trend of growth through schism.

Current trends in LDS evangelism and apostasy in Mexico are also rich sources for scholarly research. Following the dissolution of the Third Convention, a period of significant growth ensued for the Latter-day Saints in Mexico. Two hundred ten stakes have been organized under local leadership, thirteen temples have been constructed, and the LDS Church lists its membership in Mexico at more than a million members.[87] But the 2010 Mexican census lists only 314,932 Mexicans who self-identified as Latter-day Saints.[88] This discrepancy in numbers of converts as opposed to the number of those who self-identify as members very likely mirrors a similar trend among evangelicals in Mexico, as reported by Kurt Bowen. Bowen notes that in the 1980s, half of those raised as evangelicals dropped their affiliation with evangelicalism as adults, and between 1980 and 1990 only 32 percent of those baptized into evangelicalism chose to retain their affiliation.[89] Clearly, opportunities for further research in apostasy studies on Latter-day Saints in Mexico continue to present themselves, and these opportunities will undoubtedly provide valuable insight to the field in general, if and when they are included in contemporary investigations.

NOTES

1. Kurt Derek Bowen, *Evangelism and Apostasy: The Evolution and Impact of Evangelicals in Modern Mexico* (Buffalo, NY: McGill-Queen's University Press, 1996), 6.
2. F. LaMond Tullis, "A Shepherd to Mexico's Saints: Arwell L. Pierce and the Third Convention," *BYU Studies* 37, no. 1 (1997–1998): 127–57.
3. Ibid., 140.
4. Roger Finke and Rodney Stark, *The Churching of America, 1776–2005: Winners and Losers in Our Religious Economy* (New Brunswick, NJ: Rutgers University Press, 2008), 232.
5. Ibid., 127–28.
6. Gerry R. Flake, "Mormons in Mexico: The First 96 Years," *Ensign*, September 1972. https://www.lds.org/ensign/1972/09/mormons-in-mexico-the-first-96-years?lang=eng.
7. Deborah Baldwin, *Protestants and the Mexican Revolution* (Urbana: University of Illinois Press, 1990), 157; Tullis, "Shepherd to Mexico's Saints," 128.
8. Baldwin, *Protestants*, 169, 177–79.
9. Tullis, "Shepherd to Mexico's Saints," 131, 141.
10. Amelia Dominguez Mendoza, "Los mormones: surgimiento, expansion, crisis y asentamiento en Mexico," *Graffylia* 1, no. 2 (Summer 2003): 133–41.
11. Ibid., 139.
12. Ondina E. Gonzalez and Justo L. Gonzalez, *Christianity in Latin America: A History* (Cambridge, UK: Cambridge University Press, 2008), 65, 299.
13. Agricol Lozano Herrera, *Historia del Mormonismo en Mexico* (Mexico City: Editorial Zarahemla, 1983) 79.
14. Margarito Bautsita, Diary, April 26, 1936. Bautista uses the phrase "de raza Mexicana" in his diary; F. LaMond Tullis and Elizabeth Hernandez, "Mormons in Mexico: Leadership, Nationalism, and the Case of the Third Convention," http://www.orsonprattbrown.com/MexicanMission/third-convention.html.
15. Tullis, "Shepherd to Mexico's Saints," 129.
16. Tullis and Hernandez, "Mormons in Mexico," 139.
17. Flake, "Mormons in Mexico."
18. Mexican Mission, *Manuscript History and Historical Reports*, May 6–8, 1937, The Church of Jesus Christ of Latter-day Saints. LR 5506 2 v. 5, Box 2, folder 2 of 2.
19. Mendoza, "Los mormones," 139.
20. Elisa Pulido, oral history interview with Daniel Taylor, December 15, 2010, transcript in author's possession. Daniel Taylor was a missionary in Mexico from 1944 to 1946. He worked a portion of his mission in the mission office as the

editor of the *Liahona*, a periodical put out by the mission. He also hired faculty for new church schools and was a driver for Arwell L. Pierce.

21. Tullis, "Shepherd to Mexico's Saints," 127.

22. Elisa Pulido, oral history interview with Arturo de Hoyos, December 12, 2010, transcript in author's possession. A native Mexican, Arturo de Hoyos served a mission in the Mexico Mission from 1945 to 1947. He was an assistant to President Arwell L. Pierce.

23. Margarito Bautista, Diary, April 23, 1936, 226–27.

24. Mexican Mission, "History of the Mission for the Three Months Ending June 30, 1936," LDS Church Archives, Salt Lake City, LR 5506 2 v. 5, Box 2, folder 1 of 2. See also Margarito Bautista, Diary, Monday, April 4, 1936, 282.

25. Mexican Mission, "History of the Mission."

26. Ibid.

27. Mexican Mission, *Manuscript History*, May 6, 1936.

28. Margarito Bautista, Diary, April 12, 1936, June 20, 1936.

29. Elisa Pulido, oral history interview with Charles W. Eastwood, November 28, 2010, transcript in author's possession. Charles Eastwood was a Mormon missionary in Mexico from 1946 to 1948. Utah State Archives and Records Service, Salt Lake City; County: *Salt Lake*; Record Group: *Salt Lake County, Third District Court Declarations of Intention Record Books, 1896–1959*; Series: *85108*.

30. Mexican Mission, *Manuscript History*, November 24, 1934, June 24, 1936.

31. Ibid., November 14, 17, and 24, 1934, and April 27, 1937.

32. Ibid., November 18, 1934.

33. Mendoza, "Los mormones," 139.

34. Tullis, "Shepherd to Mexico's Saints," 139.

35. Pulido, oral history interview with Charles W. Eastwood, November 28, 2010, January 16, 2013, transcripts in author's possession.

36. Fernando Gomez, *From Darkness to Light: The Church of Jesus Christ of Latter-day Saints and the Lamanite Conventions* (Mexico City: MHMM, 2004), 39.

37. Ibid., 140.

38. Pulido, oral history interview with Charles W. Eastwood, November 28, 2010.

39. Pulido, oral history interview with Daniel Taylor.

40. Ibid.

41. Ibid.

42. Ibid.; Pulido, oral history interview with Arturo de Hoyos.

43. Pulido, oral history interview with Arturo de Hoyos.

44. Richard B. Summerhays, "How Temple Worship Helps the Living," *Improvement Era* 39, no. 4, April 1936.

45. George Albert Smith, Dedicatory Prayer at the Idaho Falls Temple, September 23, 1945.

46. Pulido, oral history interview with Daniel Taylor. Pierce's prediction was accurate, as by 2013 there were thirteen temples in Mexico, located in Ciudad Juárez,

Chihuahua; Colonia Juárez, Chihuahua; Zapopan, Jalisco; Hermosillo, Sonora; Mérida, Yucatan; México City, Mexico City; Monterrey, Nuevo León; Oaxaca de Juárez, Oaxaca; Madera, Tamaulipas; Tijuana, Baja California; Tuxtla Gutiérrez, Chiapas; Boca del Rio, Veracruz; and Villahermosa, Tabasco.

47. Tullis, "Shepherd to Mexico's Saints," 145.

48. Pulido, oral history interview with Daniel Taylor.

49. Tullis, "A Shepherd to Mexico's Saints," 143.

50. Ibid.

51. David O. McKay, *Gospel Ideals: Selections and Discourses of David O. McKay* (Salt Lake City, UT: The Improvement Era, 1953), 81. As the Mormon prophet, McKay increased the church's missionary force from 3,000 to 13,000 and built temples in London, New Zealand, and Switzerland. See Newell G. Bringhurst, "The Private versus the Public David O. McKay: Profile of a Complex Personality," *Dialogue* 31, no. 3 (1998): 11–32. McKay also had evangelizing aspirations for China and the nations of the Soviet Bloc, well before the dismantling of the Iron Curtain. See also McKay, *Gospel Ideals*.

52. Author unknown, "The Life and Ministry of George Albert Smith," in *Teachings of the Presidents of the Church: George Albert Smith* (Salt Lake City, UT: The Church of Jesus Christ of Latter-day Saints, 2010), xi–xl.

53. In 1935, Margarito Bautista made repeated attempts to have an interview with then Mexican president Lázaro Cardenas, but was unable to bring a meeting to fruition. See Margarito Bautista, Diary, April 17, 1935, October 4, 1935, October 9, 1935, November 7, 1935, November 9, 1935, March 23, 1936.

54. Elisa Pulido, oral history interview with Laurie Teichert Eastwood, November 28, 2010, transcript in author's possession. Laurie Teichert Eastwood was a missionary in Mexico from 1946 to 1948. To distinguish her from her husband Charles W. Eastwood, she is referred to as "Teichert" in this essay. Arwell L. Pierce, "La Mision Mexicana en una Epoca Histórica," *Liahona* (July 1946): 272; F. LaMond Tullis, *Mormonism in Mexico: The Dynamics of Faith and Culture* (Logan: Utah State University Press, 1987), 137. The hymn sung by attendees at the conference is the LDS hymn "We Thank Thee O God for a Prophet."

55. Museo de Historia de Mormonismo en Mexico, oral history interview with Agricol Lozano Herrera, 1997, transcript with the Museo de Historia de Mormonismo en Mexico.

56. Tullis, "Shepherd to Mexico's Saints," 147.

57. Pulido, oral history interview with Charles W. Eastwood, January 16, 2013.

58. Tullis, "Shepherd to Mexico's Saints," 149–50.

59. Ibid.

60. Pulido, oral history interview with Charles W. Eastwood, November 28, 2010.

61. Pulido, oral history interview with Charles W. Eastwood, January 16, 2013; Pulido, oral history interview with Laurie Teichert Eastwood, January 16, 2013.

62. Pulido, oral history interview with Daniel Taylor.
63. Pulido, oral history interview with Charles W. Eastwood, November 28, 2010; Pulido, oral history interview with Laurie Teichert Eastwood, November 28, 2010; and Pulido, oral history interview with Daniel Taylor.
64. Pulido, oral history interview with Charles W. Eastwood, November 28, 2010; Pulido, oral history interview with Laurie Teichert Eastwood, November 28, 2010; and Pulido, oral history interview with Daniel Taylor.
65. Pulido, oral history interview with Charles W. Eastwood, November 28, 2010; Pulido, oral history interview with Laurie Teichert Eastwood, November 28, 2010; Pulido, oral history interview with Daniel Taylor; and Pulido, oral history interview with Charles W. Eastwood, January 16, 2013.
66. Pulido, oral history interview with Daniel Taylor.
67. Hugo Nutini, "Native Evangelism in Central Mexico," *Ethnology* 39, no. 1 (Winter 2000): 29–54.
68. During this era, many LDS missionaries in Mexico used the term "convencionistas" to describe all dissenters who had originally split from the LDS Church at the time of the Third Convention, whether they were still affiliated with the Convention or not.
69. Laurie Teichert Eastwood, Missionary Journal, June 7, 1946, Cuautla-Morales, Mexico. Unpublished, in author's possession.
70. Teichert, Missionary Journal, July 14, 1946, Cuautla-Morales, Mexico.
71. Ibid., September 10, 1946.
72. Pulido, oral history interview with Laurie Teichert Eastwood, January 16, 2013.
73. Elisa Pulido, oral history interview with Ruth Torres, January 6, 2011, transcript in author's possession. Torres was a Mormon missionary in Mexico.
74. Ibid.
75. Pulido, oral history interview with Laurie Teichert Eastwood, January 16, 2013.
76. Ibid.
77. Ibid.
78. Teichert, Missionary Journal, October 16, 1946, Cuautla-Morales, Mexico.
79. Ibid., October 20, 1946.
80. Pulido, oral history interview with Ruth Torres.
81. Thomas W. Murphy, "'Stronger Than Ever': Remnants of the Third Convention," *The Journal of Latter-day Saint History* 10 (1998): 1, 8–11.
82. Gomez, *From Darkness to Light*, 40.
83. Pulido, oral history interview with Charles W. Eastwood, January 16, 2013.
84. Miguel A. De La Torre and Gaston Espinosa, introduction to *Rethinking Latino(a) Religion and Identity*, ed. Miguel A. De L Torre and Gaston Espinosa (Cleveland, OH: Pilgrim Press, 2006), 1–12.
85. Ibid., 1.
86. Robert Wuthnow, *Boundless Faith: The Global Outreach of American Churches* (Berkeley: University of California Press, 2009), 247.

87. "Mexican Mormons Reflect on Church Growth, Temples," Church of Jesus Christ of Latter-day Saints, October 16, 2008. http://beta-newsroom.lds.org/additional-resource/mexican-mormons-reflect-on-church-growth-temples.

88. "LDS Membership by Mexican State: 2010 Mexican Census." ldschurchgrowth. blogspot.com/2011/08/lds-membership-by-mexican-state-2010.html.

89. Bowen, *Evangelism and Apostasy*, 218.

CHAPTER SIX

Queso y gusanos

The Cosmos of Indigenous Mormon Intellectual Margarito Bautista

STUART PARKER

FOR THE LEADER of a relatively small movement never numbering more than a thousand people, polygamist Mormon schismatic Margarito Bautista (1878–1960) has received a surfeit of attention from scholars of Mormon studies with a sociological perspective.[1] Yet, from other perspectives, Bautista's valuable corpus comprising thousands of pages of books, pamphlets, correspondence, and journal entries is underappreciated. Fundamentally, there are few examples in any time and place of non-elite, indigenous people leaving such a comprehensive and fulsome archive describing a vast synthetic world view comprising a cosmology, historiography, religion, politics, and moral philosophy. From it, religion scholars have learned much about the cultural translation of Mormonism, but there is more still to learn from Bautista by following Jason Dormady's lead, contextualizing Bautista as a *callista* enthusiast.[2] Such an approach casts light on the possibilities of Mexican Revolutionary imagination and the dimming of Revolutionary optimism at the folk level. The approach I bring to this project is that of cultural microhistory, drawing on the methodologies of Carlo Ginzburg—one that seeks to tease out the origins and elements of a "folk substratum" missed in elite-focused engagements with intellectual and religious history.

This kind of rich non-elite theological-cosmological synthesis is what Ginzburg used to develop his method in *The Cheese and the Worms*.[3] This field-changing work, which examines the cosmology of Menocchio, a sixteenth-century Italian miller, focuses on elements of his thought that were, at once, at obvious variance with the mainstream and orthodox thinking of his era and, at the same time, congruent with the thinking of another Italian miller, Pighino, who appears never to have met Menocchio.[4] In *The Cheese and the Worms*, Ginzburg uses these points of congruence to highlight elements of what he terms early modern Europe's "folk substratum." To use Bautista's corpus as an access point to a Mexican substratum, I perform a similar operation. This necessitates that I locate a Mexican contemporary to be the Pighino to Bautista's Menocchio; for this role, I choose government minister, philosopher, and presidential candidate José Vasconcelos.

Unlike Bautista, who came from humble origins in a Nahua-speaking village and whose only claim to fame comes from his founding of a schismatic branch of a marginal religion in Mexico, 1929 presidential candidate and former secretary of public education José Vasconcelos (1882–1959) could never be considered non-elite.[5] But despite the differences of race, class, and political affiliation separating them, similarities in the two men's life narratives and their subjective understandings thereof can help us to elucidate the Mexican thought of their day, through the confluences between an indigenous villager's Mormonism and a presidential contender's idiosyncratic philosophy. Such a comparison can also help us to better understand the optimism and shattered hopes of Mexican revolutionaries who yearned for a more ambitious and radical project of social transformation.

To begin, it is necessary to make the case that the two men generated their corpora independently, especially given Vasconcelos's elite status and the substantial reach of his publications. It could be that Bautista's work is simply derivative. Fortunately, a generic feature of Bautista's works provides us with a substantial accounting of what he did and did not read. Like those of Anglo Mormons of his day, Bautista's tracts are replete with lengthy excerpts from every text with which he interacts, whether arguing against it or using it as a legitimation prop. And so it is noteworthy that, despite the appearance of Vasconcelos in a pivotal episode in his first and longest work, *La evolución de México: sus verdaderos progenitores y su origen; el destino de América y Europa*, Bautista never quotes him. Taken together with the absence of any distinctively Vasconcelan terminology, it seems doubtful that either man ever read the other's work.

THEMES IN THE EARLY AND LATER CAREERS
OF BAUTISTA AND VASCONCELOS

Both men began their careers in the first decade of the twentieth century as advocates for US-based interests, and they focused much of their early work on representing to fellow Mexicans the desires of their American patrons.[6] A period of intense Revolutionary optimism followed with respect to the changes unleashed through the processes of nationalization and emancipation underway in 1910. Both spent much of the period from 1910 to 1940 in America's Hispanic southwest borderlands, which Bautista termed "External Mexico," the place where Vasconcelos was educated (he attended primary school in Eagle Pass, Texas) and where much of both men's thinking gelled.[7] External Mexico was not just a place but a demographic reality, numbering more than a million Mexican citizens who continued to participate in the Mexican state through consulates as both migrant laborers and as exiles, Bautista falling into the latter group from 1912.[8] Vasconcelos campaigned exclusively in this region in the first months of his presidential campaign and Bautista directed the majority of his missionary efforts there between 1910 and 1935.[9]

And it was here that the only encounter between the two took place, at a campaign rally for Vasconcelos in California in 1929. In Bautista's account, he attended the event expecting to hear a speech celebrating the candidate's career as education minister. Instead he was treated to "dark and horrifying storm" of negativity concerning the Maximato of Plutarco Elías Calles, which brought Bautista to his knees and triggered a deep existential crisis that he likened to Jonah's experience in the belly of the whale. Upon emerging from his metaphorical whale but while still in self-imposed exile, Bautista penned his first and best-known work, *La evolución*, as a direct response to Vasconcelos and "dedicated to the heroes of our Mexican Revolution."[10]

Bautista made clear that *La evolución* reacted not to Vasconcelos, the revolutionary, but to Vasconcelos, opponent of former president and power broker Calles.[11] In the times in which Bautista wrote, writers of patriotic Revolutionary histories engaged in similar intellectual sleights of hand as they sought to create a hagiography of the revolution: redescribing enemies and rivals as friends and allies in a shared project of liberation and bifurcating the careers of Revolutionary heroes who had fallen out of favor with the regime. These histories created for the former a good and patriotic past and for the latter a disappointing and disloyal present.[12] The state-sponsored hagiography that transformed Zapata, Villa, and Caranza into allies in Revolutionary nationalism substantially leavened Bautista's early writings. In *La evolución*, there is no Mexican leader (other than Porfirio Díaz and Hernan Cortés) whom Bautista does not praise as a national hero, describe in superlative terms, and depict as allied with their predecessor, up to and including Pascual Ortiz Rubio (1930–1932), who held office when most of the book was written.[13] And Vasconcelos is not the only national hero whose career is split into two phases; Álvaro Obregón (1920–1924) is declared a fallen national hero following his split with the Calles clique, although Bautista explains this as resulting from his war against the racially elect Yaqui.[14]

If one were to narrate Bautista's own life from an orthodox Mormon perspective, one could apply a similar periodization, bifurcated by his break with the LDS Church. Like Vasconcelos, his career also reached its crescendo in leading ultimately unsuccessful reform movements in the first generation after the revolution.[15] And he, too, later concluded that the 1910 Revolution had failed, and blamed the shattered hopes of that failure on his former allies.[16] Bautista similarly descended into a literarily prolific yet socially marginal period of crankish political and religious conservatism, characterized by anti-Semitism, conspiratorial thinking, and an understanding of Mexicans as a "fallen people."[17]

For Bautista, the pivot point was the failure of a movement called the Third Convention. After seeking the official LDS Church's endorsement of *La evolución* and being rebuffed, Bautista returned to Mexico in 1934 and aligned himself with a group of Mexican converts chafing under Anglo-Mormon ecclesiastical domination, demanding that a person of Lamanite Mexican descent (*pueblo lamanita mexicano*) become the next head of the LDS Church in Mexico.[18] This movement for autocephaly, named for the meeting at which the schism had taken place, drew one-third of the Mexican members out of the LDS Church. Existing from 1936 to 1946, the Third Convention comprised two factions: a moderate majority advocating simple leadership by mestizo or indigenous Mexican citizens and a radical group, led by Bautista, whose set of demands only grew as the schism deepened.[19]

La evolución is concurrently a Mexican nationalist text and an early, possibly cognate, Lamanite text. Lamanite is an identity category derived from the Mormon scripture, adopted by many converts to the Mormon religion

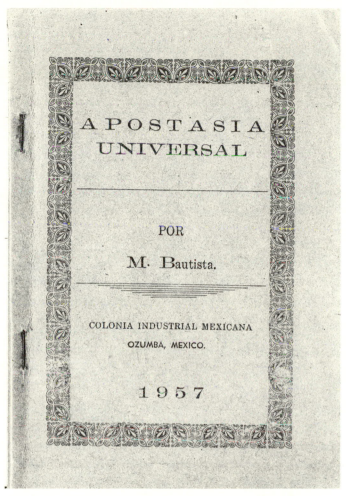

Apostasia Universal is one example of the many brochures produced by Margarito Bautista after his split with the LDS Church. Photo courtesy of Stuart Parker.

who are of Polynesian and Amerindian descent.[20] Early Mormons understood the term "Lamanite" as a pejorative, as the Lamanites were described as a fallen people given to savagery and, in nineteenth-century Mormonism, unproblematically conflated with American Indians. Bautista's writings are among the first by self-identified Lamanites that instead argue the identity to be a prophetically exalted one, based on scriptural prophecies concerning the group's millennial conversion and resulting pivotal role at the *eschaton*.[21]

This millennial optimism in the early parts of Bautista's writing mirrors that of Vasconcelos. In the first period, both wrote about Mexico as an elect nation (due, in large measure, to its special racial makeup), whose Revolutionary innovations would make it both the envy of the world and the state that would lead the whole of Latin America in a vast project of political integration and global leadership.[22] While both spoke admiringly of Mexico City as a capital, each placed the millennial state capital outside Mexico's national borders.[23] Vasconcelos proposes the creation of a new city in the Amazon Basin, "Universopolis," while Bautista hews close to Mormon scripture that places Zion, capital of the millennial kingdom, just outside of Kansas City, Missouri.[24] This is likely because Mormon prophecies of Christ's millennial rule centering on Jackson County, Missouri (where the LDS members were based from 1832 to 1838), are among those most closely entwined with prophecies concerning the exaltation of the Lamanites at the eschaton, their mass conversion and demographic resurgence, and the construction of the temple from which Christ will rule.

TIME, RACE, AND THE FUTURE OF MEXICO

Both Bautista and Vasconcelos subscribe to dispensational theories of history that they fashioned out of the ideologies and texts with which they were familiar. I use the term "dispensational" in its general religious-studies (as opposed to specifically Mormon) sense. Dispensational understandings of history are rooted in a religious cosmology that organizes time into distinct ages or dispensations, often ending in a cataclysmic or reordering event. Examples include Hesiod's Gold, Silver, and Iron Ages, or the Five Suns of Nahua thought. Using Auguste Comte, Herbert Spencer, and Pythagoras as support, Vasconcelos's *Raza cósmica* offers a three-age system culminating in the dawning third utopian age of aesthetics, while Bautista eschews traditional Mormon dispensationalism that posits a seven-millennium human history in favor of his own tripartite system of the Age of the Jews, the Age of the Gentiles, and the Age of the Lamanites.[25] For both, the terminal dispensation centers on Mexico because of its racial makeup.[26] Vasconcelos, in *The Cosmic Race* (published in Spanish as *La raza cósmica*), envisions a race in which all inferior and prior races will be subsumed through a process of *mestizaje*, facilitated by a new eugenics of aesthetics—beauty-based natural selection.[27] In Bautista's case, the reassertion of Lamanite blood will do the job. While Vasconcelos posits the fundamental superiority of the Hispanic people in whom other races' flaws will be diluted or annihilated, Bautista makes the same argument for the Mexicans and others he terms "Nahuatl-speaking Chichimecs," the best and most authentic Lamanites.[28] For both men, there is a Mexican race, even if it comprises racial and lineage groups of unequal value that, forged through the revolution into a cohesive race, will go forth and lead the world.[29]

Both dispensational systems also invoke a lost Christian Golden Age in America. For Vasconcelos this age stretches from Cortés's providential arrival at Veracruz, prior to which there was no Mexico and, ergo, no Mexican history, to the inauguration of the Bourbon reforms in the eighteenth century.[30] During this period, Hispanic civilization unified America through extraordinary Renaissance men like Cortés with accomplishments as scholars, poets, warriors, and noble leaders.[31] For Bautista, the lost Christian Golden Age is the two-century period described in the Book of Mormon, between AD 34 and 234, when a society founded by the risen Christ excelled the whole world not just in holiness and virtue but in science, education, the arts, economics, and political organization.[32]

Despite their continued affiliation with US-based organizations (in Vasconcelos's case, a number of large corporations for whom he served as legal counsel and adviser, and, in Bautista's case, the LDS Church and, later, Mormon fundamentalists) their respective early writings are suffused not merely with a belief in an elect Mexico, but with anti-US nationalism.[33] Bautista is critical of American land ownership in Mexico and sees government expropriation of American mineral and agricultural holdings as a divinely mandated process that will convert the Revolutionary state into Christ's millennial reign, by what he calls the Law of Restitution.[34] Both men foresee an ultimate victory of Mexicans over their Yankee oppressors, arising from the natural superiority of Christian values to those of unfettered capitalism, and effected through nonviolent means—specifically, demographic growth and cultural exchange, for Vasconcelos, and, for Bautista, divine intervention.[35] This victory would bring about a total global reordering based around a novel transformative Mexican episteme.[36]

Within the small community of Mexican Hispanic Mormons, Bautista's *Evolución* exerted an extraordinary impact and became the text around which the Third Convention rallied. The church's largely mestizo base of converts in southern and central Mexico praised the book, as it exalted them over the Anglo Mormons of Utah as the most proximate to the Lord in the impending millennial kingdom. But, for obvious reasons, the Utah Church's hierarchy failed to appreciate the book, leading to their decision to suppress it and Bautista's decision to throw his lot in with the Third Convention.[37]

For the post-convention Bautista, Mexico was no longer the millennial kingdom in embryo but a fallen state that had missed its chance at greatness. But, as for Vasconcelos following his electoral defeat, Bautista's shift in perspective was pessimistic but stopped short of despair. While the vast majority of Lamanites, as exemplified by the Third Convention, had failed to heed the prophetic call, a few years yet remained, in which some small remnant might still fulfill their historical destiny.[38] For this reason, Bautista promotes "procrastination" as the worst of all human sins, noting that the hour to build the temple and create the kingdom may already have passed.[39] These views closely paralleled the evolution of Vasconcelos's thought concerning Universopolis.[40]

Beginning in the late 1940s, not long after Vasconcelos's anti-Semitic turn (contemporaneous with his elevation of African decolonization to a threat equal in magnitude to that of the International Zionist Conspiracy), Bautista also suddenly began foregrounding the most antiblack and anti-Semitic Mormon doctrines and nondoctrinal folk beliefs, identifying Africans as an accursed people controlled by evil spirits, who merited eternal enslavement.[41] But this embrace did not entail any newfound appreciation of Gentiles (or cause Vasconcelos to warm to indigenous people). Cortés and the conquistadors were now conflated with Yankee imperialist corporations, an incorrigible people, used by God only as a scourge when his chosen peoples have let him down.[42] It is also around this time that both corpora took on a more generalized nostalgia. Vasconcelos increasingly looked to the Catholic Church's anti-modernist period, when it generated the *Syllabus of Errors*—the 1864 papal document that condemns earlier ideas on religion, philosophy, and society that were previously supported by the Vatican.[43] Bautista similarly fixed on the views that he espoused at the time of his conversion, exalting polygamy and economic communalism, both of which had been abandoned by the LDS Church by 1935.[44]

Neither Vasconcelos nor Bautista labeled themselves as *indigenistas*, yet their visions of Mexico could easily be characterized as part of the discourse of *indigenismo* that verged on a hegemonic status in the Revolutionary state.[45]

The social science of Mexican anthropologist Manuel Gamio (1883–1960) and others reconciled the supposedly benighted state of indigenous peoples in the present with the classical past and future greatness of the Mexican Indian. This movement simply recast a long-held Mexican belief, continuous through the Porfiriato, dating back to Las Casas's *Apologética Historia Sumaria*, in social-scientific terms, amplifying the tradition of comparing the pre-Columbian past to Europe's classical past, celebrating past but not present Indian greatness.[46] Bridging classical greatness to imminent future greatness was exemplified in discourse of the Agrarian Reform, connecting pre-Columbian communalism to cutting-edge collective farming.[47]

Both men's refusal to engage with social-scientific terminology allows us to see a folk substratum more clearly in their work, one reflective of a heritage of baroque Franciscan thought. By the end of the sixteenth century, during the age of *congregación* (the process by which indigenous peoples were resettled in planned utopian communities created by religious officials), ideas of an Edenic Indian past and present gave way to this tripartite periodization as the dominant Spanish understanding of the encounter with the Mexico's Central Valley civilization.[48] This metanarrative arose from Joachim of Fiore's three-dispensation, Trinitarian system that situated his time at the dawn of the terminal third "Age of Spirit."[49] The first age constituted a glorious imperial, so-called classical past of high culture, arts, science, and technology paired with imperial greatness, followed by a dark age of barbarism and ignorance, followed, in turn, by a future quasimillennial age of renewal, enlightenment, and conversion.[50]

Congruence between the thinking of early baroque (1521–1580) Franciscan missionaries to Mexico Bernardino de Sahagún and Toribio de Benavente, aka Motolinía, is particularly notable in Bautista, who shares the former's claim that Maya and Nahua peoples descended from Israelite migrants during the first millennium BCE and the latter's claim that, while Mexico would be the site of an elect millennial state that would trigger the third age, its new converts would create a new global capital outside Mexico's borders (usually Jerusalem).[51] As centuries wore on, the present remained at the same point in the millennial teleology, at the degenerate nadir with just the first glimmers of the third age over the horizon, with the hopes for the millennial third age affixed to a long series of political and religious projects of which the revolution emerged as the latest.[52] Throughout their respective careers, even as they declined into pessimism, both Vasconcelos and Bautista offered a near-identical periodization, celebrating the Toltec past as a golden age,

understanding the state of indigenous peoples during the Porfiriato as one
of degradation, and foreseeing a utopian future, in which the Indian will be
fully integrated and greatness will be restored.[53]

Like indigenismo, the anti-clericalism of the Maximato can be misunder-
stood when justified through the social-scientific language of the time; as
Dormady points out, "separation of church and state" actually masked an
ongoing competition between church and state over key social functions in
Catholicism.[54] The work of Bautista and, to a lesser extent that of Vasconcelos,
articulates instead of masking the undesirability of church-state separation
in the thinking of many Mexicans. Continuous with the Porfiriato, the governments of Madero, Carranza, and Obregón paid lip service to the 1857 and
1917 constitutional limitation of foreign clergy, public worship, and church
involvement in politics and land ownership.[55] Calles's regime, on the other
hand, attempted systematic enforcement—not to achieve separation but
rather nationalization.[56]

This nationalization (versus secularization) project helped to attract
Bautista to *callismo* and inspired his self-funded extension of his two-year
Mormon mission into a pro-Calles speaking tour of External Mexico beginning in 1926, a generosity reciprocated in 1935 by printer and high-ranking
presidential ally Apolonio Arzate, who published *La evolución*.[57] It is during
this extended tour that Bautista developed his distinctive take on church
nationalization, seeing it as a means to draw Mexicans away from an apostate
Catholicism and toward a true and liberal faith, a take not so different from
that of the contemporaneous efforts by the presidency and four pro-
Maximato state governors who created the short-lived Mexican Apostolic
Church.[58]

As with his views on the Agrarian Reform and the "gathering of Israel,"
Bautista understood the establishment of a single, state-organized Mexican
church as one of the key means by which the Revolutionary state, Zion in
embryo, would bring about the millennial kingdom. (Indeed, state-sponsored
efforts to repatriate Mexicans living abroad could therefore be understood as
the "literal Gathering of Israel.[59]) This church would be established by a
"National Religious Convention," in which representatives of every faith
would deliberate under the neutral auspices of the state to discover the true
and correct religion for the Mexican people, throwing off, in the process, the
creeds "we have received from Europeans."[60] Because Mormonism to
Bautista was both indigenous to Mexico and based on the "science of priesthood," patriotic, educated, and scientific men, devoid of egotism and

personalism, could guarantee the church's success.[61] In this vision, the Calles clique, the "true shepherds [of the] national flock," not only reintegrated Mexicans living abroad, as per the "gathering," but absorbed all Mexicans into a cohesive, monolithic, national community, encompassing all lands, resources, institutions, and people in a new theocratic order.[62] Such a vision not only resonated with the highest aspirations of pre-1890 Mormonism but also with early Franciscan dreams of Mexico as an ideal indigenous Christian theocracy and beacon to all nations.[63]

One of the most intriguing convergences of Bautista's and Vasconcelos's thought about both the past and future of Mexico is their engagement with the Victorian Quetzalcóatl myth. Mormon apologist Paul Hanson offers a classic elaboration of the myth, arguing that Mesoamerican iconography and myth reveals Quetzalcóatl as a "white and bearded man born of a virgin, introducing religious rites, working miracles, prohibiting blood sacrifice, establishing an order of priests, disappearing without suffering death, leaving a promise to return at some future date, ascending to heaven, and worshipped as the creator."[64] Fusing the nascent discipline of archaeology with a new interest in Conquest-era proto-ethnographies like those of Sahagún, this understanding of Quetzalcóatl retained considerable popularity and credibility, especially early in Bautista's career, who gives the mythological figure extensive proof text in *La evolución*.[65] Given the ubiquity of the Quetzalcóatl myth, its employment by Bautista and Vasconcelos reveals little.[66] What is noteworthy is that while mainstream narratives work to conflate multiple narrative episodes and divinities into a single man and mission, Bautista and Vasconcelos effectively fill Mexican history with multiple Quetzalcóatls, extending for centuries or millennia both backward and forward from the time of writing. Bautista, furthermore, disassociates the myth of the ancient leader/god from the "returning white gods" myth of the Conquest. [67]

While Anglo Mormons used the myth to support their claim that Jesus Christ had come to the New World and conducted a highly successful ministry in AD 34 and 35,[68] Bautista rejected the association with Christ, the conflation of divinities, and the "returning white gods" myth.[69] Instead, he drew on the rich local, much-studied Anglo-Mormon folklore of the Three Nephites, virtuous men who were conferred immortality by Christ during his American mission and were tasked with ministering to people in the Western Hemisphere through prophecy, healing, and teleportation, among other miracles, which chronicled in literally hundreds of sightings beginning in the 1850s.[70] Importing this tradition to his Spanish-speaking audience in *La evolución*, Bautista uses this to explain the Lamanites' loss of the knowledge of their true origins and history and consequent creation of "Huitzipochtlis and Quetzalcóatls [*sic*]" to explain their pre-Columbian visitations.[71]

For Vasconcelos, plural Quetzalcóatls evolved to constitute a crucial structuring element in his historical thought, rivaling the three-age system itself. This can be viewed as an entailment of his amplification of the very element of the Quetzalcóatl myth that Bautista most strongly rejects: the returning white gods. Unlike other proponents of this theory, he views this perception as true, figuratively and literally fulfilling an ancient prophecy.[72] This prophecy is not so much an oracular truth as an observation of the dialectic of Mexican history, a succession of Quetzalcóatls, enlightened, cultured leaders opposing barbaric practices, deposed by a succession of bloodthirsty, tyrannical Huitzipochtlis.[73] Quetzalcóatl was not the first of these, nor Madero, the last.[74]

This kind of periodic recurrence of a historical figure, like the three-age system, is similar to medieval historical typology, elaborated most extensively by Joachim de Fiore, the important thinker for sixteenth-century Franciscans.[75] The three-age system is, in many respects, an entailment of his typological methodology compiled as *The Figurae of Joachim of Fiore*.[76] Unlike modern allegorical thinking, allegorized historical personages and episodes, in typological thinking, are not placed outside profane time but instead have their literal ontology/historical facticity magnified, to the point where it echoes through all time.[77]

From this point of view, we can see Vasconcelos's Quetzalcóatl as a type or figure, possessing both a specific and an infinitely recurring ontology; and his status as lawgiver, his failures, and his untimely death render him a type of Moses.[78] Even prior to the twentieth-century Mormon revitalization of historical typology a generation later, we find a number of types/figures in Bautista, such as President Benito Juárez (1858–1872).[79] He is also typologically related to Moses, but not in the manner one might expect. While Moses gave the Israelites a coercive, inferior law, Juárez gave them the so-called perfect law of free agency, rendering Moses a prophetic forerunner of Mexican liberalism. Like King Mosiah of Mormon scripture, it is Juárez who is the superior representative of the type, presiding, as he did over the transition from a coercive to a consensual social contract.[80]

CONCLUSION

Historian Terry Rugely and others argue that folk Porfirian-Mexican religious thought continued to bear the substantial imprint not merely of sixteenth-century Catholicism but of a specifically Franciscan vision thereof.[81] This world view's exaltation of new collectivities and placement of the dispossessed concurrently in sacred and profane time is strongly reflected in Bautista's writing and mirrored in Vasconcelos's. Their terminological and discursive distance from global frames in which post-Revolutionary thinkers placed themselves allows us to see their work as highly suggestive of what one might term "revolutionary Franciscan thought." Even Bautista's engagements with indigenismo, the Victorian Quetzalcóatl myth, callismo, nationalism, anti-Americanism, and other Gilded Age intellectual currents seem to betray this, especially in his rejection of conventional bounding categories in favor of a totalizing moral, political, economic, institutional, and, most importantly, prophetic order with a place for everything and everything in its place. In this way, his ethos does resemble the sixteenth-century vision of the original *atlpetl* (the pre-European ethno-political entity) that the Franciscans sought to recreate, in Christian terms, through processes of congregación.[82]

In the tradition of Ginzburg, such a suggestion is necessarily tentative. At the very least, this comparison of the works of Vasconcelos and Bautista helps to reveal the breadth of yearning on the part of some Mexicans for a revolution more radically ambitious and comprehensive in forging a new national reality than that imagined by its most enthusiastic mainstream apologists, and also the magnitude of disappointment suffered when those hopes were dashed.

NOTES

1. Thomas W. Murphy, "From Racist Stereotype to Ethnic Identity: Instrumental Uses of Mormon Racial Doctrine," *Ethnohistory* 46, no. 3 (1999): 451–80; Thomas W. Murphy, "Other Mormon Histories: Lamanite Subjectivity in Mexico," *Journal of Mormon History* 26 (Fall 2000): 179–214; Thomas W. Murphy, "'Stronger Than Ever': Remnants of the Third Convention," *Journal of Latter-day Saint History* 10 (1998): 1, 8–11; F. LaMond Tullis, *Mormons in Mexico: The Dynamics of Faith and Culture* (Salt Lake City, UT: Utah University Press, 1987);

and Armand L. Mauss, *All Abraham's Children: Changing Mormon Conceptions of Race and Lineage* (Chicago, IL: University of Illinois Press, 2003), 147–49.

2. Jason Dormady, *Primitive Revolution: Restorationist Religion and the Idea of the Mexican Revolution, 1940–1968* (Albuquerque: University of New Mexico Press, 2011).

3. Jason Dormady, "Opening Remarks," Mormon Research in Latin America Panel, Rocky Mountain Council for Latin American Studies conference, Park City, UT, March 29, 2012.

4. Carlo Ginzburg, *The Cheese and the Worms: The Cosmos of a Sixteenth-Century Miller,* trans. John and Anne Tedeschi (Baltimore, MD: Johns Hopkins University Press, 1980), 118–24.

5. José Vasconcelos, *A Mexican Ulysses,* trans. and ed. W. Rex Crawford (Indianapolis: Indiana University Press, 1963), 37; Dormady, *Primitive Revolution,* 64.

6. Luis A. Marentes, *José Vasconcelos and the Writings of the Mexican Revolution* (New York: Twayne Publishers, 2000), 3; Dormady, *Primitive Revolution,* 70–71. For Bautista, this was the LDS Church; for Vasconcelos, it was US business interests.

7. Dormady, *Primitive Revolution,* 71; Marentes, *José Vasconcelos and the Mexican Revolution,* 11–14; and Vasconcelos, *Mexican Ulysses,* 24–31.

8. George J. Sánchez, *Becoming Mexican American: Ethnicity, Culture and Identity in Chicano Los Angeles, 1900–1945* (New York: Oxford University Press, 1993), 111–15; Dormady, *Primitive Revolution,* 67.

9. Marentes, *José Vasconcelos,* 14, 150; Dormady, *Primitive Revolution,* 69.

10. Margarito Bautista, *La evolución de México: sus verdaderos progenitores y su origen; el destino de América y Europa* (Mexico City: Arzate Brothers, 1935), title page, 80–82; Dormady, *Primitive Revolution,* 71.

11. Bautista, *La evolución,* 80.

12. Thomas Benjamin, *La Revolución: Mexico's Great Revolution and Memory and Myth* (Austin: University of Texas Press, 2000), 99–100, 123–27, 146.

13. "Presidente Francisco I. Madero y los que le han sucedido . . . han sido fuentes vivas y verdaderos baluartes de nuestra patria" (*La evolución,* 84). *La evolución* identifies the following "heroes": Moctezuma II (41), Benito Juárez (55), Pascual Ortiz Rubio (63), José Morelos (64, 141), Cuauhtémoc (65), Emiliano Zapata (68), Madero (84), Álvaro Obregón (84, 86), Calles (85–86), Miguel Hidalgo (141), and Mariano Matamoros (141).

14. Bautista, *La evolución,* 84–85; Marentes, *José Vasconcelos,* 32.

15. Marentes, *José Vasconcelos.* In Bautista's case this is well illustrated in the tone of his later writings such as his repeated, lengthy rehearsals of his split with the LDS Church focusing on interpersonal conflicts, instances of personal betrayal and hypocrisy, and dire predictions as to the fate of specific individuals in the LDS Church who sided against him. Margarito Bautista, *Canje de verdades* (Mexico

City, 1944), 8–34; Margarito Bautista, *En defensa de los derechos de la casa de Israel [I]* (Ozumba, Mexico: Colonia Agricola Industrial Mexicana, 1958), 2–6; and Margarito Bautista, *Dedicado a la época histórica* (Ozumba, Mexico: n.p., 1946), 8–30.

16. Bautista, *Dedicado*, 43, 45; Marentes, *José Vasconcelos*, 64.

17. Bautista, *Dedicado*, 32, 43, 45, 53, 170–71, 183; Margarito Bautista, *En defensa de los derechos de la casa de Israel [II]* (Ozumba, Mexico: Colonia Agricola Industrial Mexicana, 1961), 10; Bautista, *La verdad que ellos me enseñaron* (Ozumba, Mexico: n.p., 1940), 129; Bautista, *¿Restituiras . . . el reino?* (Ozumba, Mexico: Colonia Industrial Mexicana, 1950), 111; Bautista, *El reino de dios en los ultimos días* (Ozumba, Mexico: Colonia Argicola Industrial Mexicana, 1960), 5; Marentes, *José Vasconcelos*, 15, 17 (although Marentes notes that the two share a stable core and many common elements); and Stuart Parker, "History Through Seer Stones: Mormon Historical Thought 1890–2010" (PhD dissertation, University of Toronto, 2010), 206–15. Bautista produced two publications prior to the betrayal, a short article entitled "A Faith-Promoting Experience" for the LDS house organ, *Improvement Era* (1920), and his magnum opus, *La evolución* (1935). But following his split with Mexican Mormonism, he produced a long series of book-like pamphlets, the longest numbering 195 pages. They include *La verdad que ellos me enseñaron* (1940), *Canje de verdades* (1944), *Dedicado a la época histórica* (1946), *¿Restituiras . . . el reino?* (1950), *Apostasia universal* (1957), *En defensa de los derechos de la casa de Israel [I]* (1958), *Contestación al agentilado de ríos y sus compañeros* (1960), *El reino de díos en los últimos días* (1960), and *En defensa de los derechos de la casa de Israel [II]* (1961).

18. Agricol Lozano Herrera, *Historia del mormonismo en México* (Mexico City: Zarahemla, 1983), 65. The meaning of "pueblo lamanita" (Lamanite people) will be canvassed shortly.

19. Tullis, *Mormons in Mexico*, 137, 141, 147.

20. Mauss, *All Abraham's Children*, 33, 80, 131–34, 146–49; Laurie F. Maffly-Kipp and Reid L. Nielson, eds. *Proclamation to the People: Nineteenth-century Mormonism and the Pacific Basin Frontier* (Salt Lake City: University of Utah Press, 2008); Richard L. Bushman, *Joseph Smith: Rough Stone Rolling* (New York: Vintage Books, 2004), 122; and Murphy, "Racist Stereotype to Ethnic Identity."

21. As extensively explored by Thomas Murphy, Armand Mauss, and others, Lamanite status is an ambivalent one within Mormonism, concurrently oppressive and empowering for converts with an indigenous identity. Mauss, *All Abraham's Children*; Murphy, "Racist Stereotype to Ethnic Identity."

22. Marilyn Grace Miller, *Rise and Fall of the Cosmic Race: The Cult of Mestizaje in Latin America* (Austin: University of Texas Press, 2004), 39; Bautista, *La evolución*, 196–97; and José Vasconcelos, *The Cosmic Race* (Baltimore, MD: Johns Hopkins University Press, 1997), 10–12, 15, 25.

23. Bautista, *La evolución*, 196–97.

24. Bautista, *Dedicado*, 41–42; Vasconcelos, *The Cosmic Race*, 25–26. The two men see these cities as centers of a larger geographical "promised land" comprising most but not all of the Western Hemisphere. Miller, *Rise and Fall of the Cosmic Race*, 31; Bautista, *La evolución*, 22.

25. Vasconcelos, *The Cosmic Race*, 28–29; Doctrine and Covenants 77:7; Bautista, *La evolución*, 42, 207; Bautista, *La verdad*, 42, 51–57, 63; and Bautista, *Restituiras*, 66.

26. Vasconcelos, *The Cosmic Race*, 13, 29–30, 34, 40; Bautista, *La evolución*, 196.

27. Marentes, *José Vasconcelos*, 91; Vasconcelos, *The Cosmic Race*, 29–30.

28. Bautista, *La evolución*, 24.

29. Ibid., 514–15. Bautista divides Mexicans into a racial hierarchy based on the type of indigenous blood they have, with Chichmecs/Lamanites on top, comprising all people descended from Nahuatl speakers who can trace their ancestry to the region north of the Mexico Valley. The middle tier is occupied by the Nahuas/Nephites/Toltecs, whom he defines as those descended from Nahuatl speakers whose origins are the Mexico Valley and areas south of there. The bottom tier is occupied by those of Maya/Mulekite blood. Those of pure European descent are excluded from Bautista's Mexico (Bautista, *La evolución*, 103, 129, 138, 219, 551). Unlike Bautista, Vasconcelos began with an egalitarian theory of Mexican race but, by late in his career, had moved to the position that pure Indians were non-Mexican and that Indian blood made one less Hispanic (Marentes, *José Vasconcelos*, 45, 61, 91).

30. Marentes, *José Vasconcelos*, 101.

31. Ibid., 15–17.

32. Bautista, *La evolución*, 36.

33. Marentes, *José Vasconcelos*, 3; Mauss, *All Abraham's Children*, 3, 32–33; Vasconcelos, *Mexican Ulysses*, 80–81; Bautista, *La evolución*, 52, 66. Margarito Bautista, *Contestación al Agentilado de Ríos y sus compañeros* (Ozumba, Mexico: Colonia Agricola Industrial Mexicana, 1960), 4.

34. Bautista, *La evolución*, 102–3.

35. Vasconcelos, *The Cosmic Race*, 29, 35; Bautista, *La evolución*, 116–17, 196, 207–8.

36. Miller, *Rise and Fall of the Cosmic Race*, 31; Bautista, *La evolución*, 248, 483.

37. Tullis, *Mormons in Mexico*, 122–25.

38. Bautista, *Dedicado*, 41; Bautista, *La verdad*, 81, 106, 110; and Bautista, *Restituiras*, 25, 126, 170;

39. Bautista, *Restituiras*, 2. Much of Bautista's emphasis is conveyed with all caps. The editors have chosen to include the quotes without Bautista's original all-caps emphasis.

40. Vasconcelos, *Breve Historia de Mexico*, 164. In *The Cosmic Race* he warns that if Mexicans did not build Universopolis as the capital of the world, the United States would certainly build its own global capital, Anglotown. Vasconcelos thus understood himself to be living through an inferior eschaton, although holding out faint hope for a Hispanic Universopolis into the 1950s. More likely, Anglotown

would rule the world and the only hope for the Mexicans would be to increase their demographic presence within the United States (Marentes, *José Vasconcelos*, 181).

41. Vasconcelos, *Mexican Ulysses*, 69; Angel Rama, *The Lettered City*, trans. and ed. John Charles Chasteen (Durham, NC: Duke University Press, 1996) 13; Marentes, *José Vasconcelos*, 31, 176, 183; Margarito Bautista, *Apostasia universal* (Ozumba, Mexico: Colonia Industrial Mexicana, 1957), 5, 7, 9; Bautista, *Defensa [II]*, 10; Bautista, *Reino*, 5; Bautista, *La Verdad*, 129; and Bautista, *Restituiras*, 111.

42. Bautista, *La verdad*, 71; Bautista, *La evolución*, 52, 66, 102–3, 207. The only shift is his redefinition of Anglo-American LDS members from white Israelites to constituting the very quintessence of the Gentile race. Bautista, *La verdad*, 36; Bautista, *Dedicado*, 63.

43. Marentes, *José Vasconcelos*, 53.

44. Bautista, *Restituiras*, 10, 13, 85, 104, 114, 176. Armand Mauss, *The Angel and the Beehive: The Mormon Struggle with Assimilation* (Chicago: University of Illinois Press, 1994), 25; Thomas G. Alexander, *Mormonism in Transition: A History of the Latter-day Saints, 1890–1930* (Chicago: University of Illinois Press, 1986), 13, 37, 291.

45. Alexander S. Dawson, "From Models for the Nation to Model Citizens: *Indigenismo* and the 'Revindication' of the Mexican Indian, 1920–40," *Journal of Latin American Studies* 30, no. 2 (1988): 279, 285; Swarthout, *Assimilating the Primitive*, 68, 72. Indeed, Vasconcelos condemned indigenismo. Marentes, *José Vasconcelos*, 70.

46. David A. Brading, *Prophecy and Myth in Mexican History* (Cambridge, UK: Cambridge University Press, 1984), 21, 23; Swarthout, *Assimilating the Primitive*, 63; David A. Brading, "Manuel Gamio and Official Ingidenismo in Mexico," *Bulletin of Latin American Research* 7, no. 1 (1988): 78; and Dawson, "From Models for the Nation to Model Citizens," 280, 283.

47. Dawson, "From Models for the Nation to Model Citizens," 289.

48. David A. Brading, *Prophecy and Myth in Mexican History*, 9, 12; Leonard I. Sweet, "Christopher Columbus and the Millennial Vision of the New World," *Catholic Historical Review* 72, no. 3 (July 1986): 373.

49. Brading, *Prophecy and Myth in Mexican History*, 14; Sweet, "Christopher Columbus and the Millennial Vision," 371; Delno West, "Medieval Ideas of the Apocalyptic Mission and the Early Franciscans in Mexico," *The Americas* 45, no. 3 (1989): 293–95; and John Leddy Phelan, *The Millennial Kingdom of the Franciscans in the New World: A Study of the Writings of Gerónimo de Mendieta (1525–1604)* (Berkeley: University of California Press, 1956): 14–15.

50. Brading, *Prophecy and Myth in Mexican History*, 9, 13; West, "Early Franciscans in Mexico," 297.

51. West, "Early Franciscans in Mexico," 310.

52. Kenneth R. Mills, "Religion in the Atlantic World," in *Oxford Handbook of the*

Atlantic World: 1450–1850, ed. Nicholas Canny and Philip Morgan (Oxford, UK: Oxford University Press, 2011), 434. Carlos María de Bustamante's historiography typifies this three-age system which, while still scripturally informed, had substituted Joachimite Trinitarian historiography with a three-age system that saw Mexicans as analogous to the ancient Israelites (Brading, *Prophecy and Myth in Mexican History*, 43). The failures of similar projects (e.g., Independence and the *Reforma*) functioned to reinforce rather than undermine this view, with their failure being incorporated into the axiomatic failures of the second age (Mills, "Religion in the Atlantic World," 435; Brading, "Manuel Gamio and Official Indigenismo," 75).

53. Vasconcelos, *Breve Historia de Mexico*, 149, 153–55; Marentes, *José Vasconcelos*, 85.

54. Dormady, *Primitive Revolution*, 12, 131–46.

55. David C. Bailey, *¡Viva Cristo Rey! The Cristero Rebellion and the Church-State Conflict in Mexico* (Austin: University of Texas Press, 1974), 14, 36; Meyer, *La Cristiada 2*, 69; and Jean Meyer, *La Cristiada vol. 2: El conflicto entre la iglesia y el estado 1926/29*, 3rd ed. (Mexico City: Siglo veintiuno editores, SA: 1974), 44.

56. Bailey, *¡Viva Cristo Rey!* 49, 59, 76. Edward Wright-Rios, *Revolutions in Mexican Catholicism: Reform and Revolution in Oaxaca, 1887–1934* (Durham, NC: Duke University Press, 2009). Bailey and Meyer characterize the Mexican anticlericalism of the century following *La Reforma* not so much as secular pluralism but the replacement of state-sponsored Catholicism with state-sponsored atheism and Freemasonry, along with intermittent institutional assistance to Protestant groups (Meyer, *La Cristiada* 2:25).

57. Dormady, *Primitive Revolution*, 67–68, 76–78.

58. Ibid., 70. Led by self-styled patriarch Joaquín Pérez, this movement sought to draw Mexico's Catholic congregations into an autocephalic church premised on continuing episcopacy yet subordinated to the state, similar to Eastern Orthodox churches and, to a lesser extent, Anglicanism, drawing scriptural legitimacy from the Pauline Epistles and the First Council of Jerusalem, purportedly described in Luke-Acts (Meyer, *La Cristiada*, 2:149–51).

59. Bautista, *La evolución*, 550. Mormonism's "literal Gathering of Israel" commands that all surviving Israelites are to gather in a single geographic location immediately prior to the eschaton (Sánchez, *Becoming Mexican American*, 125; Bautista, *La evolución*, 72, 80; and Article 10 of the LDS 13 Articles of Faith).

60. Bautista, *La evolución*, 141. He proposes that a group of key Mexican leaders, "under the most excellent inspection and protection of our government," would be charged with determining which churches would attend and the size of their delegations (197).

61. Ibid., 195–201. Like many other nineteenth-century religious and social movements, Mormonism, like the Comtian positivism of the Porfiriato, attempted to reunite the increasingly disarticulated categories of science and religion. Arturo Ardao, "Assimilation and Transformation of Positivism in Latin America,"

Journal of the History of Ideas 24, no. 4 (1963): 521; Parker, "History Through Seer Stones," 43.

62. Bautista, *La evolución*, 72.

63. Ibid., 196; Ramón Gutiérrez, *When Jesus Came, the Corn Mothers Went Away: Marriage, Sexuality, and Power in New Mexico, 1500–1846* (Stanford, CA: Stanford University Press, 1991), 107–9; and Sweet, "Christopher Columbus and the Millennial Vision," 370.

64. Paul Hanson, *Jesus Christ Among the Ancient Americans* (Independence, MO: Herald Publishing House, 1959), 165. I use the term "Mormon" to refer to all religious groups using the Book of Mormon in their canon. Hanson was a member of the Reorganized Church of Jesus Christ of Latter-day Saints, the second-largest Mormon denomination.

65. R. Tripp Evans, *Romancing the Maya: Mexican Antiquity in the American Imagination, 1820–1915* (Austin: University of Texas Press, 2004), 13, 35; Parker, "History Through Seer Stones," 82–87, 278–87; and Bautista, *La evolución*, 25–28, 75–77, 520–22. Luis Perez Verida's *Historia de México* is another popular source Bautista mentions in *La evolución* (50, 522). Like English authors, Verida and Perez and Torres conflate disparate Andean and Mesoamerican divinities to produce a composite picture.

66. Vasconcelos, *Breve historia*, preface.

67. Camilla Townsend, "Burying the White Gods: New Perspectives on the Conquest of Mexico," *American Historical Review* 108, no. 3 (June 2003): 659.

68. Brigham H. Roberts, *New Witnesses for God*, vol. 3 (Salt Lake City, UT: Deseret Book Company, 1951), 6. Quetzalcóatl was not the only myth to refer to Jesus's first-century mission; the myths of Kukulcan, Zamná, Votan, and Viracocha did so as well.

69. These were not to be confused with culture heroes; Zamná, Votan, and others are specifically identified, through imaginative etymology, as historical figures in the Book of Mormon (Bautista, *La evolución*, 218, 262, 443). Instead, Bautista explains that the Book of Mormon, the scripture of the heroes' ancestors, specifically predicted the arrival of "WHITE AND BEARDED MEN" (a favorite and always-capitalized refrain of Bautista's) as a scourge that would destroy their nation, a scourge they had been dreading for more than a thousand years (Bautista, *La evolución*, 29, 30–31, 42–45, 51–53, 116, 134, 139–41, 269–70, 466–67).

70. Jan Harold Brunvald, *The Vanishing Hitchhiker: American Urban Legends and Their Meanings* (New York: Norton, 1981), 35; 3 Nephi 28; Hector H. Lee, *The Three Nephites: The Substance and Significance of the Legend in Folklore* (Albuquerque: University of New Mexico Press, 1949), 31, 47, 49, 55–56. So frequent were the Nephites' appearances that LDS apostle James Talmage wryly observed that they were "the most overworked men" in Mormondom. Philip L. Barlow, *Mormons and the Bible: The Place of the Latter-day Saints in American Religion* (Oxford: Oxford University Press, 1991), 136.

71. Bautista, *La evolución*, 37, 507. It is noteworthy that, as in Vasconcelos, these two divinities are not just paired but concurrently pluralized (e.g. Bautista, *La evolución*, 1, 21).

72. Townsend, "Burying the White Gods," 666–69; Vasconcelos, *Breve historia*, 52.

73. This process will continue because of the unresolved character of the dialectic powering Mexican history and will only end at the eschaton when Universopolis is constructed and the total religious, racial, cultural, and political unification of the Americas is achieved. Vasconcelos, *Breve historia*, 164, 529.

74. Ibid., 52, 150, 154–55.

75. Beginning with the Christian Church father Tertullian, or possibly Jewish theologian Philo of Alexandria, typological or figural historical thinking flourished during late antiquity and the Early Middle Ages and continued in widespread use into the early modern period. Marie-Dominique Chenu, *Nature, Man and Society in the Twelfth Century: Essays on New Theological Perspectives in the Latin West* (Chicago, IL: University of Chicago Press, 1968), 186; Erich Auerbach, *Scenes from the Drama of European Literature* (Minneapolis: University of Minnesota Press, 1984), 28–32, 36, 52; and Henri de Lubac, *Medieval Exegesis: The Four Senses of Scripture*, trans. E. M. Macierowski (Edinburgh: T&T Clark, 2000), 2:13, 16.

76. Morton W. Bloomfield, Review of "The 'Figurae' of Joachim of Fiore" *Speculum* 50, no. 1 (1975): 148.

77. Erich Auerbach, *Scenes from the Drama of European Literature* (Minneapolis: University of Minnesota Press, 1984), 34; de Lubac, *Medieval Exegesis*, 2:3, 41, 59. Important events have not only happened but also allegorize one or more events located at other points in time. Augustine renders this idea as "prophesying by means of things done . . . [or] deeds done . . . prophetically" and Bede as "allegory of the deed" as opposed to the word (De Lubac, *Medieval Exegesis*, 2:87).

78. Vasconcelos, *Breve historia*, 154.

79. Ibid., 20; Parker, "History Through Seer Stones," 54.

80. Bautista, *La evolución*, 55–58.

81. Terry Rugely, *Of Wonders and Wise Men: Religion and Popular Cultures in Southeast Mexico, 1800–1876* (Austin: University of Texas Press, 2001), xix.

82. James Lockhart, *The Nahuas After the Conquest: A Social and Cultural History of the Indians of Central Mexico, Sixteenth Through Eighteenth Centuries* (Stanford, CA: Stanford University Press, 1992), 14, 15, 20, 28–30; Townsend, "Burying the White Gods," 666–69.

CHAPTER SEVEN

Calls to War, Calls to Peace

Mormons among New Mexicans in 1880s Arizona

DANIEL HERMAN

IN BLOOD OF THE PROPHETS, Will Bagley suggests thast Mormon prophet and church president Brigham Young set the stage for the Mountain Meadows Massacre of 1857, wherein Mormon militia members slaughtered some 120 emigrants on their way to California. Young gave fiery sermons that promoted violence, told Mormons to close emigrant trails in southern Utah, and promised Paiute allies that if they attacked emigrants they could take their stock. Other scholars tell us there is no evidence that Brigham Young approved the massacre in advance. Here I argue that the question about Brigham Young's role is a distraction. It distracts from Bagley's larger argument about a "culture of violence" among 1850s Mormons. It distracts, moreover, from understanding how Mormon culture evolved in a border-lands context where identities and alliances blurred and shifted, and where Mormons became divided on questions of violence.[1]

According to Bagley, church leaders embraced the concept of Mormon innocence amid non-Mormon depravity. Everywhere Mormons settled prior to Utah, they encountered hostility that they themselves did much to foster by arriving—and voting—in blocs. They overwhelmed non-Mormon locals. Each conflict yielded greater anger on both sides. Each conflict, moreover, reinforced Mormons' belief in their own innocence, a notion that they carried to Utah. When in 1857 US troops threatened to replace Mormon theocracy with a more conventional territorial government, church leaders—especially Brigham Young—gave vent to inflammatory rhetoric intended to rouse Mormons to resist. Because Mormonism was hierarchical—obedience to priestly authority was key to being a saint—rank-and-file Mormons often moved on cues from above. "When early Mormons received 'counsel,'" writes Bagley, "it was not simply advice: it was an order from God." Having sworn oaths to avenge the murder of their first prophet, Joseph Smith, church leaders veered toward violence in 1857.[2]

Critical to an assessment of Bagley's culture of violence argument is understanding that Mountain Meadows was not the only instance of holy violence in LDS history. In earlier years, both Danites (a secret organization) and the Nauvoo Legion (a Mormon militia) had taken vengeance on non-Mormons, including the Missouri governor who had issued a so-called extermination order against Mormons. In Utah, authorities continued to sanction violence even before the 1857 crisis. In rare instances, Mormons exacted blood atonement, decapitating those deemed to have sinned so greatly that only their own blood could earn them mercy. Mormons also killed the occasional apostate who, they feared, would seek to discredit the church. Brigham Young, moreover, instructed the faithful to execute dangerous criminals. Mormon leaders may have also directed Indians, or Mormons costumed as Indians, or both—to attack the 1835 Gunnison survey sent to Utah by the Army Corps of Topographical Engineers.[3]

Settling the question of whether Brigham Young did or did not order attacks on emigrants in 1857, or for that matter, attacks on the Gunnison party in 1853, does not negate Bagley's thesis about a culture of violence. The evidence suggests that a culture of violence did exist. Other cultures of violence, one hastens to add, existed in other parts of the United States. Indeed, Utah's 1850s culture of violence likely yielded fewer homicides and attacks—discounting Mountain Meadows—than contemporary cultures of violence in the Midwest, South, and other parts of the far West. To stop at those conjectures without further studies of how Mormon history unfolded, however, is to hide truths rather than reveal them.

Before we explore this subsequent history, there is one additional aspect of Bagley's thesis to consider. The culture of violence he locates had its genesis in crises. First came crises in Missouri and Illinois, then came the crisis of US invasion in 1857. What I argue here is that the culture of violence that developed in the 1840s and 1850s quickly dissipated in later years. Through examining conflicts between Mormons and non-Mormons in Arizona in the 1880s, moreover, I contend that there was a pacifist strain of Mormonism—a strain derived from the church's early history—that competed with its impulse to violence. I argue, finally, that not all Mormon violence flowered from church doctrine. In Arizona, Mormons absorbed some of the toughness—the honor—of their non-Mormon enemies. Mormons sometimes rejected and sometimes participated in a culture of violence that came not from within, or at least not solely from within, but also from without.[4]

COLONIZATION, CONFLICT, AND RAPPROCHEMENT

Mormons first came to east-central Arizona in the 1870s, when Brigham Young sought to expand Deseret—the vast western region colonized by Mormons—by opening a corridor to Mexico. The colonists immediately met hardship. After the torturous journey across the Grand Canyon and the Colorado Plateau, they created small communities in the Little Colorado River Valley, where fierce windstorms blistered their faces and where flood alternated with drought. Being a farming people, Mormons quickly built small dams and irrigation networks. Again and again, floods washed out the dams, forcing Mormons to rebuild.[5]

Climate, however, was not the only adversary. In communities near the New Mexico border, Mormons ran up against Hispanic New Mexicans who had begun to settle Arizona only a decade earlier after Navajos were removed to Bosque Redondo. New Mexicans came largely as sheepherders. They found lush pasture in the White Mountains and the Mogollon Rim uplands that stretched all the way to the San Francisco Peaks near modern Flagstaff. Though Mormons principally farmed, they also brought cattle and sheep that competed with New Mexican stock. One particularly prominent sheep-herding family, the Candelarias—four brothers and their kin—instructed herders to drive away Mormon stock even on federal land called free range. In response, Nat Greer—member of a prominent Mormon family who had converted in Texas—"raided every sheep camp that he found and threatened to shoot the Mexican herders." Greer's brothers and hired men assisted. When Greer found a New Mexican riding one of his family's horses, he lassoed the man, then offered him a choice between death and mutilation. When the man chose the latter, Greer cut cattle marks into his ears.[6]

Greer's act of violence, it seems, had little to do with church teachings or orders from above, and nothing at all to do with blood atonement or aveng-ing prophets. More likely it had something to do with his upbringing in Texas, where youths learned a code of honor. Honor—a term used by anthro-pologists and historians—meant physical assertion, even intimidation, including gunplay and lynching. It also meant gambling, drinking, and bragging. Honor was an emotional posture in a struggle for resources. It

flourished particularly in frontier areas in the South and lower Midwest—
and later the far West—where single men, most of them young, far outnum-
bered women. Other Mormons—few of whom came from Texas or the
South—refused to condone Greer's act. Indeed, they insisted he was not a
true member of the church.[7]

The cutting incident was part of a pattern of conflict that became more
pronounced as Mormon numbers increased. To accommodate new settlers,
Mormons bought the area in and around St. Johns—along with water rights
to the Little Colorado River—from a Jewish merchant named Solomon
Barth. Though married into a sheepherding family, Barth apparently took no
counsel from his fellow New Mexicans before making the deal. Without
warning, New Mexicans found themselves surrounded by Mormons.[8]

In response, thirty New Mexicans handed the new bishop of the St. Johns
Ward, David Udall, a petition on October 26, 1880, explaining that "all the
world knows that the members of the Mormon sect live under blind obedience to their leaders," and that those leaders had sent settlers to St. Johns
with the "intention of surrounding and oppressing us." Mormons, explained
the petitioners, sought to block them from lands lying north and west of
town, lands needed for pasturage and expansion. Citing New Mexican legal
tradition, they pointed out that "Catholic" settlements had rights to surrounding lands (unfortunately, those rights did not apply under American
law). The New Mexicans announced that they would use every means in their
power "to impede the establishment of the Mormons in the surroundings of
this town."[9]

Udall immediately sought to call a public meeting to explain that
Mormons had no intention to bother New Mexicans. Mormons, he claimed,
only wished to live alongside New Mexicans, not drive them out. Privately he
blamed Barth for selling the settlers' squatter rights—rights that Barth somehow claimed as his own—without telling them. But it was likely that the
Mormon land agent, Ammon Tenney, had asked Barth to keep the deal quiet
in order to forestall resistance. In fact, Apostle Wilford Woodruff had
instructed Tenney to do just that.[10] Despite Udall's protestations, Mormon
leaders did seek to keep New Mexicans from expanding.

Apostle Wilford Woodruff—who was living in Arizona under an
assumed name to elude prosecution in Utah for polygamy—insisted that the
Saints "must hold St. Johns at all costs, or it will become a second Carthage
to our people in Northern Arizona." Carthage was the Illinois town where a
mob had murdered Joseph Smith after he was jailed. "We would rather buy

Solomon (*standing*) and Jacob Barth (*seated with cup*) with New Mexicans, drinking. Date and photographer unknown. Courtesy of the Apache County Historical Society.

out the place," Woodruff told Tenney in 1879, "so as to make a Mormon town of it, and not be mixed with Jews, Mexicans and Gentiles [non-Mormons]." "Take all the desirable places as fast as the brethren come," he continued. "I do not intend to let daylight, dark night or grass grow under my feet to stop me trying to do my duty of helping to settle Arizona or New Mexico or bringing the House of Israel into the Kingdom of God." Whether he realized it or not, Woodruff's directive promised to repeat the very scenario that had led to violence in earlier years, when Mormons, arriving en masse, had overwhelmed whole counties in Missouri and in Illinois.[11]

It was not just Mormon numbers that promised to create conflict; it was Mormon prejudice. The "blood of Cain," insisted Jesse Smith, president of the Eastern Arizona Stake of Zion, "was more predominant in those [New] Mexicans than that of Israel." New Mexicans, he suggested, carried not just the blood of Spanish and Indians, but also the blood of Africans. Mormons—like other Americans—presumed Africans to be Cain's descendants. God,

claimed Mormons, had marked Cain and his descendants with dark skin
after he killed his brother, Abel. "If we do not settle Arizona," continued
Smith, "someone else will. . . . The Mexicans will come in here and get fat
without the blessings of God." Joseph Fish, the Mormon diarist and store-
keeper, called the New Mexicans of St. Johns "renegade[s]" who had fled their
native country after committing crimes. Nor were non-Mormon whites in
the area any better. According to Apostle Woodruff, they were the same
Missourians who had driven Mormons out of that state in earlier decades.[12]

Udall must have been aware of Mormon animus toward New Mexicans
and non-Mormon whites. Nevertheless, he did not view Mormons as aggressors. New Mexicans, he recalled, "did not realize that we had no intention of
molesting them; rather they looked upon us as enemies, who had come to
encroach upon their old 'San Juan' settled by them in 1873. The Mexicans
resented us and we did not blame them very much." Udall insisted that New
Mexicans' "'squatters' rights' . . . had not been properly respected by those
[Barth and his associates] who sold the land to our people."[13] Those words—
written in later years, when Mormons and New Mexicans had long since
come to terms—seem to put a self-serving gloss on events. Certainly they
harken back to the idea of Mormon innocence. The fault, suggested Udall,
lay with a few non-Mormon cheats. He ignored his own people's assertion
and racial bias. Nevertheless, he spoke a certain truth: he and his fellow
St. Johns Mormons—in concert with New Mexicans—eventually did seek
rapprochement.

In the short term, however, conflict increased. On a popular New Mexican
holiday in 1882—St. John's day—a contingent of so-called cowboys comprised
of the Greers and their hired hands (only one of whom, it seems, was a
Mormon in good standing) strode into town carrying guns. According to
some versions of events, they had come to watch a New Mexican bullfight.
Other versions suggest that they merely wanted to buy supplies or a meal. One
wonders whether they carried guns to make a statement. Though the town's
sheriff asked them to disarm, they refused. A short time later, the cowboys
found themselves subjected to a hail of shots coming from the vicinity of
Solomon Barth's hotel. Taking refuge in an unfinished building, they fired
back. Several were wounded; one was killed.[14]

To prevent further carnage, a Mormon elder named Nathan Tenney—
Ammon Tenney's father—entered the house where the cowboys had taken
cover and tried to convince them to give up their guns. "For God's sake, quit
firing," he shouted to both Mormons and New Mexicans. The firing

temporarily ceased. From among the New Mexicans, however, came a shot that hit Tenney in the head, killing him instantly. The fighting did not resume, only because the Mormons put themselves in the sheriff's custody.[15]

Tenney died as heroic peacemaker. It may be that he was simply trying to save Mormon lives, but he risked his own life to do it. He had had other options, after all. He could have gathered Mormons from the area to defend the cowboys. He could have simply let the fight continue, given that most of the men under siege were not Mormons or, at least, not Mormons in good standing. Instead he ran between the two sides and lost his life. In doing so he illustrated a Mormon emphasis on restraint and nonviolence.

Despite—or because of—Tenney's death, conflict continued. In 1883, Mormons found themselves locked in conflict over town lots. Because owners could claim land via possession and paltry improvement—mere stakes in the ground could suffice—conflict was bound to ensue. New Mexicans, suspecting that Mormons wanted to take control of the town, quickly contested claims. "The spirit of bloodshed seemed to be in the very air," recalled Udall's second wife, Ida Hunt Udall.[16]

In one case, New Mexicans sought to drag an existing structure onto a lot held by Mormons. "In no time," recalled Udall, "Mormons, Mexicans, Jews, and 'Gentiles' assembled on the spot and feelings ran riot." Udall considered returning home to fetch his gun. One of his friends, however, put his hand on his shoulder and told him, "*Bishop, you must keep cool. Much depends on you today.*" Udall accepted his timely counsel and told Mormons to disburse, thus heading off a potentially bloody conflict. He took the added precaution, however, of using a flag to signal Mormons outside town to rush to the defense of those in town in case of trouble.[17]

It is possible that Udall simply avoided a battle that would have led to fatalities on both sides. Neither side stood to win in a melee. Udall's subsequent actions, however, show not just pragmatism but a tendency toward moderation and restraint. "To all human appearances," averred Joseph Fish, "it would be a death struggle, yet by the blessing of God, it was averted."[18] It was not God, however, that prevented a death struggle; it was an active effort by David Udall and others—including New Mexicans—to achieve rapprochement.

Non-Mormons, meanwhile, circulated a rumor that Mormons were recruiting Indians to drive out their enemies, just as they had done at Mountain Meadows. Mormons vigorously denied any role in the 1857 massacre, despite John D. Lee's 1876 conviction for ordering it. The fact that Mormons had generally spoken of Indians as the "battle ax of the Lord" gave non-Mormons fodder for their fears. Jesse Smith used the same phrase in 1883 when he urged the Saints to redouble their missionary efforts among Arizona's "Lamanites" (the Book of Mormon's term for Indians). Elsewhere, Smith called for forbearance. In May 1884, Smith insisted, "We must intercede with the Heavens and thus fight our battles. We should cultivate a spirit of forbearance and not fight with carnal weapons. The people here should go ahead minding their own business and not give way to a spirit of fear." Brigham Young Jr.—a visiting apostle—added, "We must let the Lord fight our battles. When we go before the Lord properly, our enemies melt away. We must trust the Lord implicitly and keep our tempers." Joseph Smith himself had preached a similar message prior to the Missouri expulsion in the late 1830s. Udall, meanwhile, called on the flock to "carefully avoid acts of violence."[19]

Despite Mormon forbearance, conflict continued in another realm: politics. A contingent of New Mexicans and white non-Mormons—including Sol Barth and his brothers and another important merchant, Lorenzo Hubbell, whose mother was a Hispanic New Mexican—established a political ring. In 1880, 1882, and again in 1884, they elected their own men to county office, freezing out Mormon candidates or any candidate sympathetic to them. They did so partly by throwing out votes from alleged polygamists. Mormons also accused the ring of stuffing the ballot box. By controlling county government, the ring controlled jury and teacher appointments, too. The ring refused to install Mormons or their sympathizers in either capacity.[20]

In 1883, the ring brought in a newspaper editor whose mission was to rid the county of Mormons. The editor, a US court commissioner named John McCarter, founded the *Apache Chief*, the weekly newspaper of St. Johns. In his "Official County Paper," McCarter began a drumbeat of anti-Mormon polemic. "How did Missouri and Illinois get rid of the Mormons?" wrote McCarter in the May 30, 1884, issue of his paper.

> By the use of the shot gun and rope, Apache county can rid herself of them also. In a year from now the Mormons will have the power here and Gentiles had better leave. . . . The Mormon disease is a desperate one and the rope and shot gun is the only cure. . . . Take the needed steps while it is yet time. . . . No Mormon should be allowed

to cast a vote. He has no rights and should be allowed none. Down with them. Grind out their very existence.[21]

One plot hatched by McCarter and two others was to castrate two Mormon apostles traveling in Arizona: Brigham Young Jr. and Francis M. Lyman. After Lorenzo Hubbell backed out, it seems, the conspirators failed to act.[22]

Castration plot or no, the ring continued to make life miserable for Mormons. In August 1884 it held an anti-Mormon convention in St. Johns. Those attending included the famous cowboy and suspected rustler Ike Clanton, who had escaped Wyatt Earp's wrath in the OK Corral gunfight of 1881. With him came his brother-in-law, Ebin Stanley, a former scout for General George Crook, winner of the Medal of Honor, and now a saloon keeper. Mormons suspected him, too, of being a rustler. The anti-Mormons put forward a list of nominees for county office including Lorenzo Hubbell for sheriff. Hubbell, wrote McCarter, was "a staunch anti-Mormon, an old tried citizen, and a heavy taxpayer and property owner."[23]

Perhaps because Hubbell's anti-Mormon party included Clanton and Stanley—as well as Hispanic New Mexicans—Joseph Fish testified that Hubbell had "entered into a compact with the leading horse and cattle thieves of the county pledging to shield them in their freebooting business for their support at the election." What also generated Fish's accusation, perhaps, were the actions of cowboys employed by the giant Aztec Land and Cattle Company—owners of a million acres on both sides of the Atlantic and Pacific Railroad who appeared in 1884. The Aztec claimed that several Mormon hamlets—including Snowflake, Taylor, Heber, and Wilford—lay on the lieu lands set aside by the US government for the railroad. Having bought the railroad's land, Aztec assumed the railroad's right to claim tracts in the lieu lands in exchange for tracts already claimed when Congress had made the railroad grant in 1872. Since Mormons placed their towns in areas with good grass and water, Aztec sought to evict them. To do that, cowboys—almost all of them recruited from Texas—jumped Mormon claims, pistol-whipped Mormon men, made death threats, cut down Mormon fences, ran off Mormon stock, and stole Mormon draft horses. Though in earlier years Hubbell and his New Mexican deputies had fought a veritable war with Texas cowboys ("outlaws") who crossed into Arizona, he did little—seemingly—to stop them from attacking Mormons.[24]

The year 1884 became a watershed for another reason, too. Empowered by Congress's 1882 Edwards Act, the anti-Mormons began to charge Mormon leaders with illegal cohabitation. Unable to locate David Udall's second wife—and thus unable to prosecute him for polygamy—they merely charged him with bearing fraudulent witness to a fellow Mormon's homestead claim. Numerous other Mormon leaders stood trial for polygamy, with members of the ring supplying most of the testimony. What resulted was desperation. Twelve men from the Eastern Arizona Stake stood trial and were convicted. Forty-eight others—often with their families—fled to Mexico, where they established new colonies. Udall, too, was convicted, then sent to a federal prison in Detroit.[25]

Whereas in May, Mormon leaders had called for forbearance, now they spoke of war. In August 1884, Apostle Erastus Snow—himself a polygamist—told Apache County Mormons that "no county more than yours has felt the hand of the oppressor. . . . The time is coming when God will call [persecutors] to account for it, but not until all [persecutors] have had a chance to stain their garments with the blood of innocence." He added that it was better to die while "enjoying liberty than live to be enslaved," and then declared that "the Saints have something to live for and something to die for. . . . If you are forced into it, fight like angels, and not like devils. Keep your powder dry, and if you have no gun, sell your coat and buy one."[26]

But no war came, or at least not immediately. Instead a revolution of a different sort took place. Made stronger by the influx of some two hundred families sent in 1884 from Utah, Mormons resolved to capture county government in the 1886 elections. To do so, they allied with non-Mormon ranchers who sought to end cowboy rustling. In Winslow—in the western part of the county—Mormon leaders met with non-Mormon allies to nominate pro-Mormon officials, including several Mormons. One non-Mormon was Commodore Perry Owens, a much-feared gunslinger and Navajo killer who had served as a bounty hunter for William Flake, founder of the Mormon town of Snowflake.[27] Owens ran for sheriff on the new People's Party ticket, a name apparently meant to call to mind the official LDS Church's People's Party that had dominated Utah politics for decades.

The new party promised to bring criminals to justice. If elected, it promised to choose English-speaking jurors who would be willing to prosecute Hispanic New Mexicans. The new county attorney, moreover, along with the new sheriff, would pursue cowboy rustlers and claim jumpers who bedeviled Mormons in the western part of the county. According to Hubbell, the People's Party would take another measure, too: it would set up a vigilante committee to lynch New Mexicans. Subsequent events would prove him right. But in the eastern part of the county, something very different was happening. Meeting in St. Johns, a separate contingent of Mormons and non-Mormons—again including Ebin Stanley—created the Equal Rights Party. The "Winslow Convention," lamented John (Juan) Milner, the Mormon editor of the St. Johns *Orion Era*, had been "captured by Anti-Mexicans." To counter it, he helped form the new party and became its chief publicist. Under Milner's guidance, the new party drew up a platform that denounced race prejudice, soft-pedaled the crime issue, and nominated Don Lorenzo Hubbell—erstwhile Mormon enemy but now a friend—for sheriff.[28]

Precisely why and how Hubbell had come to terms with Mormons—and why and how Mormons had come to terms with him—is mysterious. David Udall, the St. Johns bishop, noted that Hubbell became a good friend to Mormons, but failed to explain the transformation. What we do know is that, in earlier years, Hubbell seems to have nixed plans to castrate Mormon leaders. By 1886, he had moved toward rapprochement. Cowboys, too, moved toward rapprochement with old enemies (both Mormon and New Mexican), at least if Ebin Stanley's presence at the Equal Rights convention is any indication. Stanley seems to have represented the Clanton brothers and their many cowboy allies (loosely referred to as the Clanton gang). All three factions—Mormons, New Mexicans, and cowboys—seemed to fear the vigilantism brewing in the west. All three seemed ready to put old animus aside and work toward a common future. All three also realized that their earlier quarrels centered on land, water, and political power, not righteousness and evil.

Bishop Udall almost certainly endorsed the new eastern-county alliance. Lay Mormons looked to their local leaders for guidance; it is highly unlikely that John Milner had acted without Udall's counsel. During his seven years as St. Johns bishop, reported Udall, the rank-and-file (though democratic) always "sustained the bishopric[,] and unity existed." Udall had another reason to support the Equal Rights Party: some of his old enemies in the ring—now Equal Rights supporters—had signed a plea to President Grover Cleveland to have Udall pardoned. Udall's "conduct," they had written in 1885, "was such as to create for him an unblemished reputation for honesty, integrity and veracity." Signatures show a who's who of ring politicians, including Hubbell; Alfred Ruiz, the district court clerk; W. B. Leonard and Ernest Tee, members of the board of supervisors; Henry Huning, chairman of the board of supervisors; C. L. Gutterson, district attorney; William M. Rudd, county judge; Dionicio Baca, county treasurer; Antonio Gonzales, county recorder; and E. C. Bunch, probate judge. Their plea succeeded—Cleveland had pardoned Udall in December 1885.

Clearly, then, the movement toward rapprochement had begun shortly after Udall's conviction and continued in 1886. Mormons and their allies in the western part of the county, however, took a contrary tack.[29]

The campaign was waged in the pages of two competing newspapers based in St. Johns, the *Herald* and the *Orion Era*. Until 1886, the *Herald* had been an anti-Mormon paper (the fiery anti-Mormon John McCarter had edited it under the title *Apache Chief* before selling it to another anti-Mormon named Henry Reed, who changed its name to the *Herald*). For the upcoming election, however, a mysterious company of cattlemen—likely the Apache County Stock Growers' Association, now controlled by western-county Mormons and their non-Mormon allies—bought the paper and installed a pro-Mormon editor. The paper lauded Mormons for good citizenship. Far from urging readers to lynch Mormons, it called on good citizens to lynch criminals, meaning Texas cowboys and New Mexicans.[30]

The split between the factions was deep and bitter. The *Herald*—in full-throated support of the People's Party—railed against "Sister Juan y Baca Milner" and his "bastard" coalition (the Bacas were a powerful New Mexican family who supported the Equal Rights party). "If Sister Milner should lay eggs and the Equalites acts as incubator," wrote Barry Matthews, the *Herald*'s new editor, "will some student of natural history tell us what name to give the birds? Judging from the smell of the nest we should they would be buzzards or winged skunks." Repeatedly the *Herald* denied Milner's manliness and attacked his "mongrel black and tan" constituency—presumably comprised of descendants of the cursed Cain—and its message of rapprochement.[31]

The *Herald* particularly harped on the idea that the Equal Rights Party countenanced criminals. "Stock thieves," announced the *Herald*, "are calling for equal rights to follow their avocation, and they will vote for it too. One week later, the Herald observed "that there is scarcely a Mormon in the County owning stock who has not suffered loss at the hands of thieves. . . . Are the Mormons prepared to say they want this state of affairs kept up? Do they or any other class of citizens desire to be continually plundered of their property without hope of redress?" If Commodore Owens were elected sheriff, promised the *Herald*, the jail would become a "popular and fashionable boarding house," adding that there were "a large number of guests from Concho and El Tule [New Mexican hamlets] who have already spoken for rooms."[32]

In November, the People's Party won every county office save one, though Commodore Owens prevailed by just 91 votes (almost precisely 10 percefnt of those cast). The Mormon towns of Snowflake, Taylor, and Woodruff—all in the western part of the county—put him over. Those towns, reported the *Herald*, were "solid for the Winslow ticket to a man." Jesse Smith, indeed—apparently having had enough of forbearance—promoted that outcome. "Went to Taylor," he reported on October 10, 1886, "and spoke on the political situation." He advised Mormons there to vote, knowing that they would move en masse to the People's Party. He may have been the "venerable Mormon patriarch" who referred to Equal Rights supporters as "dishonorable" men who had "dug their own graves."[33]

Once elected, the new pro-Mormon county attorney went to work with grand juries to drive out alleged rustlers and criminals. They also went after former officials from the ring, including Sol Barth. In 1887, a jury convicted him in of forging county warrants and his brother of jury tampering. It also convicted the county treasurer, Dionicio Baca, of robbing the county safe. Baca's claim that masked men forced him to open the safe earned him no reprieve. His alleged attackers had left no tracks, it seems, on the frozen ground. Baca, however, was probably telling the truth. Decades later, one of Baca's kidnappers admitted the deed to a Mormon missionary named Evans Coleman.[34]

The new men in office even ran out one of the preeminent American naturalists of the nineteenth century, Edward Nelson. After his heroic survey of the Arctic, Nelson retired to Apache County to recuperate from tuberculosis. There he served briefly in county government before the Mormon-Democrat faction (another name for the People's Party) threatened to prosecute him and the former county recorder, Alfred Ruiz, for pocketing forty-eight dollars worth of county bonds. To escape persecution, Nelson moved to New Mexico.[35]

After the election, Mormons in the western part of the county talked more openly of violent reprisals against enemies. In August 1887, at least two Mormons, both from the Snowflake area, asked stake president Jesse Smith to approve their plan to murder a cowboy persecutor. He told them not to act, promising that their enemies would soon be out of the way. A week later, their persecutor was dead, killed in the first battle of the so-called Pleasant Valley War. Among his killers was James Tewksbury, who had worked for William Flake as a range detective (in effect, a paid spy).[36] Perhaps Smith knew that the Tewksbury faction in Pleasant Valley was about to go to war against Aztec cowboys and their allies. Likely he also knew about vigilante cells organized throughout the region.

To the dismay of his backers, however, Commodore Owens—despite deputizing men who acted as vigilantes—proved reticent about arresting some of his range pals, particularly a braggart and blusterer named Andy Cooper who was wanted for stealing Mormon horses. Under pressure from the Stockman's Association, the new county supervisors—all members of the People's Party—called in Owens to berate him and threaten to have him fired if he did not arrest Cooper. Indeed, they carried guns into the meeting in case he grew testy.[37]

Shortly thereafter, Owens went alone to Cooper's family's house in Holbrook and placed him under arrest. Eleven people, most of them women and children, were crammed inside. Apparently fearing that Owens would turn him over to a lynch mob, Cooper refused to go. Owens immediately shot him in the gut, then shot two of brothers (apparently in self-defense) and another cowboy (who may or may not have had a gun).[38] Only one of the wounded men survived.

Owens and his associates—including deputized stock detectives who, it seems, waged a campaign of assassination—were not the only forces in operation. "Vigilante committees," recalled one Mormon observer, "were organized by both Mormons and non-Mormons throughout the area," stretching from St. Johns to Pleasant Valley. The committees gained intelligence from two paid spies: James Houck, an erstwhile anti-Mormon, and Hook Larson, a Mormon who had fallen away from the faith. Larson, like Nat Greer—or for that matter like Commodore Owens—remained good friends with the Flakes and other Mormons nearby. He and Houck "spent weeks watching trails to and from Pleasant Valley." They would periodically "meet with everybody"—including Snowflake-area Mormons Charles Ballard, Lehi Heward, and A. Z. Palmer (William Flake's brother-in-law)—to share information. The vigilantes "meant business."[39]

On at least one occasion, Larson killed an alleged Mexican (likely New Mexican) horse thief and turned over two of the man's comrades to lynchers. Houck, for his part, arrested three white men—cowboys—accused of horse theft and gave them to another group of lynchers. Eight of the approximately twenty-eight members of the latter group were non-Mormon ranchers from Yavapai County; the others seem to have been Mormons from the Snowflake area. Elsewhere, New Mexicans ambushed another of William Flake's paid spies, Carr Blassingame, apparently to repay him for assassinating sheepherders. As Lorenzo Hubbell had warned, the People's Party planned to fight criminals not only via legal means but also via murder. In all likelihood, the vigilantes knew that the People's Party men who now controlled county government would neither investigate them nor prosecute. The territorial governor himself—Conrad Meyer Zulick—may have secretly offered the vigilantes free rein.[40]

"God heard our prayers," wrote Lucy Flake, one of William Flake's wives. "Our enemies 'fell into the pits they had digged for us' as the Lord promised they would." She estimated that Commodore Owens had killed between eight and ten outlaws. Another Mormon put the figure at thirty-eight, adding that Owens had frightened many more out of the county. "The Lord said if the Saints do right He will fight our battles," wrote a Mormon settler on New Year's Day 1888. "It is said," he added, "that New York, Boston & other places would be destroyed in the near future." The destruction of Apache County persecutors, it seems, signaled a larger cleansing in the works.[41]

In 1918 Owens died and Mormons baptized him posthumously, recalling that he had been "providentially sent." By then, much had changed. Mainstream Mormons had abandoned polygamy. The United States Forest Service regulated the range, parceling out specific sections to ranchers in order to reduce competition for grass and water and to end the killing that competition generated. The territory—along with many towns—also regulated guns.[42]

MORMONS AND VIOLENCE, MORMONS AND PEACE

Encapsulated in Apache County's bitter political struggle in the 1880s—and the terror that came with it—is a story about Mormons and borderlands violence. On the western side of the county, where Mormons lived in isolation from New Mexicans but in close proximity to Texas cowboys, Mormons decided to fight fire with fire by electing a gunslinger as sheriff and by establishing vigilante committees. Undoubtedly some Mormon voters from the eastern side of the county voted with them. Owens and the People's Party nominees, after all, promised to arrest and convict New Mexican troublemakers and criminal—or supposedly criminal—county officials. Support for gunslinger law and freewheeling vigilantism, however, came mostly from the western part of the county. Mormons there resorted to violence, even if they themselves seldom engaged in it directly.

From one perspective, western-county Mormons harkened back to the 1850s culture of violence described by Will Bagley. It is possible—though far from certain—that they knew of Brigham Young's 1853 recommendation that thieves be put to death "on the spot," or his subsequent statements that criminals deserved death.[43] Young's statements, however, did not necessarily yield a vigilante culture. Though Mormons had sometimes engaged in vigilante violence in Utah in the 1850s and 1860s—years of crisis and acute stress—such events were relatively few. Religious fervor, perhaps mixed with a more traditional Western and Midwestern propensity for "rough justice," gave rise to occasional attacks on apostates, schismatics, adulterers, and backsliding criminals whose activities embarrassed Brigham Young. Even so, Utah's lynching rate in its violent decades was far lower than that of contemporary California.[44]

Insofar as the Mormons of western Apache County embraced vigilantism, then, they were not necessarily embracing the religious violence of 1850s Utah. Those who voted for Commodore Perry Owens and participated in vigilantism were not avenging the prophets, promoting blood atonement, or attacking apostates. Certainly they had brought with them the old Mormon tale of a godly people under assault by sinners. They sometimes suggested—rightly—that cowboy attacks were part of a larger attempt to drive them away. In electing a gunslinger sheriff and joining vigilante groups, however, Mormons chose to make alliances with non-Mormons whose ideas about using violence had nothing to do with LDS doctrine. In making those alliances, Mormons identified their enemies not as religious persecutors, but as mere criminals and enemies to law and order throughout the county.

What seems clear, finally, is that Apache County Mormons, at least those on the western side of the county, embraced the same violent sensibilities— the same Western honor—that inspired both their non-Mormon allies and their non-Mormon enemies. In joining with non-Mormons to attack common enemies, Mormons in the western part of Apache County were becoming, quite simply, more Western.

That observation brings us to another point. Despite a few scholars who insist, based on limited evidence, that violence was no more endemic in the nineteenth-century far West than in other parts of the United States, the West—and the borderlands in particular—was indeed a violent place. In Texas, families and their allies prosecuted feuds against other families and their allies. Sometimes former Confederates fought former Unionists. They struggled, too, for grass and water. Range wars occurred in California, New

Mexico, Wyoming, Washington, and elsewhere. In rough mining camps like Bodie, California, homicide rates were astronomical. Frontier California, indeed, was a veritable sea of violence, some of which took the form of robbing and murder, and some of which took the form of lynching. One might argue—as scholars sometimes do—that law-abiding Westerners had to resort to lynching to clean up their settlements, since courts and sheriffs were too weak to do so. Though there is some truth in that statement, it yields much mystification. It hides the fact that vigilantism and lynching had a racial dimension even in the West. Its victims were often nonwhite.[45] It also obscures the fact that robbery, rustling, and homicide shared with vigilantism and lynching a common sociological source. All of them were acts of a so-called manly assertion of honor that evolved amid a vast struggle for resources. Lynchers and gunmen shared a common sociological mother.

One wonders whether the events of 1886 to 1888 shaped Apache County Mormons permanently, or only temporarily. History suggests the former. In 1887, the LDS Church ratified the breach between Mormon settlers—at least administratively—by breaking the Eastern Arizona Stake into two. Jesse Smith retained leadership over wards in the western part of the county, now called the Snowflake Stake. David Udall became president of the new St. Johns Stake in the eastern part of the county. Clerical segregation, however, was not enough. Over the next few years, those in the western part of the county fiercely lobbied the state legislature to gain political independence from St. Johns (Will Barnes, erstwhile organizer of the People's Party and subsequently a territorial legislator, called it "the fight of my life"). In 1895, the legislature agreed, making the western half into its own county, Navajo County. The new county chose Commodore Perry Owens—who had lost his bid for reelection in Apache County in 1888 thanks to his reputation as a killer—to be its first sheriff.[46]

Twentieth-century Mormon politicians from Navajo County—including Osmer Flake (who served in the legislature in the early twentieth century), Jake Flake (who served in the legislature in more recent decades), and Jeff Flake (recently elected to the United States Senate)—have been law-and-order conservatives. William Flake's son, Osmer, indeed, thought his greatest accomplishment in the state legislature was getting Arizona's death penalty reinstated in 1918.[47] One might also include in that list the Pearce brothers, Lester and Russell (author of controversial Arizona Senate Bill 1070, a stern law-and-order measure directed at undocumented immigrants that Arizona adopted in 2010), whose ancestor James Pearce had founded the

Mormon town of Taylor and had battled Aztec cowboys. In Navajo County, it seems, honor echoed across generations. The ferocity of 1880s vigilantism, one might argue, shares something with the fervor of anti-immigrant efforts in the early 2000s.

In what remained of Apache County occurred a different dialectic. There, Mormons lived side-by-side with New Mexicans. Partly because Mormons needed peace in order to prosper and partly because they took seriously their duty to convert the whole of the Americas to the LDS faith—including dark-skinned people who spoke Spanish—Mormons built bridges with ethnic others. Far from perpetuating Bagley's culture of violence, they sought rapprochement. Their history shows that Mormons veered toward peace as well as toward violence. In post-1888 Apache County elections, Mormons and New Mexicans seem to have regularly voted for one another and traded county offices. Interestingly, Hispanic New Mexicans held the sheriff's office continuously between 1901 and 1915. Politics, it seems, lost its rancor. In a sense, Mormons in eastern Apache County set the stage for later Mormon efforts to launch vast missionary projects in Latin America (it was Ammon Tenney who led the church's early missionary efforts in Mexico). Though historians often focus, rightly, on violence as an outgrowth of borderlands contestation, we do well to remember that negotiation and rapprochement were equally possible outcomes.[48]

It should not surprise us, then, that some of the most famous Mormons in politics came from eastern Apache County. Those politicians include David Udall's son, Levi (the Arizona Supreme Court justice who, in 1948, wrote the decision guaranteeing American Indians the right to vote) and Levi's sons, Morris (a long-time US congressman and, in 1976, a candidate for president) and Stewart Udall (a US congressman and secretary of interior). Morris's son, Mark, and Stewart's sons, Tom—both US senators—carry the family legacy of civil rights and liberalism into the present. Stewart Udall went so far as to write a book decrying Western violence, arguing that those who "won" the West were not those who wielded guns, but rather those like David Udall who worked hard and built communities.[49]

Perhaps the question of whether the conflict of 1886 and 1887 left an imprint on a few Mormon families is less important than the question of which tendency—violence or peacefulness—was typical of Mormons in the late nineteenth century. Further studies of Mormons and their Western neighbors would help answer that question. What is important to remember, however, is that contrary to Bagley's culture of violence of the 1850s, Utah

Mormons engaged in very little vigilantism and lynching in the last decades of the nineteenth century. Though a lynching belt ran from Texas to New Mexico and Arizona, thence north through Colorado, Wyoming, and Montana in the late nineteenth century, the belt did not include Utah. Generally speaking, the lynching belt followed the cattle herds—and the people—who migrated north and west from Texas and the South. The belt also followed mineral strikes and the rough miners who flocked to them; mining camps became hotbeds of vigilantism. In late nineteenth-century Utah, however, lynching rates were remarkably low (according to one report, Utah had no lynchings between 1885 and 1925).[50] If we look only at late nineteenth- and early twentieth-century Utah—from perhaps 1870 to 1925— one might argue that a culture of peacefulness prevailed.

Arizona Mormons, too, often opposed lynching. Though Brigham Young himself had suggested in the 1850s that Mormons assassinate hardened criminals, that attitude does not seem to have persisted. When the "rougher element" had invited David Udall to a "necktie party" in the early 1880s, for example—in the St. Johns courthouse no less—he refused to attend and spoke bitterly of being asked to do so. John Hunt, similarly, who served as bishop of the Snowflake ward in the 1880s, is said to have stood "like a stone wall" against Apache County lynching.[51] Given that he lived in the western part of the county—where vigilantism thrived in 1887 and 1888—perhaps somewhere along the line he changed his mind. Or perhaps he didn't; perhaps his anti-lynching counsel simply fell on deaf ears. No records tell the story. The point is simply that, although Mormons did sometimes participate in vigilantism, it is far too simple to suggest that they invariably embraced Western codes of rough justice. Some did; some did not. On the whole, they probably did not. Their particular brand of Christian Perfectionism—a perfectionism that even before the Civil War had led non-Mormon reformers to oppose dueling, drinking, gambling, and slavery, and even capital punishment—did not fit easily with rough justice.

If Mormons developed a culture of violence in 1850s Utah, then, they developed very different sensibilities in later decades. In Apache County—as in New York, Ohio, Missouri, and Illinois in earlier decades—some Mormons veered toward violence whereas others veered toward peace.[52] In Arizona, however— unlike those earlier settings—both routes brought Mormons into alliance with non-Mormons around them. Mormons in western Apache County became more like the hardened ranchers and cowboys with whom they allied (a similar phenomenon may have occurred on Deseret's other peripheries, too).[53]

Mormons in eastern Apache County may or may not have become more like
their New Mexican allies and neighbors, but they certainly formed friendships.
Like Jewish Zeligs, Mormons sought to fit in. They became less dedicated to a
tribal "we against them" sensibility and more dedicated to making allies—or
smiting them, but only with non-Mormon help. The Zelig phenomenon, one
might argue, shaped Mormonism in the twentieth century—when church
leaders actively sought to bring members into the American mainstream—far
more than did the culture of violence of the 1850s.

NOTES

1. Will Bagley, *Blood of the Prophets: Brigham Young and the Massacre at Mountain
   Meadows* (Norman: University of Oklahoma Press, 2002), 378 ("culture of violence"), 378–81. For a critique of Bagley, see Ronald W. Walker, Richard E. Turley Jr.,
   and Glen M. Leonard, *Massacre at Mountain Meadows* (New York: Oxford
   University Press, 2008). See also Will Bagley, "Blood of the Prophets: Brigham
   Young and the Massacre at Mountain Meadows, Presented to the 8th Annual
   Ex-Mormon Conference, October 5, 2002, Salt Lake City, UT, with a September
   2007 update by the historian," http://www.salamandersociety.com/interviews/
   willbagley.
2. Bagley, *Blood of the Prophets*, 13 (quotation), xv, xviii, 6–19, 377–78. D. Michael
   Quinn buttresses Bagley's thesis in "The Culture of Violence in Joseph Smith's
   Mormonism," *Sunstone* 164 (October 2011), 16–37. "Culture of violence" or no, at
   least some of those ordered by superiors to carry out the massacre at Mountain
   Meadows—perhaps even most—blanched at the thought of murdering inno-
   cents. Superiors told them, however, that refusal would preclude salvation. Or it
   might earn them "blood atonement" (ritual decapitation), which some Mormons
   believed to be the only way to earn forgiveness for the most terrible of sins.
   Bagley, *Blood of the Prophets*, 21, 50–52; Bagley, "Blood of Prophets"; Polly Aird,
   Jeff Nichols, and Will Bagley, eds., *Playing with Shadows: Voices of Dissent in the
   Mormon West* (Norman, OK: Arthur H. Clark Company, 2011), 49–54. It is critical to consider, however, that Mormonism also contained messages of peace.
   Though the Book of Mormon rivals the Old Testament in narrating stories of
   violent clashes, it also celebrates warriors who lay down their weapons. More to
   the point, Joseph Smith imparted no message of violence in revelations or teachings in the church's early years. Attacks by non-Mormons—mob actions, tarring
   and feathering, seizure of property—led Mormons to veer toward violence in the
   late 1830s and 1840s, when Danites and others organized to fight enemies. The
   result in Missouri and then Illinois was a whirlwind of bitter rhetoric—by both
   Mormons and their enemies—that spawned bloodshed and dispossession. To
   understand that cycle, see Richard Lyman Bushman, *Joseph Smith: Rough Stone
   Rolling* (New York: Knopf Doubleday, 2007), 235, 249, 352–72, 529–33, 537–50.

3. Mormon jurors tried and exonerated the Indian warriors allegedly involved in the Gunnison Massacre (the jury convicted only three elderly scapegoats, all nearly blind). The United States, however, was unable to conduct a thorough investigation of its own. Colonel Dick Kindsfater (retired), "The Gunnison Massacre," http://westernamericana2.blogspot.com/2010/05/gunnison-massacre-by-dick-kindsfater.html, article posted May 5, 2010. See also David L. Bigler, *Forgotten Kingdom: The Mormon Theocracy in the American West, 1847–1896* (Logan: Utah State University Press, 1998), 82–88, 90–92. Bigler finds neither evidence nor motive for Mormon involvement in the Gunnison killing. Bigler does, however, describe other religiously motivated killings in early Utah. See Bigler, *Forgotten Kingdom*, 123–33. See also Kenneth L. Cannon, "'Mountain Common Law': The Extralegal Punishment of Seducers in Early Utah," *Utah Historical Quarterly* 51, no. 4 (Fall 1983): 308–27; Polly Aird, "'You Nasty Apostates Clear Out': Reasons for Disaffection in the Late 1850s," *Journal of Mormon History* 30 (Fall 2004): 129–207 (see particularly 173–92); William P. MacKinnon, "'Lonely Bones': Leadership and Utah War Violence," *Journal of Mormon History* 33, no. 1 (Spring 2007): 171; Ardis E. Parshall, "'Pursue, Retake & Punish': The 1857 Santa Clara Ambush," *Utah Historical Quarterly* 73, no. 1 (Winter 2005): 64–86; and Aird, Nichols, and Bagley, eds., *Playing with Shadows*, 49–54. Some of those murdered at Mountain Meadows may have been apostates who had joined the Fancher-Baker wagon train en route to California. See Bagley, *Blood*, 147. See also Craig L. Foster, "The Butler Murder of April 1869: A Look at Extralegal Punishment in Utah," *Mormon Historical Studies* 2 (Fall 2001): 308–27; and Aird, Nichols, Bagley, eds., *Playing with Shadows*, 50. Some historians argue that violence in Utah was part of a broader Western pathology that included homicide and vigilantism. See, for example, Walker et al., *Massacre at Mountain Meadows*, viii–ix, 7–8. See also Scott K. Thomas, "Violence across the Land: Vigilantism and Extralegal Justice in the Utah Territory" (master's thesis, Brigham Young University, 2010). Though Thomas finds a typically Western pattern of violence in early Utah Territory, he notes that homicides and vigilantism of any sort became rare in Utah after 1870. One suspects that Walker, Turley, and Leonard, as well as Thomas, too readily discount the religious underpinnings of Utah violence in the 1850s. Thomas admits, however, that Mormon leaders at times countenanced vigilantism as a way to deal with crime, particularly in the 1850s and early 1860s. In early Utah, it seems, rough justice and religiously sanctioned violence blended and merged. On the concept of "rough justice," see Michael J. Pfeifer, *Rough Justice: Lynching and American Society, 1874–1947* (Urbana: University of Illinois Press, 2004).

4. On the nonviolent currents in early Mormonism, see Bushman, *Smith*, 235, 249. Scott Thomas similarly argues that Mormons on Utah's periphery—especially in Genoa County, which is now part of Nevada—engaged in patterns of violence common throughout the West, patterns that had little to do with Mormon beliefs. See Thomas, "Violence," 42–55. Though Thomas shows that at least some

of Genoa County's violence was prompted by quarrels over land and resources—the same sort of quarrels that appeared throughout the West—his discussion does not systematically examine the extent to which Mormons initiated violence (as opposed to taking defensive action against aggressors), the degree to which incidents of violence had a strong religious basis, or the rate of violence in Genoa County compared to other Utah counties. Nevertheless, his work, like mine, suggests that Mormons sometimes absorbed the culture of violence of those they encountered, particularly where Mormons and non-Mormons contested land and resources.

5. Charles S. Peterson, *Take Up Your Mission: Mormon Colonizing Along the Little Colorado River, 1870–1900* (Tucson: University of Arizona Press, 1973).

6. Evon Z. Vogt, "Intercultural Relations," in Evan Z. Vogt and Ethel M. Albert, *People of Rimrock: A Study of Values in Five Cultures* (Cambridge, MA: Harvard University Press, 1966), 52–54; Edward H. Peplow Jr., *History of Arizona* (New York: Lewis Historical Publishing Company, 1958), 2:147; James T. LeSueur, "How St. Johns Was Settled," George S. Tanner Collection (GSTC), University of Utah, Box 5, folder 25, 3; John H. Krenkel, ed., *The Life and Times of Joseph Fish, Mormon Pioneer* (Danville, IL: Interstate Printers & Publishers, 1970), 259; John Ray Hamblin, *Outlaws of Apache County* (n.p.: n.p., n.d.), 2; and George S. Tanner and J. Morris Richards, *Colonization on the Little Colorado: The Joseph City Region* (Flagstaff, AZ: Northland Press, 1977), 86.

7. Joseph Fish, "History of Eastern Arizona Stake of Zion; Early Settlement of Apache County [and] Stake Clerk's Records & Journal, 1878–1912," handwritten MS, Arizona State Library Division of Archives and Public Records (ASLAPR), 36. On honor and its constituents, see Sheldon Hackney, "Southern Violence," *American Historical Review* 74 (1969): 906–25; Bertram Wyatt-Brown, *Southern Honor: Ethics and Behavior in the Old South* (New York: Oxford University Press, 1982); Bertram Wyatt-Brown, *Yankee Saints and Southern Sinners* (Baton Rouge: Louisiana State University Press, 1985); Kenneth S. Greenberg, *Honor and Slavery* (Princeton, NJ: Princeton University Press, 1996); Richard E. Nisbett and Dov Cohen, *Culture of Honor: The Psychology of Violence in the South* (Boulder, CO: Westview, 1996); Grady McWhiney, *Cracker Culture: Celtic Ways in the Old South* (Tuscaloosa: University of Alabama Press, 1988); Dick Steward, *Duels and the Roots of Violence in Missouri* (Columbia: University of Missouri Press, 2000); and Timothy H. Breen, "Horses and Gentlemen: The Cultural Significance of Gambling among the Gentry of Virginia," *William and Mary Quarterly* 34, no. 2 (1977): 239–47. The racialized codes of honor that prevailed among Arizona settlers came with immigrants from Texas, the South, and the lower Midwest, and rooted themselves in the fertile soil of resource competition. See Daniel Justin Herman, *Hell on the Range: A Story of Honor, Conscience, and the American West* (New Haven, CT: Yale University Press), chapters 1, 5, 9.

8. Joseph Fish, "The Fish Manuscript, 1840–1926," ASLAPR, 575; Evans Coleman, "St. Johns Purchase," TS, GSTC, University of Utah, Box 5, folder 24, n.p.; and Peterson, *Take Up Your Mission*, 33.

9. The petition appears in David King Udall, *Arizona Pioneer Mormon: David King Udall; His Story and His Family* (Tucson: Arizona Silhouettes, 1959), 77–78.

10. C. Leroy Wilhelm and Mabel R. Wilhelm, *A History of St. Johns Arizona Stake* (Orem, UT: Historical Publications, 1982), 28, 30; Udall, *Arizona Pioneer Mormon*, 77–80.

11. Udall, *Arizona Pioneer Mormon*, 74–75; Lewis Allen [Wilford Woodruff] to A. M. Tenney, Sunset, Apache County, Arizona, November 24, 1879, GSTC, Box 5, folder 20.

12. John W. Tate, "Journal of John W. Tate, Oct. 1880 to July 1881," TS, GSTC, Box 5, folder 23, 37 (December 20, 1880); Jesse Nathaniel Smith, "Journal," Jesse N. Smith Papers, Harold B. Lee Library (HBL), Brigham Young University, Box 1, folder 2, 347 (May 16, 1884), 363 (September 26, 1884); Fish, "Eastern Arizona Stake," 1–2; Peterson, *Take Up Your Mission*, 34–35, 166; Robert Carlock, *The Hashknife: The Early Days of the Aztec Land and Cattle Company, Limited* (Tucson, AZ: Westernlore Press, 1994), 15. On how the Missouri and Illinois persecutions helped create Mormon identity—and shaped subsequent Mormon relations with outsiders—see David Grua's fine thesis, "Memoirs of the Persecuted: Persecution, Memory, and the West as a Mormon Refuge" (master's thesis, Brigham Young University, 2008).

13. Udall, *Arizona Pioneer Mormon*, 77.

14. Hamblin, *Outlaws*, 2–3; Jo Ann F. Hatch, *Willing Hands: A Biography of Lorenzo Hatch Hill, 1826–1910* (Pinedale, AZ: Kymera Publishing Company, 1996), 165–67; 277–78; Fish, "Eastern Arizona Stake," 36; Wilhelm and Wilhelm, *A History of St. Johns*, 45; and James Warren LeSueur, "Autobiography," TS, GSTC, Box 5, folder 10, n.p. On the absence of guns among Apache County settlers prior to the arrival of Texas cowboys, see William N. Miller to Will C. Barnes, Darlington, Idaho, July 20, 1936, Will C. Barnes Collection (WCBC), University of Arizona Special Collections, Box 2, folder 18.

15. William N. Miller to Will C. Barnes, Darlington, Idaho, July 20, 1936.

16. Miller, "St. Johns's Saints," 82.

17. Udall, *Arizona Pioneer Mormon*, 92–93.

18. Fish, "Fish Manuscript," 630.

19. Bagley, *Blood of the Prophets*, 26, 163; Udall, *Arizona Pioneer Mormon*, 93–94 (quoting Smith); Peterson, *Take Up Your Mission*, 214; Smith, "Journal," 320, 341, 347 (March 25, 1883; January 18, 1884; and May 17, 1884); John Henry Standifird, "Journal of John Henry Standifird," GSTC, I, 230 (May 18, 1884); Miller, "St. Johns's Saints," 90 (Udall quotation); and Bushman, *Smith*, 235, 249.

20. Fish, "Eastern Arizona Stake," 24, 36; Fish, "Fish Manuscript," 575, 631–32, 644–50; Albert Levine, ed., *The Life and Times of Snowflake, 1878–1978* (n.p.: compiled

by The Centennial Committee, Snowflake, Arizona, 1978), 35–36; Smith, "Journal," 294 (undated entry from November 1880); Mark E. Miller, "St. John's Saints: Interethnic Conflict in Northeastern Arizona, 1880–85," *JMH* 23, no. 1 (Spring 1997): 79; Tanner and Richards, *Colonization on the Little Colorado*, 110; and Fish, "Eastern Arizona Stake," 43.

21. Fish, "Eastern Arizona Stake," 37 (McCarter quotation); *Apache Chief* (*AC*), May 9, 1884.

22. Fish, "Fish Manuscript," 630–31.

23. Ibid.; *AC*, May 9, 1884; Rita Ackerman, *OK Corral Postscript: The Death of Ike Clanton* (Honolulu, HI: Talei Publishers, 2006), 51.

24. Fish, "Eastern Arizona Stake," 39; Herman, *Hell*, chapter 4; and Thomas Edwin Farish, *History of Arizona*, vol. 6 (San Francisco, CA: Filmer Brothers Electrotype Company, 1918), 281–82.

25. John H. Krenkel, ed., *The Life and Times of Joseph Fish, Mormon Pioneer* (Danville, IL: Interstate Printers & Publishers, 1970), 29. On the Mexican colonies, see Thomas C. Romney, *The Mormon Colonies in Mexico* (Salt Lake City: University of Utah Press, 2005); and F. LaMond Tullis, *Mormons in Mexico: The Dynamics of Faith and Culture* (Logan: Utah State University Press, 1987).

26. Smith, "Journal," 355 (September 25, 1884).

27. Les Flake, *Tales from Oz* (n.p.: n.p., n.d.), 35; S. Eugene Flake, *James Madison Flake, November 8, 1859–February 4, 1946: Pioneer, Leader, Missionary* (Bountiful, UT: Wasatch Press, 1970), 83; and Leland J. Hanchett Jr., *The Crooked Trail to Holbrook: An Arizona Cattle Trail* (Phoenix, AZ: Arrowhead Press, 1993), 53, 61.

28. Larry D. Ball, "Commodore Perry Owens: The Man Behind the Legend," *Journal of Arizona History* 33, no. 1 (Spring 1992), 34; *Saint Johns Herald* (*SJH*), September 28, 1886.

29. *SJH*, October 21, 1886; Udall, *Arizona Pioneer Mormon*, 95–96, 132–33; and Peterson, *Take Up Your Mission*, 237.

30. *SJH*, April 15, April 22, May 6, 1886; April 7, April 14, May 26, July 28, August 11, 1887.

31. *SJH*, October 21, October 28, 1886.

32. *SJH*, October 1, October 21, October 28, 1886.

33. Carlock, *Hashknife*, 107; Smith, "Journal," 406–7 (entries for September 12, 1886 and October 10, 1886); and *Apache County Critic* (*ACC*), October 21, 1886.

34. Evans Coleman, "Reminiscences of an Arizona Cowboy" (chapter 12), Evans Coleman Collection (ECC), Arizona Historical Society/Tucson, Box 6, folder 61, 224; Ackerman, *OK Corral*, 47–48; *SJH*, August 12, August 24, December 16, 1886; and *ACC*, October 21, 1886, July 17, 1887.

35. E. W. Nelson to [illegible] Donnelly, Wallace, New Mexico, February 23, 1890, photocopy, Rita Ackerman files; "Edward William Nelson—Naturalist," *The Auk: A Quarterly Journal of Ornithology* 52, no. 2 (April 1935): 135–48. It was presumably Nelson whom the *Herald* had mocked as "some student of natural

history." Nelson went on to conduct a vast zoological survey of Mexico before directing the US Bureau of Biological Survey.

36. Joseph Lorenzo Petersen, "Life Sketches of Niels Petersen and Mary Mortensen Petersen," in "Biography of Joseph Lorenzo Petersen," TS, GSTC, Box 10, folder 1, 9–10; Smith, "Journal," 416 (entry for May 27, 1887); James Warren LeSueur, "The Trouble with the Hash Knife Company," TS, James Warren LeSueur Collection, Arizona Historical Society/Tucson, Box 1, folder 10, 2; Peterson, *Take Up Your Mission,* 170; George S. Tanner, *Henry Martin Tanner: Joseph City Pioneer* (n.p.: n.p., 1964), 51; Anonymous, "Wilford," Delph Collection (DC), North Gila County Historical Society, Box 1, folder 2, 6–7; and Anonymous, "'Old Brigham City' and Wilford," DC, Box 1, folder 2, 2.

37. Will C. Barnes, "Commodore Perry Owens," TS (photocopy), WCBC, Box 10, folder 68, 5; Will C. Barnes, *Apaches & Longhorns: The Reminiscences of Will C. Barnes,* ed. Frank C. Lockwood (Tucson: University of Arizona Press, 1982), 146–47.

38. Barnes, "Owens," 13. For details of the gunfight, see Herman, *Hell,* chapter 7.

39. *ACC,* June 18, 1887; *SJH,* November 29, 1888; George S. Tanner, *Henry Martin Tanner: Joseph City Arizona Pioneer* (n.p.: n.p., 1964), 52; and "Miscellaneous Notes," TS, GSTC, Box 12, folder 15, unnumbered.

40. Fish, "Eastern Arizona Stake," 80 (entry for July 15, 1889); *SJH,* December 23, 1886; *ACC,* December 30, 1886. On the lynching of the three white cowboys— Jamie Stott, Jim Scott, and Jeff Wilson—see Herman, *Hell,* chapter 8. On the possibility that Zulick endorsed vigilantism, see *Arizona Journal-Miner,* September 7, 1887; Martha Houck, "An Arizona Pioneer's Reminiscences: A Report on Pioneer Life in Arizona, Based on Information Given by Mr. and Mrs. J. D. Houck, including Relations with Indians, and the Pleasant Valley War," TS dated 1916, Arizona State University, Department of Archives and Manuscripts, 5; and Leland J. Hanchett, *Arizona's Graham-Tewksbury Feud* (Phoenix, AZ: Pine Rim, 1994), vii. Those citations suggest that Zulick permitted the Tewksbury faction in Pleasant Valley to kill off the supposedly criminal Grahams. What is important to consider is that the Grahams were closely allied with the Hashknife cowboys who plagued Mormons. Zulick—noteworthy for his sympathy to Arizona's Mormons—likely endorsed the vigilante campaign not just in Pleasant Valley, but in Apache County, too. The two campaigns were closely linked, if not one and the same. On Zulick's sympathy for Mormons, see Herman, *Hell,* 145.

41. Roberta Flake Clayton, ed., *To the Last Frontier: The Autobiography of Lucy Hannah White Flake* (n.p.: n.p., 1976); LeSueur, "Hash Knife," 5; Minutes of the Little Colorado Stake, TS, GSTC, 212 (entry for November 11, 1886); and Andrew Locy Rogers, "Diary of Andrew Locy Rogers, 1882–1902," TS, HBL, 81, 83, 84.

42. Preston Bushman, Diary (entry for June 9, 1920), cited in George S. Tanner, *Henry Martin Tanner: Joseph City Arizona Pioneer* (n.p.: n.p., 1964), 55. On Forest

Service regulations and the decline of range competition—and the violence it entailed—see Herman, *Hell*, chapters 9–11.

43. Thomas, "Violence," 42, 60, 65, 79, 88.

44. Pfeifer, *Rough Justice*; Thomas, "Violence," 42, 60, 65, 79, 88. Richard Maxwell Brown found 101 lynchings in California in the 1850s and 1860s but none in Utah. Brown, *Strain*, 306–7, 318. Ken Gonzales-Day has located additional lynchings in California, which would make the lynching rate higher than Brown's figures suggest. Utah's rate, too, was higher than Brown's figures suggest. But even if we add the scattered cases of lynching discussed by Thomas and others, Utah's rate comes nowhere near California's. On lynching in California, see Ken Gonzales-Day, *Lynching in the West, 1850–1935* (Durham, NC: Duke University Press, 2006); Roger D. McGrath, *Gunfighters, Highwaymen, and Vigilantes: Violence on the Western Frontier* (Berkeley: University of California Press, 1984); and Lori Lee Wilson, *The Joaquín Band: The History behind the Legend* (Lincoln: University of Nebraska Press, 2011).

45. Those who argue that the West (excluding Indian wars and massacres) was no more violent than other parts of the United States include W. Eugene Hollon, *Frontier Violence: Another Look* (New York: Oxford University Press, 1974), x; Robert R. Dykstra, "Body Counts and Murder Rates: The Contested Statistics of Western Violence," *Reviews in American History* 31, no. 4 (December 2003): 554–63; Robert R. Dykstra, *The Cattle Towns* (New York: Knopf, 1968); and Frank Richard Prassel, *The Western Peace Officer: A Legacy of Law and Order* (Norman: University of Oklahoma Press, 1972). On range wars, see Herman, *Hell*; C. L. Sonnichsen, *I'll Die Before I'll Run: The Story of the Great Feuds of Texas* (1951; repr., Lincoln: University of Nebraska Press, 1988); Robert M. Utley, *Billy the Kid: A Short and Violent Life* (Lincoln: University of Nebraska Press, 1989); Bill O'Neal, *Cattlemen vs. Sheepherders: Five Decades of Violence in the West, 1880–1920* (Austin, TX: Eakin Press, 1989); Bill O'Neal, *The Johnson County War* (Austin, TX: Eakin Press, 2004); Daniel Belgrad, "'Power's Larger Meaning': The Johnson County War as Political Violence in an Environmental Context," *Western Historical Quarterly* 33, no. 2 (Summer 2002): 159–77; and Cecilia Rasmussen, "Castaic Range War Left Up to 21 Dead," *Los Angeles Times*, April 15, 2001. See also Peter K. Simpson, *The Community of Cattlemen: A Social History of the Cattle Industry in Southeastern Oregon, 1869–1912* (Moscow: University of Idaho Press, 1987). Though Simpson does not chronicle a range war, he does chronicle frictions between big and small operators in southeastern Oregon that led to murder. On violence in early California, see McGrath, *Gunfighters*. On violence in 1850s California, see Wilson, *Joaquín Band*. On the racial component of vigilantism, see Gonzales-Day, *Lynching*; and William D. Carrigan, *The Making of a Lynching Culture: Violence and Vigilantism in Central Texas, 1836–1916* (Urbana: University of Illinois Press, 2004).

46. Larry D. Ball, "Commodore Perry Owens: The Man Behind the Legend," *JAH* 33, no. 1 (Spring 1992); Barnes, *Apaches & Longhorns*, 166.

47. Les Flake, *Tales from Oz* (n.p.: n.p., n.d.), 7–8.

48. Apache County Sheriffs, http://genealogytrails.com/ariz/apache/sheriffs.htm. On Ammon Tenney's missionary work in Mexico, see Jared M. Tamez, chapter 4 of this volume. For another story of borderlands negotiation and compromise, see Juliana Barr, *Peace Came in the Form of a Woman: Indians and Spaniards in the Texas Borderlands* (Chapel Hill: University of North Carolina Press), 2007.

49. Stewart L. Udall, *The Forgotten Founders: Rethinking the History of the Old West* (Washington, DC: Island Press/Shearwater Books, 2002). The history of race and politics in Apache County after 1890 remains to be written. It is a particularly interesting locale for research insofar as it was populated not just by Mormons and New Mexicans but also by Navajos. In the first half of the twentieth century, Apache County elected a mix of Mormon and Hispanic supervisors and state representatives. In the late twentieth century, it also elected Navajos to county office. Some whites, however, protested—indeed some called for the abolition of reservations—given that Indians could vote on the allocation of county funds without themselves being subject to county taxes. Daniel Herman, "Apache County's Indian War" (master's thesis, Columbia University Graduate School of Journalism, 1985).

50. James Brooke, "Memories of Lynching Divide a Town," *New York Times*, April 4, 1998; Stephen J. Leonard, *Lynching in Colorado, 1859–1919* (Boulder: University Press of Colorado, 2002), 7. See also the University of Missouri at Kansas City's "Lynching Statistics by State and Race," http://law2.umkc.edu/faculty/projects/ftrials/shipp/lynchstats.html. Utah, according to the UMKC figures, had eight lynchings between 1882 and 1968. New Mexicans seem to have learned the art of lynching from Texans. Capital punishment of any kind was rare in colonial New Mexico. Robert J. Tórrez, *The Myth of the Hanging Tree: Stories of Crime and Punishment in Colonial New Mexico* (Albuquerque: University of New Mexico Press, 2008), 3–4. On the honor culture—and violence—of Texas cowboys, see Herman, *Hell*, chapter 5. On cowboy revelry and violence generally, see Jacqueline M. Moore, *Cow Boys and Cattle Men: Class and Masculinities on the Texas Frontier, 1865–1900* (New York: New York University Press, 2009), chapters 4, 6. On violence in Texas generally, see Gary Clayton Anderson, *The Conquest of Texas: Ethnic Cleansing in the Promised Land, 1825–1870* (Norman: University of Oklahoma Press, 2005); and Carrigan, *Lynching Culture*; Sonnichsen, *I'll Die Before I'll Run*.

51. Udall, *Arizona Pioneer Mormon*, 93–94; "The Life of John Hunt (1833–1917)," in Roberta Flake Clayton, ed., *Pioneer Men of Arizona* (n.p.: n.p., 1974), 238.

52. Patrick Q. Mason, "The Possibilities of Mormon Peacebuilding," *Dialogue: A Journal of Mormon Thought* 37, no. 1 (Spring 2004): 12–49.

53. On the nexus between Mormon and non-Mormon violence in Genoa County— an area originally part of Utah Territory, but now part of Nevada—see Thomas, "Violence," 42–55.

CHAPTER EIGHT

Colonia Díaz and the Railroad That Almost Was

The Deming, Sierra Madre and Pacific, 1887–1896

BRANDON MORGAN

Deming is on the eve of another boom, J. W. Young, the boss Mormon railroad
builder is figuring for purchase of the D. S. M. & G. road and proposes to push the
work to completion. Large colonies of the L.D.S. are being established in Mexico,
and this road is being built for their convenience.

—*Deming Headlight*, January 17, 1891

THE SACRAMENT MEETING on the last Sunday of September 1892 in Colonia
Díaz, Chihuahua, was far from typical. Just days previously, Bishop William
Derby Johnson Jr. had learned that the railroad project he had championed
since late 1889 was bankrupt. As the local ecclesiastical leader and treasurer
of the railroad company, Johnson worked tirelessly to enlist the help of his
fellow colonists to build the rail line that promised a much faster and reliable
connection with Deming, New Mexico—the colony's base for supplies and
main port of entry to the United States. Yet, with Johnson's dreams of a modern transportation lane for his colony shattered, he found himself in a difficult position. Many of the Díaz colonists had become critical of his dedication
to the rail project, which he had maintained at the expense of his duties as
bishop, and that of many others who had sacrificed their own precious time
and resources to support the railroad. As Bishop Johnson stood before his
ward that September day, his heart was extremely heavy. As he recalled, "I
spoke thirty minutes and said if I had done wrong, I asked their forgiveness."
He also specifically pled for the forgiveness of his counselors for having
"been so much away from home that I had neglected my duty as a bishop but,
with the help of the Lord, I would now stay at home." Joseph H. James, one

159

of the bishop's two counselors, vouched for Johnson, saying, in essence, that if Johnson had wronged the members of the colony "it was a mistake of the head and not of the heart." With such sentiments, the colony began to heal deep personal rifts created by the failure of the proposed Deming, Sierra Madre and Pacific Railroad (DSMP).[1]

The Díaz colonists were not the only people in the region devastated by the failure of the project. Promoters and entrepreneurs of Deming, New Mexico, had been working toward the construction of the line for an even longer period of time. On July 4, 1889, the focal point of the town's Independence Day celebrations was the laying down of the line's first rails, ceremoniously driven into the freshly graded landscape with four silver spikes. The editor of the *Deming Headlight* heralded the event over a week in advance, emphasizing that this would be perhaps the world's only railroad inaugurated with silver spikes. The spikes were forged locally from silver extracted from nearby mines and from metal taken from donated Mexican coinage. In late June, Demingites were afforded the opportunity to view the spikes on display at the offices of McKeyes & Washington, a law and real estate firm. At the ceremonies, the railroad's chief engineer, Ladislao Weber, promised locals that they could "take a free ride with him to Mexico [on the completed railroad] about the middle of September." The dream of a good road south to Mexico, a priority of capitalists since the town's inception in 1881, seemed to be a near reality. Of course, the road was not completed by September 1889, and continued efforts to create the line that repeatedly promised to open up the exploitation of untouched resources in northern Chihuahua had still failed to produce results by 1892.[2]

The story of the Deming, Sierra Madre and Pacific Railroad project is not merely the tale of a failed business venture. As the historian Richard White points out in his recent work on the transcontinental rail lines of North America, the railroads "created modernity as much by their failure as by their success." In his study, White emphasizes that even as the railroad companies themselves folded time and again, they solidified a system of finance capitalism that allowed the presidents and boards of such companies to continue to reap a fortune from such failures.[3] The modern form of finance capitalism that came of age in the transcontinental ventures was very much present in the attempts to create the DSMP. Additionally, the Mexican state was heavily involved in creating the atmosphere in which corporations, both foreign and domestic, backed colonization and development projects throughout the nation. The infamous *compañías deslindadoras* (land

demarcation or surveying companies) took advantage of the Porfirian government's desire to transfer *terrenos baldíos* (unimproved public lands) to
private hands as a means of modernizing the country. In more than just a few
cases, the rights to newly surveyed lands were attached to concessions for
colonization and development rights (including railroads, telegraphs, mines,
etc.).[4]

In the case of the DSMP, Mexican and American capitalists came together
with local businessmen in Deming, as well as prominent colonists of Colonia
Díaz, and they laid out plans to secure the capital and resources necessary to
complete the railroad and develop the vast tract of land that adjoined its proposed route. As new colonists continued to stream into Colonia Díaz between
1886 and 1892, residents worked to build permanent homes and community
buildings. The completion of a railroad that would connect the colony to
Deming thus had a twofold appeal: first, it would allow greater ease of migration south, and second, it promised to channel building materials and other
needed supplies into the colony in a more regular fashion. Concurrently,
Deming merchants and entrepreneurs welcomed the prospect of creating a
consistent market for their wares. And, the capitalists connected to the compañías deslindadoras and colonization companies also invited the prospect
of commerce in the region nearest to their land concessions. This set of dove-
tailing interests meant that the residents of Colonia Díaz allied themselves
early on with economically influential groups in their immediate transnational region. Leaders like Bishop Johnson forged connections with the elites
of Deming that outlasted the failure of the railroad company and linked
colonists to their neighbors to the north who supported their prosperity in
the 1890s, as well as their dark hour of necessity when they were forced from
their community in the summer of 1912. Out of the ashes of the DSMP
demise came the construction of a regional community that straddled the
New Mexico–Chihuahua international boundary.

By exploring in detail the socioeconomic context of the small transnational region in which Colonia Díaz was founded, this essay illuminates a
side of the Mormon colonies that is often overlooked in scholarly and other
historical literature. Works such as Annie R. Johnson's *Heartbeats of Colonia
Díaz* and Nelle Spilsbury Hatch's *Colonia Juárez: An Intimate Account of a
Mormon Village* exemplify studies that were written by local Mormon historians.[5] These works present an insider's perspective and tend to emphasize
the insular nature of the various Chihuahua and Sonora colonies. Scholarly
treatments of the colonies generally follow this trajectory. Thomas Cottam

Romney's 1938 *The Mormon Colonies in Mexico* is the treatise of a scholar who also grew up in the colonies.[6] Romney places the colonists within the context of the racial, social, and economic ideas of their (and his) time to indicate why the colonists usually kept their Mexican neighbors at arm's length. B. Carmon Hardy's dissertation, "The Mormon Colonies in Northern Mexico: A History, 1885–1912," expands on the theme of cultural isolation to explain the reasons that the colonists were forced from their homes by Mexican revolutionaries in the summer of 1912.[7] Of works that focus directly on the colonies, Bill L. Smith's dissertation, "Impacts of the Mexican Revolution: The Mormon Experience, 1910–1946," steps outside the framework of isolation.[8] Using archival sources from Mexico City, Smith examines the perceptions that Mexican political elites held about the Mormon colonists. He aptly describes the controversy between pro-Porfirian policies (favoring Mormon colonization) and anti-Porfirian policies (opposing it) at the national level. Finally, borderlands scholars and historians of the Mexican Revolution often mention the Mormon colonies in their treatment of the Chihuahua-Sonora border region.[9] Yet none of these histories examine in much depth the direct connections forged between Mormon colonists and their neighbors in the immediate region in which they lived.[10] A discussion of the failed DSMP illuminates the local historical context in which the first of the Mormon settlements, Colonia Díaz, was founded. Díaz's story belongs within the history of nineteenth-century Mexican land and modernization policies. In framing the colony's history in this way, its intricate economic and social connections with other nearby communities on both sides of the international boundary become clear.

A close examination of the attempts to build the DSMP highlights the social and economic complexities of the transnational border region from Deming, New Mexico, to La Ascensión, Chihuahua. On both sides of the international line, few attempts were made to develop the area's resources until the 1880 defeat of Mimbres, or Chihene, Apache headman, Victorio. For Victorio and other Apache peoples the border provided a means of escape from American and Mexican military campaigns that sought the subjugation of indigenous peoples. For the Mimbres people specifically, their homelands stretched from the Black Range and Mimbres River Valley of southern New Mexico into the plains near the Palomas Lakes and into the Sierra Madres of northwestern Chihuahua. Their ability to elude capture, coupled with a lack of formal cooperation between American and Mexican forces during the 1870s, prevented development projects from taking root along the New Mexico–Chihuahua border. For all intents and purposes, Victorio's band controlled the region. But US and Mexican forces refused to abandon their goal of confining Apaches to reservations in order to open the region's resources to development. In October 1880 the cycle of violence left Victorio dead at Tres Castillos, Chihuahua, and his band scattered on both sides of the border.[11]

During the same general time period, several communities were founded in the Mimbres' traditional homeland. The border communities of La Ascensión, Deming, Colonia Díaz, Las Palomas, and Columbus (founded in 1872, 1881, 1886, 1888, and 1891, respectively), were (and are) all tied together by physical geography and spatial proximity. The distance between La Ascensión and Deming, the furthest points south and north in the region under scrutiny, is only about one hundred miles. Although boosters of the Deming, Las Palomas, and Columbus town sites boasted an "inexhaustible" artesian water supply that promised to support the cultivation of crops ranging from alfalfa to corn to canaigre (also known as Tanner's Dock, cultivated for tannin), the reality of the local environment was starkly different.[12] Physically, the region is defined by desert landscapes dotted with yucca and cactus and broken by small mountain ranges. The Mimbres River runs south from the Black Range in New Mexico and then becomes an underground aquifer that feeds the Palomas Lakes a few miles south of the border. Its water supply was crucial for the survival of local communities, but it was hardly the agricultural engine promised by regional promoters. This landscape, however, provided (and provides) continuity across the arbitrarily drawn international boundary line, and the homogeneous physical geography indicates the region's interconnected history.

On the Mexican side of the line, the region was peopled in the 1870s and 1880s through the colonization policies of the Mexican government under Porfirio Díaz. Although efforts to attract Mexican repatriates from the US Southwest were initiated almost immediately after the signing of the Treaty of Guadalupe-Hidalgo in 1848, promised funds to support relocation to northern Mexico were not forthcoming. The only successful repatriate colonies were those comprised of people who were able to shoulder the costs of migration without government support. This pattern continued throughout the latter half of the nineteenth century; the colony of La Ascensión was settled by Mexican repatriates from La Mesilla, New Mexico, who fled following a violent election riot on August 27, 1871, that left between six and nine people dead (reports vary). With little support from Mexico City, despite its promise of aid for repatriates, La Ascensión grew. By 1883 it was a small but thriving community, although contested surveys fostered land disputes that culminated in a violent revolt on January 6, 1892.[13]

From the moment of their arrival in the region, Díaz colonists relied upon the people of La Ascensión for their livelihood. Juan Holguín, La Ascensión's municipal leader in 1885, provided the first colonists with a campsite on his own lands in the northwestern section of the colony. This site, so close to town, provided protection from Apache bands who continued their struggle to hold on to their traditional lands in the area through the mid-1890s. Holguín allowed the colonists, whose number grew week by week, to remain camped on his land until the Mormons' land negotiations were finalized in mid-1886. Other Asensionenses supported the Mormons' right to colonize the area when the acting governor of Chihuahua and some minor regional authorities ordered their immediate expulsion in May 1885. In 1886 and 1887, the colonists negotiated with Anastacio Azcarate and Zacarías, Pedro, and Juan Zozaya for access to the Palotada spring as well as access to the nearby Ojo Caliente. Water rights had been lacking in their land purchase contracts, so Azcarate and the Zozayas's assistance in this matter was crucial for the colony to sustain its population and eventually flourish.[14]

Additional colonists trickled into Colonia Díaz throughout the rest of the decade, and Bishop Johnson worked with colonist Alexander F. McDonald and LDS officials in Mexico City to create the Díaz Colonization Company to manage the continued migration and settlement of their compatriots. During negotiations with Mormon representatives in Mexico City, Porfirio Díaz raised concerns over the Mormons' desire to hold land so near the border, but the incorporation of the colony's landholdings allowed them to overcome this potential obstacle to their expansion in northwestern Chihuahua.[15] As the historian Rachel St. John points out, American citizens were able to acquire lands in the forbidden zone along the international boundary by forming Mexican corporations. By taking that route, they could maintain their American citizenship status as individuals while simultaneously gaining corporate Mexican citizenship privileges. St. John states that "any company incorporated under the laws of Mexico carried all the rights of citizenship, save voting."[16] The Mormon colonists thus formed various companies, including the Mexican Colonization and Agricultural Company and the Díaz Colonization and Dublán Land and Water Corporations, to gain legal access to land and water rights in their adoptive country.[17] Additionally, the first Mormon representatives to Mexico had been interested in northwestern Chihuahua as a prime colonization site because of the prospect of a proposed railroad that "from Deming will pass up this valley to Casas Grandes and Chihuahua and connect with the Mexican Central R.R."[18]

The rail line that was under discussion in Deming and La Ascensión as early as 1885 was not proposed in concrete form until a few years later. In 1887, Luis Huller, a wealthy Mexican national of German origin, received several different railroad concessions from the Secretaría de Fomento for lines throughout Mexico. Among his various rail concessions was the Sonora, Sinaloa y Chihuahua grant which provided Huller and his companies with the right to build a rail line from Guaymas, Sonora, through the Sierra Madres "at the most practicable points," and to Ciudad Chihuahua where the line would connect with the Mexican Central Railroad.[19] He also contracted with the Secretaría de Fomento, Colonización e Industria to construct a line from Ciudad Chihuahua, through Guerrero, and northward through "Colonias Juárez, Porfirio Díaz y Palomas to a point convenient to the boundary line with the United States."[20] In connection with this last leg of the proposed rail line, on June 4, 1888, Huller signed a colonization contract in Mexico City that bound him to establish at least five hundred colonists on his Palomas tract within three years. Sixty percent of the colonists were to be repatriates from the US Southwest. In all, he gained control of 2.6 million acres of land in northwestern Chihuahua.[21]

As early as November 1887 he began to forge ties with entrepreneurs in Deming who supported his Deming, Sierra Madre and Pacific Railroad Company. At about the same time, he disclosed his plans to create a new town called Las Palomas (identified as "Palomas City" in US newspaper reports) about thirty-eight miles south of Deming, directly on the proposed rail line, and about four miles south of the international line.[22] The creation of the town of Las Palomas was the first step in Huller's plans to develop and populate the region. Newspapers on both sides of the border heralded the town's official founding on November 17, 1887 (about seven months before the colonization contract), and the people of Deming took interested notice. Over the next few years Deming merchants provided the bulk of the supplies for the physical construction of the fledgling colony. Settlers in southern New Mexico recognized the potential of the colony to make their region an important port of entry and trade point between the two nations, and they put all of their support behind the success of Las Palomas and the railroad that would connect the two towns.

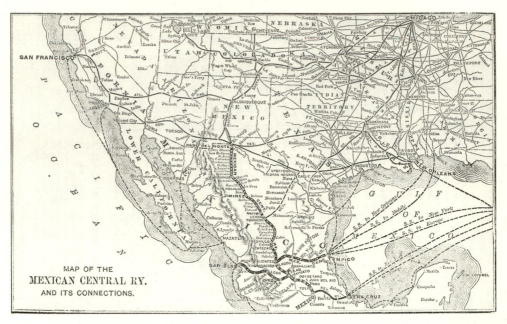

Poor's Mexican Central Railway and its connections, 1891. Wikimedia commons, public domain.

Although the town grew slowly, the Palomas project was certainly well advertised and staffed, and it gave rise to most of the key development efforts along the Chihuahua–New Mexico boundary during the late 1880s and 1890s. The twin border towns of Las Palomas and Columbus were founded as a direct result of efforts to colonize and modernize the Palomas tract, and the DSMP seemed constantly to be at the point of near completion (or near construction) during that same period. The Palomas tract and its various railroad, colonization, mining, and water concessions also provided reasons for residents of the communities on both sides of the border to come together. Broadsides and the short-lived weekly newspaper *El Eco de Palomas* advertised the region's bright future, with a special focus on attracting repatriates from the southwestern United States. Although the total number of settlers drawn to Palomas from the United States is unclear, wealthy entrepreneurs from both nations invested in the town. Ladislao Weber was initially in charge of the developing township; later he also carried the title of chief engineer for the proposed railroad. Colonel Andrew O. Bailey, a Massachusetts native and veteran of the US Civil War, was also drawn to the town. He headed up the ranching enterprises on the Palomas tract and later replaced Weber as Huller's point man in the colony. Despite the fact that the effort to build the railroad ultimately failed and that Palomas never became a thriving urban center, during the attempt the Díaz colonists forged ties with the communities of Deming and Columbus that might not have materialized otherwise.[23]

Although in 1887 and 1888 hopes were high for the speedy construction of the DSMP line, the venture was unstable from its onset. Locals in Deming (and later Colonia Díaz and Columbus) viewed Luis Huller, George H. Sisson, and Ladislao Weber as men who were fully dedicated to the cause of their railroad and colonization projects. Yet Huller and Sisson, as agents of the Connecticut-based International Company of Mexico, had overextended their efforts. In railroad concessions alone (not counting land grants and purchases, colonization projects, or shipping rights-of-way that Huller also owned), Huller and Sisson—sometimes on behalf of the International Company, sometimes as individuals—received rights and subsidies to build lines in Baja California, Sonora, Sinaloa, Chiapas, and Chihuahua. In all, these commitments meant that they had to build at least six different roads in Mexico.[24] In addition, in January 1889 a London firm purchased the International Company, and Huller had a falling out with the new corporate leadership that briefly landed him in a Mexico City prison on charges of embezzlement. He cleared his name but broke with the company. Fortunately for the Deming investors, Huller retained many of the railroad concessions that had been made in his name rather than explicitly granted to the corporation.[25]

In Deming, local reports began to tie the town's future to the success of the coming railroad. On February 25, 1889, the Chihuahua and Sierra Madre Railway Company was officially Charles H. Dane & Sons, a local construction enterprise, positioned itself to receive the surveying and grading work for the line.[26] Following on the heels of the company's inauguration, stories ran in the *Santa Fe New Mexican* and *St. Louis Republic* announcing that work on the new railroad into Mexico was to "begin at Deming about April 15."[27] These developments led to the ceremonious laying of the silver spikes on July 4, 1889. The level of excitement remained high through the month of July, but fits and starts on construction had not ended. Another lull set in when the financing from Huller's German sources failed to materialize. Once again grading teams halted their work and laborers and machinery stood idle. In early November, the word in Deming was that work was going to shortly begin anew on the road. In this instance another newcomer to the project, John W. Young, was rumored to be the spark that would renew the work. Young was reportedly "an extensive and successful railroad contractor and builder" and one of the sons of Mormon prophet Brigham Young. When business negotiations to transfer the railroad company to Young became public knowledge in mid-November, Demingites dared to think that actual rail construction might soon be carried out.[28] And, for the first time, Mormon colonists in Colonia Díaz had a direct link to the venture.

Interestingly, just prior to John W. Young's connection to the railroad project, Deming began a shift in its attitude toward the Mormon colonists. An examination of the pages of the *Deming Headlight* in the period 1888 to 1890 indicates this change.[29] Mormons had been transiting through Deming, stocking up on supplies, verifying their loads with the Mexican Consul, and checking in at the customs house there from the initial founding of Colonia Díaz in the fall of 1886. Between September 1888 and late 1889, the colonists were rarely mentioned in the paper, despite accounts from the colonists themselves that indicate their regular passage through the town.[30] When they did appear, it was usually in passing—in relation to the route of the proposed railroad, for example—or in negative light. The January 11, 1889, edition derided and condemned "the president's recent pardon of five convicted Mormon adulterers."[31] In early March, however, stories about colonists and the Mormon people in general began to appear much more regularly. In the March 15 *Headlight*, the Mormon colonists were described as "well-to-do, having fine stock and comfortable, well put up outfits." Instead of reporting in horrified tones on the colonists' practice of polygamy, the paper now focused on their economic standing as well as their uncanny ability as colonizers. The Díaz Mormons were also characterized as the people who "have in two years turned the country in the neighborhood of La Ascensión from a barren waste into a garden."[32]

Beginning in December 1889, the references in the *Deming Headlight* to sizable groups of Mormon colonists passing through Deming toward their new homes in Colonia Díaz increased markedly in number. The December 14 issue reported that "twenty-three wagons filled with the families and goods of Mormon people from Utah and Colorado, have passed through here during the past week en route for Díaz and La Colonias [sic], in Mexico." Again, of particular note in these types of announcements was the fact that the colonists "did considerable buying while in town." From January to November 1890 (when John W. Young took control of the railroad company) similar references to Mormon migration, ingenuity, and buying power appeared on a regular basis. Reports mentioned Mormon leaders, such as Bishop William Derby Johnson and Alexander F. Macdonald, making extended visits to Deming as representatives of the colonies' business affairs.[33] On April 12 the *Headlight* ran an extended feature titled "Another Mormon Hegira." This story emphasized the Mormons' adherence to law, order, and hard work and made no mention of the issue of polygamy—the very practice that had caused the recent conflicts between members of the faith and US federal officials. An August 16 report called out the federal government for enacting laws that suppressed the rights of Mormons, forcing them to "find some freer country than the United States" in which to reside. Through the *Headlight*, Deming businessmen thus worked to overpower negative reports so common at the time about the Mormon practice of polygamy and to recast the Mormons as upstanding people and excellent neighbors. Indeed, their business had the potential to enrich and support Deming's mercantile industry, and by November 1890 it seemed that the Mormons would be the impetus needed to complete the DSMP.

In early January 1891, Huller and Young met in Deming and the former officially transferred all the railroad property to the latter. Bishop Johnson began to spend much more of his time in Deming at that point because Young had singled him out for a prominent position in the rail venture. Johnson had acted as Young's agent for land purchases north of Colonia Díaz in which young secured 150,000 acres near the Casas Grandes River. At about the same time, Huller extended 20,000 acres of his lands near the town of Nuevo Casas Grandes for the settlement of Mormon colonists. Although Huller's creditors (he was never financially in the clear during the early 1890s) refused to allow the Mormons to take possession of the tract, it was acquired by them years afterward. The settlement that became known as Colonia Dublán was initially dubbed Colonia Huller because of these dealings between the wealthy German-Mexican and the agents of the Mormon Mexican Colonization and Agricultural Company. In 1889 the company, which enjoyed the support of the First Presidency of the LDS Church, purchased 28,000 acres from Young that were added to Colonia Díaz.[34] In these transactions, Johnson served as the representative on the ground while Young was away schmoozing wealthy investors in New York City in support of his several rail and land ventures in northern Mexico and the western United States. This type of relationship continued between the two men during Young's tenure as president of the railroad company.

During an early trip to New York in his capacity as an agent of the railway company, Johnson gave an interview to the *New York Saturday Globe* that was subsequently excerpted in the *Deming Headlight*. Despite the efforts by Deming elites to incorporate the Mormon colonists into their regional society and economy, the *Headlight*'s treatment of that interview indicates that some Demingites had reservations. Editor Edmund G. Ross used the opportunity to emphasize the idea that the Mormons in Mexico were in no way practicing polygamy. In introducing Johnson's statement that polygamy could not exist in the Mormon colonies because it was contrary to Mexican law as well as the 1890 proclamation of LDS President Wilford Woodruff that expressly ended the practice among adherents of the faith, Ross highlighted Johnson's "very emphatic language, which ought to be satisfactory to all reasonable people." The actual continuance of polygamous marriages in the colonies, however, calls into question the success of Ross's attempts at persuasion.[35]

With all of its usual flourish and bravado, on February 21, 1891, the *Headlight* announced that "a new star was born in the railway firmament on Thursday last" when the enterprise was officially reorganized as the Mexican Pacific Railway Company with John W. Young as its controlling officer. Johnson, Andrew O. Bailey, and the Deming investors placed their faith in reports that seemed to prove John W. Young's aptitude as a business leader and railroad builder. With little personal knowledge of Young or the details of his other ventures, they pledged their time and money to the cause. The March 7 *Headlight* reported that the Deming townsite company, a McKeyes and Burnside interest, had "transferred to J. W. Young, president of the Deming, Sierra Madre & Pacific railroad, a quarter interest in all their town property"—a gesture of good faith meant to tie Young to the interests of the locale. Additionally, many of the Díaz colonists threw their support behind the projected railroad. Ammon M. Tenney, a Díaz colonist and a longtime Mormon missionary in Mexico, partnered with Bailey to secure funds for the line. Bailey put in $80,000 of his own money for the railroad because he believed that it would spur the growth and importance of his Columbus townsite. Tenney received a contract to complete the grading for a ninety-mile stretch of the line from Las Palomas to Corralitos, and he promised to raise $40,000 through personal connections in Utah and elsewhere. Colonists Joseph H. James, Erastus Beck, and Andrew C. Peterson organized mule teams and hired Mexican helpers, presumably from La Ascensión and Las Palomas, to aid in the grading work.[36]

Entire families were engaged in work on grading the rail route. Both of John Adams's wives served as cooks for the laborers and many others followed suit. Anyone connected to the project would have quickly noticed that whether or not new polygamous marriages were discontinued among the Mormons, polygamous families that had already formed were commonplace in the Díaz colony. Yet such considerations did not hamper the growing business connections between Deming and Colonia Díaz. From the colonists' perspective the women created an atmosphere of religiosity and morals that kept the men in line at the worksite. Colonists remembered that one non-Mormon supervisor felt that he had to watch his mouth because his typical jobsite vocabulary didn't "fit in with the oathless and clean conversation about him." Entire families freely gave their time to the venture because the future prosperity of the colony seemed to be ensured by the progress of the railroad. Many dreamed that the railroad, with its promise to bring to the colony a modern shipping connection, would bring an era of more luxurious homes, new supplies and machinery, and better schools for their families and the community at large. Reportedly, the youngest members of the effort were four- and six-year-old Charles and Rhoda Merrill, "who had been hired to pick up kernels of corn spilled by the horses while eating." Through the effort and commitment of the colonist families, seventy-five miles of grading work were completed south of the border by May 29, 1891.[37]

The renewed confidence that came along with the organization of the Mexican Pacific Railway Company thus seemed well founded in early 1891. Salvador F. Maillefert, Mexican Consul in Deming, recognized the potential of the railroad both to develop lands and to continue the migration of Mormon colonists to northern Chihuahua. In connection with Alexander F. MacDonald and the Mexican Colonization and Agricultural Company, Maillefert secured 700,000 acres in the Galeana District of northwestern Chihuahua (southwest of the Palomas tract and La Ascensión) from Carlos Pacheco, Secretario de Fomento, in Mexico City. As part of the deal, Maillefert became the official colonization agent for the tract, as well as all other colonies established in the Galeana District. His contract stipulated that he was to settle six hundred colonists on the lands granted to him and the colonization company. Certainly, his partnership with the Mormons made the venture's success seem a foregone conclusion. Back in Deming in late February, Maillefert reported on his dealings and announced that he had also acquired lands in Sonora and Durango as well. He advertised 5 million acres for sale.[38]

Andrew O. Bailey also considered John W. Young's tenure with the railroad venture to be a sign that the time had come for the completion of the DSMP line. By late March 1891, work to expand Bailey's small border town of Columbus hit full stride. Accompanying his heavy investments in the railroad, therefore, Bailey put up funds "for the erection of new buildings at Columbus." He also reached out to Deming investors who understood the possibilities of growth for Columbus should their railroad investment pay off this time around. As stated in the *Deming Headlight*, "We trust Columbus, on the border, will grow into a lively town. Every new building erected there is of benefit to Deming."[39] This was not only due to the increased potential for transnational commerce that came with the new town, but also the fact that most of the lumber, hardware, and other building materials to construct Columbus were sold by Deming merchants. For promoters and investors in the region, prospects could not have appeared brighter.

Despite the revelry and high confidence of the first half of 1891, ominous signs for the railroad project began to accumulate. As grading proceeded from Deming to Las Palomas and beyond, officials of the Mexican Pacific Railway Company and Maillefert renewed the push for an official independent customs house at Las Palomas. As the situation stood, customs were assessed in the town of La Ascensión—even for goods destined for Las Palomas. The result was a 140-mile round trip from the border to the customs station and back. Additionally, colonists Peter McBride and Wilford Webb levied complaints of wrongful confiscations against La Ascensión customs agents in the spring of 1891. Although the relocation of the customs house to the border made sense to colonists and railroad investors, the Mexican secretary of hacienda and existing customs administrator, Francisco Raymundes, did not readily agree.[40]

The customs-house dispute went back and forth through official channels in the Secretariat of Hacienda from June 1891 through March 1892. As the fight dragged on, the fortunes of the Mexican Pacific Railway Company evaporated. With or without the construction delays caused by the unresolved customs issue, John W. Young had apparently overextended his finances by June 1891. The previous April, rumors began to circulate that Young was on the verge of selling the railroad venture. The *Deming Headlight* reported on June 13 that Young had gone to London to close a financing deal with an English syndicate. As hundreds of Mormon colonists continued to pour into Colonias Díaz, Juárez, and Dublán, Bishop Johnson attempted to maintain confidence in Young's ability to fund his various projects. Along with his interest in the DSMP, Young also presided over several railroad projects in Utah and had invested in several different ventures in New York City. Only one of his proposed railroads, a short line between Salt Lake City and Coalville, Utah, was ever completed. The status of Young's various projects seemed to elude public knowledge along the New Mexico–Chihuahua border. Although he maintained communications with his representative in Deming, Young never returned to the town after his trip to England was announced. Johnson made several trips to New York and London to meet with Young and prospective backers, but the bulk of the capital that Young had promised when he signed the rail concession never materialized.[41]

In late July 1891, Mormon contractors with the grading project began receiving late payments for their work. By August they received nothing at all. Bishop Johnson promised to rectify the situation by holding Young's land in the region, large sections of which were also in Johnson's name, as a security until the contractors were paid. Young had acquired so many debts, however, that he was unable to make good on all of them. Despite attempts in Deming to indict him for fraud, Johnson was able to maintain the company's office there through the fall of 1892. Although no construction took place after August 1891, hope that the railroad might be redeemed died hard. In November the secretary of hacienda made the official decision to relocate the customs house to Las Palomas by no later than March 1 of the following year. Demingites heralded this action as the spark that would reignite construction on the railroad. When election violence erupted in La Ascensión on January 6, 1892, and Díaz colonists with Joseph H. James's "peace committee" helped to suppress the group that rose to arms, the decision to relocate the customs house was solidified.[42]

Ironically, by March 1892 the conditions desired by the railway company and Consul Maillefert were in place but the finances of John W. Young and his Mexican Pacific Railway Company were in shambles. When Bishop Johnson left London on September 16, 1892, after a meeting with Young, he was forlorn. Only 40,000 acres of Young's northern Chihuahua lands remained as security for the Díaz colonists who had invested their time, money, and resources into the effort. Although the debt for unpaid supplies and services was almost $90,000, Johnson estimated that the land was only worth about $20,000. He feared that when it was subjected to forced sale it would only garner about half of that amount. Johnson was faced with the dismal task of informing the Díaz colonists and the Demingites that the railroad company had folded.[43]

Deming investors were also left with nothing to show but debts for their efforts to support the railroad. Andrew O. Bailey, as the company's general manager, retained piles upon piles of unused ties outside of his Columbus ranch house. Ammon Tenney was unable to supply the $40,000 that he had promised Bailey for the railroad effort. When the project dissolved in late 1892, Bailey was granted control of the DSMP's assets in Deming, which he attempted to sell in an effort to pay off some of his debts. Yet confidence in the growth of his Columbus town site dwindled as well. The post office there was discontinued in 1893 and Columbus existed in name only until 1903 when it was resurrected by the new El Paso and Southwestern Railroad that connected Phelps-Dodge smelters in Douglas, Arizona, to the industrial hub of El Paso.[44]

The towns of La Ascensión and Las Palomas were also left in shambles. Following the 1892 revolt, Asensionenses found themselves under the constant scrutiny of Mexican federal forces. Between fifty-five and sixty of the participants were exonerated of the charges brought against them and several others fled to southern New Mexico where they claimed US citizenship as a means of eluding arrest. Their town lost its customs house, but its roughly two thousand inhabitants continued to make their living as small-scale farmers, and most of the unclear and corrupt land surveys were resolved favorably for the Asensionenses. Las Palomas continued to exist primarily because it was the site of the customs house, and its small population remained in a poor and destitute state. The majority of those who remained in the town were repatriates from various places in New Mexico and Texas. The capitalists who had first constructed large estates and elaborate houses, however, had vacated the colony. The historian Jane-Dale Lloyd provides an apt assessment of the status of Las Palomas in the 1890s: the false promises of the colonization project "abandoned on the tract a few impoverished Mexican families, who had hoped to work rich agricultural lands that did not exist."[45]

The long-awaited boom for the region failed to materialize, yet its people forged ahead. For the Díaz colonists, although the collapse of the railroad taxed relationships within their own community, it created important ties with people in Deming, Columbus, and even La Ascensión. Despite the lack of rail transportation, Colonia Díaz thrived during the mid-1890s. The colonists constructed mercantile institutions, grist mills, and irrigation canals that allowed them to cultivate large orchards and various crops. Beginning in September 1894, Colonia Díaz initiated an annual fair that provided an outlet for the Mormons to showcase their agricultural produce as well as their community. For months prior to the event, the *Deming Headlight* ran lengthy promotional stories and advertisements. Each year, large groups of people from Deming came together to make the trip to Colonia Díaz to participate in the fair. The 1896 fair generated more than the usual fanfare as the colonists marked the ten-year anniversary of the colony; Demingites turned out en masse to help them celebrate. An invitation was sent to President Porfirio Díaz, but due to other commitments, he deferred to Chihuahua governor Miguel Ahumada who did attend. Other officials from La Ascensión and Ciudad Chihuahua also took part in the festivities, praising the colonists for their ingenuity and great ability to transform a desert into a blooming rose.[46]

Cooperation didn't always typify the Díaz colonists' relations with other people in their region. Various conflicts with neighbors in Mexico— including skirmishes with Apache bands and Mexican *revoltosos*—and continued hardships due to isolation also marked the 1890s and the first decade of the 1900s. Yet the relationships with residents of Deming and Columbus that began during episodes such as the attempt to build the railroad proved crucial in the summer of 1912 when *Colorado* forces under José Ines Salazar forced the Mormon colonists to flee their homes for the safety of the American side of the border. From Colonia Díaz, colonists escaped along the route that had been graded in anticipation of the DSMP two decades earlier. Some former Díaz colonists, such as Peter K. Lemmon, Ernest V. Romney, and Zeno Johnson (son of William Derby) made permanent homes in the Columbus-Deming area. Lemmon and Romney established a store in Columbus in the fall of 1912 and the Johnson family remained in Columbus through the early 1930s. The episode of the DSMP venture illustrates that the Mormon colonists in Díaz were not merely refugees in a foreign country but actors in a transnational regional community.

NOTES

1. Annie R. Johnson, *Heartbeats of Colonia Díaz* (Mesa, AZ: self-published, 1972), 96–97; Joel H. Martineau Papers, Box 1, folder 3, Church of Jesus Christ of Latter-day Saints Church History Library and Archives, Salt Lake City, UT [hereafter CHLA].
2. *Deming Headlight*, June 28 and July 5, 1889.
3. Richard White, *Railroaded: The Transcontinentals and the Making of Modern America* (New York: Norton, 2011), xxi, xxv.
4. Robert H. Holden, "Priorities of the State in the Survey of the Public Land in

Mexico, 1876–1911," *Hispanic American Historical Review* 70, no. 4 (November 1990): 579–81; Rachel St. John, *Line in the Sand: A History of the Western U.S.-Mexico Border* (Princeton, NJ: Princeton University Press, 2011), 72–82. José Angel Hernández, *Mexican American Colonization During the Nineteenth Century: A History of the U.S.-Mexico Borderlands* (New York: Cambridge University Press, 2012), argues convincingly that Porfirian colonization projects were also driven by the government's desire to repatriate Mexican people from the southwestern United States as ideal colonists, especially along the border. See pages 62–63 and chapters 5–7.

5. Johnson, *Heartbeats of Colonia Díaz*; Nelle Spilsbury Hatch, *Colonia Juarez: An Intimate Account of a Mormon Village* (Salt Lake City, UT: Deseret Book Company, 1954).

6. Thomas Cottam Romney, *The Mormon Colonies in Mexico* (1938; repr., Salt Lake City: University of Utah Press, 2005).

7. B. Carmon Hardy, "The Mormon Colonies of Northern Mexico: A History, 1885–1912" (PhD dissertation, Wayne State University, 1963); Hardy, "Cultural 'Encystment' as a Cause of the Mormon Exodus from Mexico in 1912," *Pacific Historical Review* 34 (November 1965): 439–54.

8. Bill L. Smith, "Impacts of the Mexican Revolution: The Mormon Experience, 1910–1946" (PhD dissertation, Washington State University, 2000). Political scientist F. LaMond Tullis also examines the history of the Mormon colonies in detail, but from the perspective of Mormon missionary efforts and relations with Mexican converts, in *Mormons in Mexico: The Dynamics of Faith and Culture* (Logan: Utah State University Press, 1987).

9. Among borderlands studies that tangentially mention the Mormon colonies, see Samuel Truett, *Fugitive Landscapes: The Forgotten History of the U.S.-Mexico Borderlands* (New Haven, CT: Yale University Press, 2006); and Miguel Tinker-Salas, *In the Shadow of the Eagles: Sonora and the Transformation of the Border during the Porfiriato* (Berkeley: University of California Press, 1997). Additionally, Moisés González Navarro's three-volume work, *Los Extranjeros en México y los Mexicanos en el Extranjero, 1821–1970* (Mexico City: Colegio de México, Centro de Estudios Históricos, 1994), discusses the development of the Mormon colonies in Chihuahua (see vol. 2). Many works on the Mexican Revolution mention the Mormon colonies, at least in passing. See, for example, Alan Knight, *The Mexican Revolution*, 2 vols. (Lincoln: University of Nebraska Press, 1986); John Mason Hart, *Revolutionary Mexico: The Coming and Process of the Mexican Revolution* (Berkeley: University of California Press, 1987); Friedrich Katz, *The Life and Times of Pancho Villa* (Stanford, CA: Stanford University Press, 1998); and Mark Wasserman, *Capitalists, Caciques, and Revolution: The Native Elite and Foreign Enterprise in Chihuahua, Mexico, 1845–1911* (Chapel Hill: University of North Carolina Press, 1984). John Mason Hart's *Empire and Revolution: The Americans in Mexico since the Civil War* (Berkeley: University of California Press, 2002) discusses the Mormon colonies in terms of their economic position relative to

the rest of northwestern Chihuahua. Its treatment of the colonies, however, is limited because it draws primarily on secondary sources that frame the colonies in terms of their isolation.

10. Notably, the Spanish-language work of Jane-Dale Lloyd defies these trends. Through the use of oral histories from the area around Colonias Juárez and Dublán, she describes in detail the colonists' relationship to local rancheros and medieros. See *El Proceso de Modernización Capitalista en el Noroeste de Chihuahua, 1880–1910* (Mexico City: Universidad Iberoamericana, 1987); and *Cinco ensayos sobre la cultura material de rancheros y medieros del noroeste de Chihuahua, 1886–1910* (Mexico City: Universidad Iberoamericana, 1987).

11. In referring to Victorio's band as "Mimbres" Apaches, I follow Dan Thrapp's characterization of social divisions within the larger group known as the Chiricahua Apaches. See Dan Thrapp, *Victorio and the Mimbres Apaches* (Norman: University of Oklahoma Press, 1974), 3–4, 12. For Apache dominance of the border region in the 1860s and 1870s as well as the pattern of escalating violence between Apaches, Americans, and Mexicans during the same period, see Thrapp, *Victorio*, 266–67, 277–80; St. John, *Line in the Sand*, 51–53; and Truett, *Fugitive Landscapes*, 60–63. The members of the particular band of Chiricahua Apaches to which Victorio belonged referred to themselves as the Chihene, or Red Paint, People. See also Kathleen P. Chamberlain, *Victorio: Apache Warrior and Chief* (Norman: University of Oklahoma Press, 2007), especially pages 5–11.

12. See, for example, *Deming Headlight*, August 9, 1890, July 4, 1891, and June 10, 1893; and Columbus & Western New Mexico Townsite Company, Hellberg & Blair, "Columbus and the Lower Mimbres Valley, New Mexico" (El Paso, TX: Columbus & Western New Mexico Townsite Company, 1912).

13. Hernández, *Mexican American Colonization*, 98–99, 177, 183–85, 192–94; Ramón Ramírez Tafoya, *Ascensión antes y después de la revolución* (Chihuahua: Instituto Chihuahuense de Cultura, 2011), 38–39; and Martín de la Vara, "The Return to Mexico: The Relocation of Mexican Families to Chihuahua and the Confirmation of a Frontier Region, 1848–1854," in *The Chicano Homeland: A Chicano History of New Mexico*, ed. Erlinda González-Berry and David Maciel (Albuquerque: University of New Mexico Press, 2000), 43–44.

14. Ramírez Tafoya, *La Ascensión*, 19–22; "Water Rights Contract, Díaz Ward, Mexican Mission," LR 2271 22, folder 1, CHLA; extracts from the journals of Alexander F. MacDonald and W. Derby Johnson Jr., March 10–October 24, 1886, Joel H. Martineau Papers, Box 1, folder 3, CHLA.

15. Extracts from the journal of Alexander F. Macdonald, April 1885, Joel H. Martineau Papers, Box 1, folder 3, CHLA.

16. St. John, *Line in the Sand*, 81.

17. The companies were key for the initial land acquisitions for the Mormon colonists, but with time many of them decided to become naturalized Mexican citizens.

18. Entry for January 8, 1885 [microfilm], A. F. Macdonald Journal, Taylor Orden Macdonald Collection, CHLA; and Romney, *Mormon Colonies in Mexico*, 65.

19. Contrato Luis Huller para su construcción, 87–22–1, Subfondo 87, Fondo Ferrocarriles, Archivo General de la Nación, México, DF [hereafter AGN].

20. Informe de George H. Sisson, 86–5-1, Subfondo 86, Fondo Ferrocarriles, AGN.

21. Letter from Garfield and Rhodes to Henry W. Anderson, Agente de la Comisión de Reclamaciones Mixtas, August 1, 1925, Correspondence relative to the Palomas Land and Cattle Company, Box 349a, Entry 125a, RG 76: International Claims Commission, National Archives and Records Administration, Washington, DC [hereafter NARA]; and Secretaría de Fomento, *Contract Entered Into Between The Secretary of Public Works, General Carlos Pacheco, and Luis Huller, Esq., for the Colonization of Lands called "Palomas," situated in the District of Galeana, State of Chihuahua* (Mexico City: Printing Office of Joaquin Guerra y Valle, 1889), 3–4.

22. *Dallas Morning News*, November 26 and December 18, 1887. Although the 1887 concession specifically stated that the railroad would also pass through the Mormon colonies Díaz and Juárez, those colonists were not a key part of the early planning and development stages.

23. *El Monitor Republicano* [México, DF], January 26, February 7, and March 16, 1888, contain extracts from *El Eco de Las Palomas*. Unfortunately, there are no extant copies of *El Eco*. Broadside "La Colonia de Las Palomas," 1888, Caja UI1350, Expediente 479, Fondo Hacienda Pública, AGN; Ray Sherdell Page, *Columbus, NM: Queen of the Mimbres Valley* (Silver City, NM: Page 1 Publishers, 2001), 6–7; Richard Dean, "Founder of Columbus, Colonel A. O. Bailey," unpublished MS, Personal Archive of Richard Dean, President of the Columbus Historical Society, Columbus, New Mexico [hereafter Dean Archive].

24. Francisco R. Almada, *El Ferrocarril de Chihuahua al Pacífico* (Mexico City: Editorial Libros de México, 1971), 73–75; International Company of Mexico, *Description of Lands in Lower California For Sale by the International Company of Mexico: Absolute Patent Title from the Federal Government of Mexico* (San Diego, CA: Ferguson, Bumgardner, 1887), 2. George H. Sisson was the International Company's Assistant General Manager, operating out of San Diego, CA. Luis Huller, a Mexican citizen, worked as the Company's Land Commissioner out of Mexico City. The various contracts for rail and land concessions issued by the Mexican Government in the 1880s specifically listed the names of Huller and Sisson.

25. *Deming Headlight*, February 22, 1889; Emilio Rabasa, *Luis Huller, acusado de abuso de confianza a la Compañía Internacional de México* (Mexico City: Imprenta del Gobierno en el Ex-Arzobispado, 1889); and "The Northwestern Colonization and Improvement Company: Juicio, jurisdicción voluntaria, testimonio de documentos," Caja 1058, Expediente 187408, Fondo Justicia, AGN.

26. For the regular visits of Huller and his associates to Deming, see *Deming*

Headlight, September 21 and 28, October 5, and November 23, 1888, as well as February 1 and 8, 1889. For the incorporation of the local railroad company, see *Deming Headlight*, March 1, 1889.

27. *Santa Fe New Mexican*, March 5, 1889; *St. Louis Republic*, March 7, 1889.

28. *Deming Headlight*, 1 and 15 November 1890.

29. There are no extant copies of the *Headlight* between fall 1882 and fall 1888, so my examination begins with the September 21, 1888, issue. The newspaper reports do not, of course, indicate how all of the residents of Deming felt about the Mormon colonists. Due to a lack of other sources, however, the newspaper provides the best available evidence about the opinions that were expressed by Deming boosters and entrepreneurs.

30. Johnson, *Heartbeats of Colonia Díaz*, 29, 54, 59; Joel H. Martineau Papers, CHLA, Box 1, folders 2 and 3.

31. For reports about the colonists in passing see, *Deming Headlight*, October 5, December 7 and 28, 1888, and January 4, 1889. For the negative remark about the Mormon practice of polygamy (as a form of adultery), see *Deming Headlight*, January 11, 1889.

32. *Deming Headlight*, March 15 and November 30, 1889. The Mormons' colonizing abilities were also noticed by papers in Las Cruces and other points in southern New Mexico. See, for example, *Mesilla Valley Democrat*, July 2, 1889. In terms of the shift away from polygamy to the colonists' economic status, a paragraph in the *Deming Headlight*, November 2, 1889, reported: "Two families of Mormons spent a few days here this week, on their way from Utah to the Mormon settlement near Ascension, Mexico. There were eleven persons in the two families, and they seemed to be comfortably stocked with worldly goods and cash. *There were no indications of polygamous practices*" (emphasis mine).

33. *Deming Headlight*, March 22 and June 7, 1890.

34. *Deming Headlight*, January 3, 1891; Romney, *Mormon Colonies*, 64–65; "Extracts from the Deed of Sale Executed by Messrs. William Derby Johnson Jr., and John Willard Young in Favor of Mexican Lands and Railway Trust, Limited," Mexican Land Transactions, 1893–1895, MS 19672, CHLA.

35. *Deming Headlight*, January 31, 1891. For the continuance of polygamy in the colonies, see B. Carmon Hardy, *Solemn Covenant: The Mormon Polygamous Passage* (Urbana: University of Illinois Press, 1992), 171–78.

36. *Deming Headlight*, February 21, 1891; *Dallas Morning News*, March 10, 1891; Johnson, *Heartbeats of Colonia Díaz*, 93–94; F. Stanley, *The Columbus, New Mexico Story* (Pep, TX: self-published, 1966), 6; Page, *Queen of the Mimbres Valley*, 8–9; and *Deming Headlight*, April 11, 1891. For reports on John W. Young's railroad acumen, see, for example, *Albuquerque Citizen*, March 5, 1891; and *Deming Headlight*, December 13, 1890 and March 7, 1891.

37. Johnson, *Heartbeats of Colonia Díaz*, 95–96.

38. *Deming Headlight*, February 28, 1891; Romney, *Mormon Colonies in Mexico*,

63–64; and "Memorandum de M. Fernández, Secretaría de Fomento," February 23, 1891, and "Letter from M. Azpiroz, Sección Consular," February 24, 1891, Archivo Historico Génaro Estrada, Secretaría de Relaciones Exteriores, México, DF [hereafter AHGESRE].

39. *Deming Headlight*, April 11, 1891.

40. Johnson, *Heartbeats of Colonia Díaz*, 94; *Deming Headlight*, June 13, 1891; Informe sobre el estado de los colonos en Las Palomas, July 1891, Caja UI1350, Expediente 479; and Informe del Visitador de Aduanas, September 12, 1891, Fondo Hacienda Pública, AGN; Letter from Secretary of Hacienda Pública to Francisco Raymundes, May 23, 1891, Caja UI1350, Expediente 1098, Fondo Hacienda Pública, AGN. The set of correspondence that outlines the calls for the Customs House's relocation is found in Caja 1350, Expedientes 1098 and 1697, Fondo Hacienda Pública, AGN.

41. Reports on the railroad company in the *Headlight* between June 1891 and September 1892 routinely rely on Johnson's knowledge of Young's efforts to secure funding in New York and London. Young's presence in the town was never again reported.

42. Orden oficial mandada a la Audana de La Ascensión, November 28, 1891, Caja UI1350, Expediente 1697, Fondo Hacienda Pública, AGN. For the election riot and Díaz colonists' participation in its suppression, see Hernández, *Mexican American Colonization*, 201–5.

43. Johnson, *Heartbeats of Colonia Díaz*, 95–97.

44. Page, *Queen of the Mimbres*, 6–9, 12; and Stanley, *Columbus, New Mexico Story*, 6.

45. Hernández, *Mexican American Colonization*, chapter 7; Ramírez Tafoya, *Antes y después de la revolución*, 60–64; and Jane-Dale Lloyd, *El Proceso de Modernización Capitalista en el Noroeste de Chihuahua, 1880–1910* (Mexico City: Universidad Iberoamericana, 1987), 32.

46. See *Deming Headlight*, August 16 and September 6, 1895, and August 21, September 18, and October 9, 1896; and Johnson, *Heartbeats of Colonia Díaz*, 128–35.

Porfirian Saints or Latter-day Revolutionaries?

Mormonism in Modern Mexico

MATTHEW BUTLER

THE MEXICAN HISTORY of the Church of Jesus Christ of Latter-day Saints (LDS) has been little studied by non-Mormon historians, with most of the literature being church- or missionary-produced, as well as testimonial and apologetic in character. These biases are reflected in their generally Anglophone, if not Utahan, character and confessional tone.[1] The appearance of a methodologically sophisticated, groundbreaking, and thoroughly researched collection of essays written from a nonconfessional perspective brings to an end long historiographical neglect, opens up promising avenues for new research, and allows historians to reconsider the significance of Mexico's Mormon experience. It is perhaps inevitable that the first achievement of the richly diverse papers assembled here is to complicate, and greatly so, our understanding of Mexican Mormondom. Previous confessional histories stressed eschatological imperatives or evangelical fervor as simple drivers of Mormon expansion southward.[2] But a highly nuanced composite picture of the Mexican LDS Church emerges here, one that varies by dint of locale, period, ethnicity, associated political commitments, and even prevailing religious beliefs and practices.

Mexican Mormonism was a bundle of contradictions, being at once locally colored and resolutely transnational, both American and Mexican (if not actually indigenous), as Revolutionary as it was Porfirian, by turns socialistic and capitalistic, as given to taking root in the center as it was to existing on the periphery. Making sense of this complexity, working with the historiographical clock stopping circa 1946, well before the main LDS boom in Mexico, is not easy. The preceding chapters collectively show the history of Mexican Mormondom as less providentially unique than contingent and highly differentiated: A plural history that begins with the narratives of interconnected if unique Mormonisms but that feeds into the broader history of religious pluralism in Mexico. In many ways, too, the history of Mexico's LDS is decipherable only when set against the secular backdrop of Mexican social and political history. The periodization employed by the volume's editors suggests this kind of affinity. Exclusively with reference to the LDS Church, the chapters span the period from 1875— when Daniel Jones led the first Mormon missionaries to Mexico—to 1946, with the healing of a schism known as the Third Convention, which tore Mexican Mormondom apart a decade before. This cycle dovetails perfectly with the classic coupling of the Porfirian dictatorship (1876–1911) and Revolutionary catharsis (1910–1940). The 1940s saw big institutional consolidations: for the LDS Church, the year 1946 saw church reunification when schismatic Mormons in central Mexico recanted before LDS president George A. Smith; for Mexico, the maturation of the post-Revolutionary regime, rebranded as the stolidly oppressive Institutional Revolutionary Party (PRI). Both for the reintegrated LDS Church and the perpetual Revolution, we might note, decades of growth lay ahead of the negotiation of their respective hegemonies. Secular and sacred history shadowed and to some extent even anticipated one another.[3]

What though, of more precise connections, and where does Mormonism fit in the wider social, political, and religious history of modern Mexico? How, too, can we characterize the roles that our principal actors—Anglo Mexican and indigenous Mormons—played in that history? In the short discussion that follows, I will offer some entirely provisional answers to these questions. First, I will make an extremely rudimentary, schematic attempt to tie the different strands of Mormon history in pre-1950s Mexico together. Second, I will set the LDS members' experience in very loose comparative perspective, venturing comparisons with other dissident (i.e., non-Catholic) groups but also referring to Catholicism where it offers better comparison. Last, I will gloss specific aspects of Mexican Mormonism arising from the many stimulating chapters here, using four basic rubrics: Mormonism as local religion; the history of LDS church-state relations, meaning Mormondom's relationship with the Porfirian and post-Revolutionary states; Mormonism's ties to political, especially Revolutionary, ideas and practices; and, to conclude, some transnational aspects of Mexican Mormonism.

PLACING MORMONISM IN MEXICAN HISTORY,
1900 TO 1950

In tentative terms, then, I suggest that one way to conceptualize the history of Mexican Mormondom is to see it as a culturally unique rendering of the more generalizable phenomenon that I have elsewhere termed a "revolution in spirit."[4] By this I mean a rapid diversification of Mexico's religious field during the late Porfirian and Revolutionary decades, especially, and, just as importantly, of the internal religious fields of many religious groups occupying the same terrain. I do not mean that Mormonism was or became a Revolutionary religion, though sometimes it appears so. Instead, the LDS colonists' experience was not isolated from broad patterns of change associated with the revolution but energized by them. The revolution was a period of violence, high mortality, and ontological anxiety, hence of religious experimentation and soul-searching. New churches also proliferated as a result of socioeconomic and political shifts that collectively pried open spaces for new religious actors: economic modernization, Revolutionary turmoil, anticlericalism, state building, and constitutional reform. Generally it can be argued that the Revolutionary reordering of Mexican society, along with developmental stresses, helped to build the foundations of the religious pluralism that today characterizes Mexico.[5]

We should at once qualify our ideas of pluralism, however, by noting that state tutelage of churches died very hard in Mexico, for all that the state claimed to be entirely secular (*laico*). As Jason Dormady has shown, in practice it was *less* so, to the extent that religious pluralism was partly administered, even created, by the regime through the informal granting of corporate privileges (e.g., ministerial licenses, property rights, party affiliation) to client groups. Mexican-style religious pluralism up to 1950 did not mean a free market in spiritual goods; instead, the old corporatist tradition of church patronage was multiplied by several factors and applied informally to growing numbers of non-Catholic groups, including Mexico's Latter-day Saints.[6] Religious institutions and identities were reconstructed in line with secular ones, therefore, with a widening number of religious groups competing for the tacit preferment of the state.

With this in mind, I would contend that Mexican Mormonism, in tandem with the state, went through a hegemonic process between 1910 and 1940.[7] Many of the chapters here suggest such a parallel, particularly given the emphasis on two points: first, growing diversity within Mormonism in a context of institutional church incapacitation, especially from 1910 to1940; second, the idea of popular agency, which links many of the chapters thematically. Running the two threads together, by 1900 we find that the Utahan LDS Church had authorized a parish (stake) structure in the north and a dependent mission in central Mexico. Both were controlled unevenly, and the mission was administered indirectly through the other. From 1910 through 1940, we see that even this control lapsed for long periods, partly because of Revolutionary violence but also due to the impact of Revolutionary-style nationalism, both legal and cultural, which encouraged outbreaks of schism and growing internal variance within the LDS Church. In the end, however, by 1940 the demise of the most extreme manifestations of Mexican nationalism and anti-clericalism made it easier for religious elites to reassert themselves in their own spheres. As already noted, this change occurred in the LDS Church in 1946, and, for the sake of comparison, in 1938 in the case of the Catholic Church.[8] Effectively, the state now ceased competing with churches for their clienteles and allowed them to run their internal affairs if they abstained from contesting state projects in the sociopolitical sphere. In this very broad sense, LDS history seems to track that of the post-Revolutionary regime. By the 1940s, indeed, Mormonism was expanding, if the continued maintenance of schools in so-called Catholic cities like Aguascalientes is any indication.[9]

Nonetheless, one can follow Elisa Pulido and other contributors in arguing that the authority of the LDS Church was more negotiated than it was simply reasserted in 1946, and that some important qualitative changes had occurred within Mexican Mormonism between 1910 and1940. For one thing, Mormonism as a fundamentally migrant, colonial enterprise was effectively dead; most northern pioneers had left, at gunpoint, and many did not return. The Revolution ensured that the future LDS Church in Mexico would either be indigenous/mestizo or irrelevant.[10] At the same time, the Revolutionary years saw increasingly desperate pleas made by indigenous Mormons that the Utahan LDS Church treat them as spiritually mature congregations, worthy of full induction into the mysteries of the faith and a genuine say in the government of their church. In part these demands for recognition were cultural legacies of the revolution, though they also stemmed from the paternalistic attitude of the pre-Revolutionary Utahan LDS Church. Arguably, too, they were persuasive factors in the achievement of reunification of 1946, which might therefore be seen as a sort of hegemonic pact reintegrating the Utahan authorities and the bases of Mexican Mormondom. The very curious term ("ratification") that was used to describe the readmission of nationalistic excommunicates to the LDS fold in 1946, without the humiliating requirement of re-baptism as church discipline theoretically required, perhaps tells its own story.

MORMONISM COMPARED

If the Mormon experience mirrored broader historical developments yet refracted these in a unique way, we would expect its history to have features in common with other religions while still remaining distinctive. This is perhaps what we find when we generally compare the LDS Church to other religious groups in Mexico. From some angles, for instance, the LDS colonies seem to belong to the first-wave dissident expansion that rolled over northern and central-southern Mexico under Porfirio Díaz, inasmuch as Mormonism, like the Protestant congregations studied by Jean-Pierre Bastian, put down roots in agrarian hinterlands that were experiencing traumatic economic modernization, especially near the US border, Gulf Coast, and Mexico City.[11] Mormons were welcomed by the Porfirian elite as farmers able to turn northern deserts into market gardens, for instance; yet the spirit of Revolutionary clubbability found in Porfirian Protestantism was absent from the Mormons, few of whom are known to have embraced Madero's 1910 uprising. Moreover, it was Protestant revolutionaries who took the lead in persecuting the Chihuahuan LDS colonists, forcing many to flee their homesteads in the exodus of 1912.

In another respect, Mormonism resembles second-wave Pentecostal-style dissidences, which cropped up in the middle years of the revolution, circa 1914. Like the Pentecostals, the LDS colonists arrived as part of a US-based, missionary church, subsequently becoming Mexicanized and spreading in small, schismatical increments. (There were at least five major schisms: those of Plotino C. Rhodakanaty, Margarito Bautista, the conventionists, Daniel Mejía, and Joel LeBaron, had occurred by the 1950s; and there were smaller breakaway movements in LDS communities encircling the Popocatépetl volcano in Puebla and Mexico State.)[12] Again, though, the link between religion and Revolutionary participation was not so explicit in the LDS Church compared to Pentecostal bodies like Luz del Mundo or the Iglesia de Dios, both of them founded by former constitutionalists. Nor was religious charisma diffused as dramatically in the LDS Church. Nor, finally, did Mormonism (yet) absorb migrant constituencies in urban settings, like Luz del Mundo: instead, it appealed to sedentary highland peasantries and pioneers.[13]

Yet another parallel exists in the eclectic third-wave dissidents whose Revolutionary work ethic or pedagogic labors won them invitations from post-Revolutionary officials. The Jehovah's Witnesses and Old Colony Mennonites, for example, both came to Mexico under state auspices in the 1920s, and in the Cárdenas years, the regime supported the Protestant fundamentalists led by Cameron Townsend. Mormons, too, benefited from tacit state support at times, yet this occurred more in the Porfiriato, not the post-Revolution era. Typically, too, Mormons had sought state sanction for specific practices: first, the right to acquire property in Mexico as US citizens, and particularly to observe the illegal practice known as celestial marriage (polygamy) without hindrance. The LDS Church thus sought to hide controversial practices in the shadows of the state, not to obscure the religious nature of its entire enterprise, which suggests a somewhat lower level of dependency. The LDS Church did not, for example, disguise itself as a philanthropical society, like the Witnesses, or as a mere language institute like Townsends's *indigenista* bible-punchers on the Hidalgo plains. Nor did it hole up in the mountains like the Mennonites.[14] Rather, Mexico's LDS Church changed in situ: beginning in Porfirian mold, it gravitated to the revolution as indigenous groups like Bautistas's community introduced a concept of Revolutionary liberty.

Lastly, perhaps most surprisingly, the LDS Church's transnationalism and vertical ecclesiology make for some interesting points of comparison with Roman Catholicism. Mormons, especially in northern Mexico, were self-consciously members of a transnational religious community that transcended the nation; not for them a reified sense of the border or any discomforting rupture between local and universal stylings of the faith, at least until they returned to the United States post-exodus and found themselves denounced as polygamists. Southern Mormons, by contrast, whose religion acclimatized to the villages of central Mexico, were disciplined by the Utahan elders via American mission chiefs who in some ways resembled the autocratic Romanized prelates then taking the Catholic episcopate by storm. In tragic fashion, Mormons endured the revolution's worst sectarianism after that faced by Catholics, and felt it first.

Mexican Mormondom thus evidenced similarities with other religions at the time in Mexcio. These traits, however, were compressed in uniquely Mormon cultural forms and revealed themselves through uniquely Mormon

Gathering of Mexican LDS members, date and location unknown, but probably a congregation in central Mexico. Photographer unknown. Courtesy of the Museum of Mormon Mexican History.

conjunctures. They included growing jurisdictional struggles in the church, particularly over the hierarchy's universalizing claims and the degrees of exceptionalism (indigenista, polygamous) claimed by local bodies; religious differences, which could originate in subaltern reinterpretations of revelation (Bautista) but most commonly involved the legitimation/proscription of practices defined as orthodox or unorthodox (polygamy, women's participation in the liturgy, petitioning Salt Lake City, hybrid devotional styles); contradictory economic approaches (United Order socialism, agrarian capitalism); and the exaltation or transcendence of the Mexican nation (Lamanite nationalism; the Anglo-American identities cultivated by Mormons on the US/Mexican border).[15]

MORMONISM AS LOCAL RELIGION

Turning to the specific themes outlined at the start, we can see that Mormonism as a normative set of beliefs and practices served only partially to contain, let alone integrate, religious divisions inside the church until 1946. In the 1910s through 1930s, in contrast, the essays here reveal that some Mormons desired to live their religion in a distinctively Mexican way, while others only hoped to preserve *in Mexico* what they saw as the Saints' so-called true religion. Making sense of this contradiction requires us to use a concept of religion, and here I would suggest that Mormonism in the first half of the twentieth century was often practiced in Mexico as a local religion. By this I mean a set of mixed, yet usually overlapping, devotional practices—some universal, others local. The relationship between the two, moreover, was not usually one of complete opposition, but more one of cooptation, and, as a final resort, disavowal and repression.[16]

The evidence clearly points to such a localization of religion, and to the idea that such divisions were both exacerbated and brought to breaking point by the Mexican Revolution. As stated, northern and central variants of Mormonism were different from inception. Though they were interconnected, in practice they frequently developed in isolation, largely because of LDS neglect until circa 1900 (when Utah was preoccupied with fighting off the polygamy charge) and subsequently because of the unstable political situation in Mexico.[17] Early efforts to reintegrate the two lines, as when southern colonists were invited to the Chihuahua colonies in the late Porfiriato, ended disastrously and left a legacy of resentment among incoming southerners.[18] Post-Revolutionary attempts were constantly frustrated by central Mexican demands for their mission to be run by a Mexican, which the Utahan LDS Church would not countenance.

It is tempting to see the northern version as more orthodox, but it, too, as Barbara Jones Brown's chapter shows, became localized because the Utahan church had changed ground on the question of plural marriage by 1904. Henceforth, both strains can reasonably be described as local Mormon religion, meaning this was not a simple division between American and Mexican, or orthodox and unorthodox, versions of the LDS Church. Rather, it was a question of social, political, and cultural forces impacting a weakly articulated Mexican Latter-day Saint movement, creating significant local variations in practice and belief in the process. From another perspective, it was a tale of initially futile Utahan attempts to manage these multiple expressions of Mormonism effectively.

Looking first at the Mexican north, we see that Mormonism was introduced in the 1870s by Anglo colonists seeking to preserve celestial marriage, a principle which, they held, readied practitioners for God's highest blessings. In this endeavor colonists *initially* embarked on an orthodox path, following the guidance of LDS presidents Brigham Young, John Taylor, and, more equivocally, Wilford Woodruff (collectively, presidents from 1847 to

1898).[19] Rebuilding a polygamous society was the essence of this kind of Mormonism.[20] Indeed, there was a twenty-five-year period, prior to the 1904 Smoot hearings and Joseph F. Smith's Second Manifesto, in which Mexico was recognized as the safe haven for polygamous Mormons. The articulation of north Mexican Mormonism as a civil and religious practice reflected this, as George Ryskamp's chapter shows through a critical reading of Mormon entries in the civil register. Mormons' civic vows, Ryskamp argues, obscured the existence of polygamous marriages (resulting offspring being registered as *hijos naturales*) while standing as a public record of Mormons' commitment to the law. In sum, Mormons strategically embraced a Mexican civic identity while tacitly reaffirming their status as polygamous Saints. More broadly, the northern colonies alone were raised to the level of a stake in 1895, by which point they had lost their missionary fervor and become polygamous enclaves. The proselytizing goals of the 1870s, which once led LDS preachers into Tarahumara and Yaqui settlements, were allowed to lapse with the closure of the Chihuahua and Sonora missions in 1899. In any case, as Daniel Jones once lamented, many of the colonists had discovered that they could not stand actual Lamanites in the flesh.[21]

US state formation propelled this type of Mormonism, therefore, after which it became successively localized, then just plain unorthodox. On the other hand, and as Barbara Jones Brown's chapter convincingly argues, it was the Mexican Revolution that inadvertently killed off polygamy, since it prompted the exodus of 1912 and forced polygamous exiles to confront their now uncomprehending brethren back in Utah. Mormon settlers in Mexico who remained true to the principle could cleave to schismatic groups like the Colonia LeBaron, but their heyday was over. Jones Brown's essay makes use of fascinating personal correspondence to recapture the emotional hardships this rejection caused to those concerned; yet the main thrust of her chapter, as with Ryskamp's, is to demonstrate how intimately connected changes in Mormon religious practice were to bigger sociopolitical shifts, both in and outside Mexico.

In the center of the country, it was a case of Mexicanized Mormondom not Mormonized Mexico. Indeed, Mormonism here followed a diametrically opposite path, starting out as a tiny urban phenomenon in 1870s Mexico City before settling in a few surrounding pueblos in the 1880s. The subsequent interaction between very patchy missionary work and village cultures generated a variety of local spin-offs in the late Porfiriato and Revolutionary decades, until this trend partly reversed itself with the reassertion of Utahan authority in 1946 and, rather later, the creation of the first stake in 1961. A common feature of the entire period, however, was that Mormonism appealed mainly to residents of indigenous pueblos in the Valley of Mexico, specifically in the hacienda-textile belt running east and southeast of Mexico City: Ozumba, at the base of the Popocatépetl, provided the first converts, but then came Ixtacalco, Tecalco, Chimal, Nopala, Chalco, and Atlautla. These were so-called Catholic communities that spiritually rebooted between 1880 and 1910, and again in the Revolutionary decades; having shown interest in political liberalism and schismatic Catholicism in the 1860s, from the 1880s they experimented with Protestantism (usually Methodism) and later honed a particular style of Mormonism.[22] This trend, we might add, was occasionally but much less frequently repeated in the Mexican north; it was roughly the case, for example, in the *municipios* of Guerrero and Namiquipa (Chihuahua) where Mormon missionaries actively disseminated the Book of Mormon, apparently with some success—though whether these converts included future *tomochitecos* (spiritual-agrarian rebels from an 1891 revolt in the town of Tomochi) or *villistas* (followers of Francisco "Pancho" Villa) remains a fascinating yet still unanswered question.[23]

A detailed understanding of the conversion process and of the early development of indigenous or peasant Mormonisms thus remains an important lacuna in the historiography.[24] Nonetheless, several chapters effectively address the subtle interactions between Mormon ideas and local culture in the 1900s and beyond, collectively revealing the significance of a grassroots, largely indigenous constituency to the long-term development of Mormonism in Mexico. Jared M. Tamez's insightful chapter on Chalco and Atlautla, for example, shows how Mormonism became entwined with highly local practices in the absence of effective supervision from the northern stake or Utah. Precisely, Tamez contrasts the records found in the mission's minute books before and after protracted periods of missionary inactivity to trace the development of a hybrid, village-style Mormonism over three decades, one premised on religious mobility and a deregulated kind of social participation. To the consternation of visiting elders like Ammon Tenney, who reactivated the mission in 1901, Mormonism here was cross-fertilized with Methodism, with the result that unseemly practices entered the tradition—impromptu services and tearful prayer sessions led by women and unordained men, for example, as well as rites peppered with hymn singing and exuberant Biblical exhortations. Second, Mormonism emerged in a less patriarchal mold. Third, and equally significant, it became entwined with secular elements of pueblo culture. Tenney considered Indian Mormons to be exceptionally religious but morally and sexually libertine. The pueblos were refractory to ecclesiastical authority, too, when this was in their interests.[25] In a word, Tamez reveals the emerging contours of a local Mormon culture, one that would assume a more antagonistic stance vis-à-vis mainline Mormonism come the revolution.

Elisa Pulido's chapter pursues this theme by showing that the colonial right of petition, refired by nationalistic indignation in the Revolutionary 1930s, was the cultural taproot of Third Convention Mormonism. The conventionist hybrid was perhaps best encapsulated in the title of its periodical, *Sendero Lamanita* (Lamanite Path), which hinted that Mormonism was developing as an Indian folkway given a patriotic Revolutionary gloss. Margarito Bautista went further than this, as Stuart Parker's essay shows, when he claimed that the Revolutionary *ejido* (a pseudo-indigenous land corporation) was of divine origin. Village fields, socialistic reforms, and Mormon theology, whether taken out of context or creatively deployed, therefore met in a local synthesis that was used to undergird the rights of the highland agrarian community. This was not so surprising given the degree of indigenous leadership that obtained in the southern LDS congregations from circa 1900, yet it returns us to the essential point that Mexico's LDS Church was a diverse organization whose assimilation with the norms of the Utahan mainline would not necessarily be straightforward.

MORMON CHURCH, MEXICAN STATE

The LDS had a complicated relationship with the Mexican state, which reflected these local differences and the sort of expectations that were associated with them. Indeed, the ties between the LDS and Mexico's state-information were as varied as the relationship between LDS orthodoxy and local religious practice, though in the end they varied on similar lines. Before discussing the variations, however, it is worth noting a line of continuity that seemingly ran through the period: Mormonism's truth claims as a universal religion administered via a divinely sanctioned hierarchy meant that the LDS Church was jealous of its control of the religious sphere and reluctant to admit state supervision of what it viewed as religious matters. A *degree* of ambiguity was therefore common in LDS dealings with the state. Polygamy was the classic case, already discussed, but there were later examples.

Foreign-born LDS missionaries visited Mexico on various occasions in the 1920s through 1940s, for instance, regardless of the constitutional ban on the exercise of religious ministry by non-Mexicans. Two US elders, Antoine R. Ivins and George F. Richards, were rapidly escorted from a meeting in February 1937 at which they planned to berate Third Conventionists as schismatic, for fear that they would themselves be arrested by government agents. The principle they had come to defend was Utahan leaders' right to nominate local leaders in Mexico and require the people to sustain them, which does not seem a million miles away from the Romanist principles of canon law.[26] All this is significant in that some Mormon missionaries (and historians) are wont to contrast the LDS's willingness to obey Mexican law with Roman Catholicism's imperiousness as a state-within-a-state. In fact, Mexican Mormon engagements with the state were contingent affairs based on the convergence or otherwise of institutional interests and authority claims.

It is this that explains the divergent postures of the LDS Church toward Mexico's state. Once again, geography was important. On the one hand, Anglo Mormons fetishized Mexico's liberal state builders, as is evident in the names given to many of the colonies.[27] This was not surprising given that the Díaz regime allowed the LDS colonists into Mexico. Just as important, however, the LDS Church endorsed the modernizing dreams of Porfirian industrialists and agriculturalists, right down to the canned fruit that Juárez colonists sent to Mexico City food fairs.[28] Northern Mormonism was more ambivalent about the post-Revolutionary state, though, and was particularly suspicious of its nationalism and agrarianism—to the extent that Mormon landowners in 1920s Namiquipa (Chihuahua) attempted to block the ejidal petitions of the local peasantry.[29] Northern Mormons in general preferred a state that was patriotic in terms of rhetoric but in practice cosmopolitan. The state's ideological content therefore mattered greatly.

In the Central Valley of Mexico, however, the LDS were associated with a radical critique of the Porfirian state's developmentalist project, as dreamed up by Plotino C. Rhodakanaty (the "Mormon Eagle") from 1876. This critique has been explored in the strong, revisionist chapter by Bill Smith and Jared M. Tamez, which shows that Rhodakanaty wanted a Mormon-style socialism based on the United Order, a theologically driven communalism endorsed by Joseph Smith and Brigham Young. In a close reading of his written correspondence, the authors demonstrate that Rhodakanaty believed in a kind of Mormonism that would solve the problems of poor workers, meaning the economically poor, not just spiritually poor gentiles. This led LDS elders to accuse Rhodakanaty of coopting their theology, prompting his excommunication. Yet again, we see how state forms could shape novel responses in Mormonism and precipitate contests of ideas and authority.

In the end, LDS members thought more in terms of specific states, support for which rested on particular ideological and cultural affinity as well as politics. Where there was some convergence with their religious values, LDS members assisted the state by assimilating some of its practices. But overall, as these two Porfirian examples demonstrate, the relationship of Mexico's LDS Church with the state was a dynamic and variegated one. This is worth stressing because it helps to clarify why, in the post-Revolutionary decades, some LDS groups became cheerleaders of the Calles and Cárdenas governments while others denounced their expropriatory politics.[30] Perhaps it also explains why—though the hypothesis is conjectural—the mainline LDS Church in Utah found the confidence to reassert itself over Mexican Mormondom post-1940, when Mexico was governed by a self-declared Catholic believer and socially moderate member of the Revolutionary elite.

THE LDS AND THE MEXICAN REVOLUTION

Mormon attitudes toward the Revolutionary project support some of these assertions. Here again, we need to distinguish LDS members as victims of Revolutionary violence from the apparently small number who took to the hills and the greater but still apparently small number who took inspiration from the ideals of the revolution. It was not the case, though, that Mormons were necessarily repelled by the idea of violent social change. As Daniel Herman's chapter shows, a "culture of violence" was a constituent part of (American) Southwest Mormonism, which in places developed a powerful theological binary of Mormon holiness and gentile depravity, and on occasions acted violently (and zealously) upon it.[31] Herman's ultimate point is a broader one, however: that multiple Mormonisms coexisted, and that the more warlike strains had often assimilated their propensities to violence from the secular cultures in which they operated. This was the case in nineteenth-century Arizona, Herman shows, where some Saints assimilated the violent norms of Western culture and resorted to shotgun justice, even hiring Rooster Cogburn–type sheriffs to tame (they alleged) Mexican cattle rustlers. Yet other Saints did no such thing and peacefully sustained the legalistic bases of a more urbane gentile society.

Though Herman does not directly make the point, the Zelig-like tendency that he observes in the American Southwest, if applied to Mexico, suggests that Mormon participation in the revolution was neither a given nor a philosophical impossibility; we might even ask ourselves why LDS colonists' exposure to frontier society did not yield a local Revolutionary culture or cultures of its own, a respectable Mormon-style *maderismo*, a rowdy, prophetic *villismo*, or both. In central Mexico, by contrast, it appears that there may have been such a thing as a Mormon-style *zapatismo*, given that some Mormons revered Zapata as an Indian messiah, even if others detested him.[32] Connections between the LDS and Revolutionary mobilization represent an interesting and an open line of inquiry therefore, especially, perhaps, for the post-Revolutionary decades. Parker gives us an insightful chapter about Margarito Bautista, the Nahua prophet who defended the Calles regime from its religious-political foes. But some other Mormons, too, were significant Revolutionary functionaries or members of affiliate organizations, and so would merit further scholarly study: Third Conventionist leader Isaías Juárez, for example, was an agrarian department employee and founder of the *cardenista* peasant league (Confederación Nacional Campesina, or CNC) whose agrarianism was radical and notorious enough for him to be exiled by the conservative regimes of the Maximato; Daniel Mejía, who led a schism in Morelos, was a worker in a sugar factory in *zapatista* Cuautla.[33] No doubt there were other comparable figures.

Such formal links are worth pursuing in the deep Revolutionary-era archives, so that we have a clearer sense of how Revolutionary ideas dialogued with Mormonism in the case of key individuals like Bautista and Juárez, Revolutionary changelings both. More broadly, we need to understand how Mormons transitioned in the medium term to life in the post-Revolutionary order, and how they participated in major Revolutionary programs like *agrarismo*, labor reform, and public schooling, as well as PRI politics. These questions matter, given that the LDS's history post-1940 remains the most obvious lacuna in the literature. Just how did a church associated with Porfirismo and resistant to Revolutionary innovation—bar its schismatical spinoffs—so find its feet in the *priísta* regime that it became Mexico's third largest religion? If some causes of this change lie tangled in the roots of the LDS's Revolutionary history, they deserve digging up.[34]

From what we know so far, we might advance two connected hypotheses. First, it may be that the reemergence after 1910 of the socially utopian type of Mormonism already discussed in reference to Plotino C. Rhodakanaty was significant in providing a bridge between Revolutionary and LDS values in the latter part of our period. Stuart Parker's methodologically artful (indeed Ginzbergian) study of Bautista's cosmic nationalism is a case in point. Although (and perhaps because) he had not seen the armed revolution in the flesh, Bautista lionized the Sonoran governments as national redeemers; he likewise inserted the LDS Church into a teleological and mystical history of his country, *La evolución de México* (1935). This vast tome ended with a call for a racially based national church: Mexico's revolutionaries were "true shepherds of the national flock," Bautista wrote, in that they freed the Lamanites from Rome and so facilitated their realization as Mormonism's superrace in a future church dubbed the National Religious Convention. This account is bizarrely original in its epistemological blending of prophecy, patriot history, and scientific theory, Parker observes, yet it appealed to his coreligionists. Thus it was that some LDS figures engaged ex post facto with post-Revolutionary ideas, eliding Mormon religion, millennial concerns, and nationalism in striking ways.

Usually, however, Mexican Zionists had more limited goals, which brings me to a second hypothesis: moderate grassroots mobilization among the LDS members may also have been significant in reframing Mormonism in ways acceptable to a wider Mexican audience. The Third Convention, for example, rested on the desire for self-respect and autonomy within the orthodox theology and structure of the LDS Church. As such it was more amenable to reintegration when the opportunity came in the 1940s and offered a more workable translation of revolutionary nationalism in a religious context. Nonetheless, as Elisa Pulido's essay expertly shows, a spirit of democratic participation drove conventionists back to the fold, as well as away from it. A key factor in the schism was Utah's stubborn, if not humiliating, refusal to grant the mission full access to religious truth in Spanish: instead, Mexican Mormons thumbed a truncated version of the Book of Mormon, known as the *Trozos Selectos*. Hence the schismatics sought recognition as mature spiritual actors and the right to study full LDS doctrine in the vernacular, not just jurisdiction.

An inclusive ethos also drove the reunification of Mexican Mormondom. Indeed, Mormons at the grassroots, women especially, had been working to reintegrate the branches of the church before mission president Arwell Pierce arrived in 1942, Pulido shows, thus setting the scene for conventionist reunification with Utah. This conclusion strongly revises the traditional historiography, which sees a top-down, Utahan solution: Tullis, for example, sees

Pierce as the Dwight Morrow of Mormon religious diplomacy and claims that he won over the rebellious Lamanites by showing them the folly of ethnic pride and showing them the way, which was to seek recognition from Salt Lake City as a stake, not revolt because they were denied a Mexican mission chief.[35] By stressing popular agency, however, Pulido suggests the emergence of a negotiated religious (as well as Revolutionary) hegemony by the 1940s. This cultural shift may help to explain why Mormonism expanded so prodigiously under Revolutionary rule, and again suggests that understanding the relationship between Mormonism and popular (religious) culture is key for future research. Analysis might also focus on the ecumenical history of the LDS Church, largely absent from the discussion here, or on state views on Mormonism as a non-Catholic religious practice. Another gap, finally, is the detailed sociology of Mexican Mormonism.

MORMONISM AS A TRANSNATIONAL COMMUNITY

In some clear ways, the patterns that we have seen in this volume can be explained by the fact that different Mormon communities were more or less transnational in character. As we have seen, central Mexican Mormonism was weakly transnational in spirit: though part of a normative belief system and an institutional framework that crossed borders, it was most conscious of local gravity's pull, a fact that at times led it into conflict with the LDS hierarchy. In the final analysis, it was assumed that Mormonism should corrugate *mexicanidad*, which again is why LDS expansionism contradicts assertions that Mormonism was religious Americanization.[36] Northern Mormonism, however, was deeply implicated in Porfirian development policies along the US-Mexico border and, from its inception, increasingly integrated in transnational networks of both a religious and nonreligious kind. Indeed, ultimately this type of Mormonism denoted an Anglo cultural identity and an associated religious identity, both of which inhabited a secondary (Mexican) civic identity. Though it is plain that the Mormonism of the Díaz colony was not simply an insular religion for communities of refugees, its relationship to northern Mexican society was of a minimalist, official kind. It is true that the Porfirian government stood behind attempts to settle northern Mexico with Mormon colonies, yet the arriving colonists' strongest and most enduring ties were transnational ones. Some of the Díaz colonists were lured into Mexico on the strength of a promised railroad boom and a

Mormon exodus southward, dreams that evaporated once the financial ambitions of the Mexican Pacific Railway Company—featuring colorful but unreliable figures such as the German-Mexican capitalist Luis Huller and a former *yanqui* colonel, Andrew Bailey—had evaporated. At the same time, the colonists were welcomed by the Demingite merchants who serviced the community and exalted by the New Mexican press as law-abiding farmers, not stereotypical bigamists. Mormons were clearly plugged into wider webs of capital and commerce and thought in transnational terms, to the extent that they reached out to collaborators further afield in an attempt to lay a railroad that would pump new migrants and supplies into the colonies. These commercial ties antagonized the repatriate Mexican community of Ascensión, which used its control of the nearest customs house to wreck the railway project by levying duties on railroad equipment and forcing the constructors to haul everything cross-country to the Díaz colony. Thus a transnational Mormonism strove to efface the border while a transnational Mexican American presence strove to reinscribe it;[37] and come the Revolutionary exodus, the Díaz colonists walked back up their abortive railroad to New Mexico. Morgan's work, like Ryskamp's, points the way toward a transnational history of the Porfirian LDS, one that might also open itself more to the history of Mexican Mormons in the United States or the role played by waves of Mexican migration in disseminating Mormonism in subsequent decades.

CONCLUSION

Just South of Zion reveals Mexican Mormonism in much hitherto unknown complexity, as a surprisingly diverse religious community that was articulated in a complex social and religious field and so quickly pulled in different directions by the interactions of state, popular cultures, geography, and local religion. A synthesis of sorts prevailed by the 1940s as Mormonism and nationalistic, post-Revolutionary Mexico learned to assimilate each other. In closing a work that sets a new standard for historical research into Mexican Mormondom, let the last word come from a voice at the grassroots, LDS Apostle Melvin J. Ballard:

> In an interview with Apostle Ballard [1938], recently he expressed pleasure at the treatment accorded his people in Mexico by the

Federal Government. While admitting that some indignities may be
perpetrated against the Mormons by the local Mexicans, they are
done without the sanction of the State or Federal Government. Every
concession possible under the law is being tendered the Mormon
people as an inducement to have them remain and build up the country. . . . The Latter-day Saints are fulfilling a great mission in Mexico,
says Elder Ballard. . . . Apostle Ballard is encouraging all of the colonists in Mexico to become citizens of that country.[38]

NOTES

1. The standard monograph that bridges the confessional and scholarly categories
   is F. LaMond Tullis, *Mormons in Mexico: The Dynamics of Faith and Culture*
   (Logan: Utah State University Press, 1987). The publication of edifying firsthand
   accounts also continues, e.g., Thomas Cottam Romney, *The Mormon Colonies in
   Mexico* (1938; repr., Salt Lake City: University of Utah Press, 2006); and Mary
   Lois Walker Morris, *Before the Manifesto: The Life Writings of Mary Lois Walker
   Morris*, ed. M. L. Milewski (Logan: Utah State University Press, 2007), see espe-
   cially "Exile in Mexico, 1902–1905," 534–74. Recent scholarly studies include Janet
   Bennion, *Desert Patriarchy: Mormon and Mennonite Communities in the
   Chihuahua Valley* (Tucson: University of Arizona Press, 2004); and Jane-Dale
   Lloyd, *El distrito de Galeana en los albores de la revolución. Rancheros y mor-
   mones: espacio regional, comercio, y un proceso de desamortización tardío*
   (Chihuahua: Gobierno del Estado de Chihuahua, 2011).
2. Mormon theology, Tullis writes at the beginning of *Mormons in Mexico* (5–13),
   foretold the "gathering"—the baptism and conversion—of the dispersed tribes of
   Israel as a prelude to Christ's second coming, and also identified indigenous
   Mexicans as "Lamanites," or descendants of the line of Joseph. As a result, Tullis
   avers, Mormon expansion in Mexico signified the imminence of the millennium:
   it was a case of "eschatological fervor" emerging via a "profoundly felt need to
   preach the gospel to the Indians," not religious colonialism.
3. Jason H. Dormady, in the introduction to this volume, alludes to the question of
   routinization: "Like the Mexican Revolution itself, Mormonism transitioned
   from a radical re-envisioning of economics and social order into a paragon of
   liberal capitalism."
4. "A Revolution in Spirit? Mexico, 1910–1940," in Matthew Butler, ed., *Faith and
   Impiety in Revolutionary Mexico* (New York: Palgrave Macmillan, 2007), 1–20.
   For an explicitly Bourdieuian survey using the religious field concept, see
   Guillermo de la Peña, "El campo religioso, la diversidad regional, y la identidad
   nacional en México," *Relaciones: Estudios de Historia y Sociedad* 25, no. 100
   (2004): 21–71.

5. For an overview of the period, see Matthew Butler, "Religious Developments in Mexico, 1865–1945," in *Cambridge History of Religions in America, 1790–1945*, ed. Stephen J. Stein (Cambridge, UK: Cambridge University Press, 2012), 2:702–26.

6. Jason Dormady, in *Primitive Revolution: Restorationist Religion and the Idea of the Mexican Revolution, 1940–1968* (Albuquerque: University of New Mexico Press, 2011), 5, advances the concept of "informal religious corporatism." See also Andrew R. Chesnut, *Competitive Spirits: Latin America's New Religious Economy* (Oxford: Oxford University Press, 2003), which sees a monopolistic Catholicism capitulating to a religious market circa 1950.

7. I borrow this formulation from Gilbert Joseph and Daniel Nugent, eds., *Everyday Forms of State Formation: Revolution and the Negotiation of Rule in Modern Mexico* (Durham, NC: Duke University Press, 1994).

8. Roberto Blancarte, *Historia de la Iglesia Católica en México* (Mexico City: Fondo de Cultura Económica, 1992).

9. Griselda Chávez Rentería, "Otra revolución cultural en Aguascalientes: la educación religiosa en las mujeres adolescentes de la Iglesia de Jesucristo de los Santos de los Últimos Días, 1940–1990," in *Revolución, cultura, y religión: nuevas perspectivas regionales, siglo XX*, ed. Yolanda Padilla Rangel, Luciano Ramírez Hurtado, and Francisco Javier Delgado Aguilar (Aguascalientes: Universidad Autónoma de Aguascalientes, 2012), 312–30.

10. In 1912 there were 4,000 Saints in nine colonies in northern Mexico, with an additional 1,000 in the central Mexican Mission; by the 1930s, however, this pattern was inverted, with the central Mexico Saints tripling in number and the northern contingent obliterated. Jones Brown, in chapter 1 of this volume, estimates that 90 percent of the 4,500 Mormons who fled during the exodus never returned. Other figures from Tullis, *Mormons in Mexico*, 56, 82, 142.

11. Jean-Pierre Bastian, *Los disidentes: sociedades protestantes y revolución en México, 1872–1911* (Mexico City: El Colegio de México, 1989).

12. On the first four, see Smith and Tamez, Parker, and Pulido, all this volume. On the Colonia LeBaron schism, see Bennion, *Desert Patriarchy*, 121–42.

13. Renée de la Torre, *Los hijos de la luz: Discurso, identidad y poder en la Luz del Mundo* (Mexico City: ITESO-CIESAS-Universidad de Guadalajara, 1995); Deyssy Jael de la Luz García, *El movimiento pentecostal en México: La Iglesia de Dios, 1926–1948* (Mexico City: Editorial Manda, 2010).

14. Harim B. Gutiérrez, "Apuntes para una historia de los Testigos de Jehová en México: Los orígenes, las primeras disidencias, y la consolidación de su movimiento, 1919–1944," *Estudios de Historia Moderna y Contemporánea de México* 28 (2004): 131–74; Todd Hartch, *Missionaries of the State: The Summer Institute of Linguistics, State Formation, and Indigenous Mexico, 1935–1985* (Tuscaloosa: University of Alabama Press, 2006); and Jason Dormady, "Rights, Rule, and Religion: Old Colony Mennonites and Mexico's Transition to the Free Market, 1920–2000," in *Religious Culture in Modern Mexico*, ed. Martin Austin Nesvig (Lanham: Rowman and Littlefield, 2007), 157–77.

15. For details, see, respectively Ryskamp, Smith and Tamez, Tamez, Morgan, Parker, and Pulido, all this volume.

16. For an application of this concept to Mexico, see Martin Austin Nesvig, ed., *Local Religion in Colonial Mexico* (Albuquerque: University of New Mexico Press, 2006).

17. Interactions between the two branches were interrupted for long periods, first from 1889 to 1901 because of church retrenchment during US anti-bigamy campaigns, and again from 1913 to 1917 because of the revolution. Another rupture occurred from 1924 to 1935 with the departure of Rey Pratt to South America and the difficulties that religious persecution caused to foreign ecclesiastical personnel in Mexico. The last break occurred from 1937 to 1946, following Utah's excommunication of the conventionists and others it viewed as schismatics.

18. Referring to this experiment, even Tullis notes that "a restrained element of Anglo-American condescension" soured ties between the northern and southern LDS (*Mormons in Mexico*, 63).

19. Woodruff's 1890 Manifesto outlawed plural marriage in mainstream LDS but permitted it to continue in Mexico. The 1904 Second Manifesto outlawed the practice everywhere.

20. Tullis writes that an "enormous effort" was made to keep polygamous families intact. Tullis, *Mormons in Mexico*, 58.

21. Ibid., 26–31, 70–71.

22. Ibid., 41–42, 77; Bastian, *Los disidentes*, 90–95.

23. Jason Dormady, personal communication regarding the mission of Daniel Webster Jones.

24. The topic of Mormon spirituality (i.e., what being a Mormon meant to different groups) is a rich topic that could be explored further. One might ask, for example, why Mormonism did not fuse with existing local practices in the north. Though it was a millenarian religion, it does not seem to have tapped into indigenous millenarian culture, which was strong in Porfirian Chihuahua, as Paul Vanderwood's work on Tomóchic shows. See Vanderwood, *The Power of God Against the Guns of Government: Religious Upheaval in Mexico at the Turn of the Nineteenth Century* (Stanford, CA: Stanford University Press, 1998).

25. On Protestant cross-fertilization and "decidedly un-Mormon" practices, see Tullis, *Mormons in Mexico*, 77.

26. For the principle, see Pulido, chapter 5 of this volume. For the incident, see Tullis, *Mormons in Mexico*, 118, 138, 144. Rey Pratt, mission president until the mid-1920s, also attended LDS meetings in Mexico but never sat on the podium and so did not violate the laws regarding religious ministry, suggests Tullis casuistically (113–16).

27. Two were named after Díaz and his home state (Oaxaca), three for obscure Porfirian officials (Dublán, Pacheco, García), and two others after conventional patriotic heroes (Juárez and Morelos).

28. Tullis, *Mormons in Mexico*, 59.

29. Daniel Nugent, *Spent Cartridges of Revolution: An Anthropological History of Namiquipa, Chihuahua* (Chicago, IL: University of Chicago Press, 1993), 111.

30. For example, see Romney, *The Mormon Colonies in Mexico*, 300–301:

> As I write these lines [1938], a revolution is on in Mexico. . . . The unsettled condition in Mexico, together with the expropriation of the oil properties of American and English capitalists have led many to fear for the future welfare and prosperity of foreigners in Mexico. What further discriminations may be enacted against them can only be conjectured in the light of what has already taken place. In the Mormon colonies within the past four months . . . certain hateful indignities have been imposed by local Mexicans against certain of the law-abiding citizens of these settlements. . . . Another colonist, the water master, was placed behind the bars for venturing to do his duty. A native Mexican had refused to release the irrigation water to an American farmer who was entitled to it whereupon the latter complained to the water master. The water was taken from the Mexican and given to the American and this resulted in the water master being placed behind the bars. If such acts of injustice and intolerance continue no one but a prophet can foretell what the future may develop.

31. The classic, if controversial, study in this regard is Will Bagley, *Blood of the Prophets: Brigham Young and the Massacre at Mountain Meadows* (Norman: University of Oklahoma Press, 2004).

32. On Mormons and *zapatismo*, see Tullis, *Mormons in Mexico*, 97.

33. On Juárez, see ibid., 158; and Tullis, "*Los Primeros*: Mexico's Pioneer Saints," *Ensign*, July 1997, 47. For Mejía, see Pulido, chapter 5 of this volume. On Bautista, see Parker, chapter 6 of this volume, as well as Dormady, *Primitive Revolution*, 63–111.

34. Even in the case of the Galeana *ejido* in Chihuahua, for example, there were complaints by the 1980s that recently arrived Lebaronites ("FOREIGN MORMONS") were acting in league with the local agrarian commissariat and starting to monopolize the *ejido*'s best irrigated lands (Nugent, *Spent Cartridges*, 112, 185n6).

35. Tullis, *Mormons in Mexico*, 154–57.

36. Dormady, *Primitive Revolution*, 63–64.

37. On Mexican American migration southward and the articulation of the border, as well as attitudes concerning the LDS, see José Ángel Hernández, *Mexican American Colonization During the Nineteenth Century: A History of the U.S.-Mexico Borderlands* (Cambridge, UK: Cambridge University Press, 2012), 29, 35, 222.

38. Romney, *Mormon Colonies*, 308–9.

Glossary of Terms Related to
Mormonism or Mexican Mormonism

bishop: The male priesthood head of a local congregation or ward. Equivalent to a parish priest in Catholicism or a pastor in Protestantism. See also **priesthood**.

chapel, or ward building: Mormons from the LDS tradition use three kinds of worship spaces: temples, chapels, and tabernacles. Chapels (also known as ward buildings) are for weekly worship services and activities, and tabernacles were used for regional and church conferences—though the construction of tabernacles ceased in the early twentieth century. See also **temple**.

convencionistas/conventionists: Members of a Mexican LDS movement called the Third Convention (1932–1946), who advocated for more mestizo leadership in wards, stakes, and missions. The resulting schism created a Mexican LDS church until it reconciled with Salt Lake City in 1946. Most active in Mexico City, Mexico State, Puebla, and Morelos.

Deseret: The vision of Brigham Young's settlement of the American West in 1847 was to create a nation called Deseret, which would either become an independent nation or an American State. Deseret, as imagined by Young, would have included parts of present-day eastern Nevada, southern Utah, Arizona, western Colorado, western Wyoming, and southeastern Idaho—all areas heavily settled by Mormon colonists. Though LDS leaders in Deseret created their own alphabet, had a limited coinage, and attempted to engage in import substitution of finished and agricultural goods, the entity never achieved complete economic or political autonomy.

elder: An office in the hierarchy of Mormon priesthood. "Elder" is also used as a title for male missionaries as well as members of the highest levels of church leadership known as General Authorities (see below). Though missionaries and General Authorities serve different functions within Mormonism, the application of the title "elder" to each of these groups is representative of the primarily evangelistic role these groups share.

First Presidency: The president of the LDS church and his two counselors. This represents the highest ecclesiastical and administrative level of authority in the organization. See also **General Authority**.

General Authority: A member of the three highest governing bodies within the LDS church: the Quorum of the Seventy, the Quorum of Twelve Apostles, and the First Presidency.

mission president: An office in the LDS church called by the Quorum of the Twelve Apostles to supervise missionaries and missionary work in a particular geographic area. In the nineteenth and early twentieth centuries they also supervised the ecclesiastical affairs of some branches, wards, and districts.

priesthood: In Mormon theology, the authorization to preside over congregations, administer church affairs, preach, and engage in certain ceremonies, ordinations, and rites are all tied to priesthood authority. Mormon offices of the priesthood are open only to men, and at regional and congregational levels they are entirely in the hands of volunteer laity. Priesthood offices are held by boys starting as early as age twelve in the modern period but were sometimes held at younger ages earlier during the nineteenth century.

Primary: Considered an auxiliary organization of the LDS Church, Primary is the children's religious education wing of the organization. Until the late twentieth century, children met on a weekday once a week for one to two hours of religious instruction, games, and music.

prophet/president: Mormon theology holds that just as in the Biblical texts, God continues to call prophets on the earth to whom revelation and guidance is given to run the administrative aspects of the church as well as to provide direction and guidance in spiritual matters or temporal welfare. In the LDS Church, the president of the church (also referred to alternately as the prophet) is the highest ranking of these prophets. In addition, Latter-day Saints also believe that there are twelve living apostles on the earth, and they, along with the church president, are referred to as prophets, seers, and revelators. The LDS apostles and First Presidency of the church have always been male. Many Mormon groups that are not LDS also have prophets and presidents of their organizations. See also **General Authority**.

Quorum of the Twelve: The Quorum of the Twelve Apostles is the second-highest level of administration and governance in the LDS Church. Apostles and the office of apostle are also present in non-LDS Mormon organizations.

Relief Society: The women's auxiliary for the LDS Church founded by Joseph Smith and headed by his first wife, Emma. The organization focuses on charitable care of the ill and poor as well as theological instruction for adult women. Until the 1970s the organization had considerable autonomy from the male hierarchy of the LDS Church. At the local level it is headed by a presidency of female leaders that reports to the congregation's bishop. At the general church level, there is a Relief Society Presidency that is supervised by the First Presidency and Quorum of the Twelve Apostles.

Seventy: An office in the LDS priesthood, in the nineteenth century these LDS members generally served as preachers and missionaries to non-Mormons in their local congregational boundaries. By 1976 the local seventies were replaced and Quorums of the Seventy were created as the third general governing body of the LDS Church. See also **General Authority**.

stake: Also "Stake of Zion." An organizational unit comprised of a varied number of individual congregations—either wards or branches. The unit is presided over by a stake president and a high council that supervise the various bishops, priesthood quorums, and auxiliaries. Organizationally, it is akin to the diocese of the Catholic Church.

temple: Temples are considered special sites of worship in Mormonism and have various uses in the history of the movement as well as between Mormon religions. Latter-day Saints are the most prolific temple builders of all Mormon sects. The LDS Church uses temples as sites where religious instruction about the nature, purpose, and destiny of humanity is taught along with a series of rituals and the use of special ritual clothing. Temple attendance is generally restricted to the most adherent practitioners of the faith in the LDS tradition.

ward/branch: The basic organizational unit of LDS Mormonism is the congregation. Large congregations are called wards and are headed by a priesthood leader called the bishop—akin to the Catholic parish and the parish priest. Smaller LDS congregations are headed by a priesthood leader called a branch president.

Zion: Drawn from the story of the Biblical prophet Enoch whose city was said to be taken up to heaven because of the righteousness of the people, Zion was used by early LDS Mormons to refer to anywhere that was the center of the church: Ohio, Missouri, Illinois, and finally Utah. When it became impractical for all converts to the LDS Church to travel to Utah to live, members were encouraged to stay in the places they were converted and "strengthen the stakes of Zion," meaning to grow their local regional units. In LDS theology, Zion is also used to mean any group that is unified in religious purpose and absent of conflict and contention. LDS scripture describes these utopian communities as follows: "And the Lord called his people Zion, because they were of one heart and one mind, and dwelt in righteousness; and there was no poor among them" (Moses 7:18).

Contributors

Matthew Butler (PhD, University of Bristol) is an associate professor of modern Mexican history at the University of Texas at Austin. He is the author of *Popular Piety and Political Identity in Mexico's Cristero Rebellion: Michoacán, 1927–1929* (Oxford University Press, 2004) and the editor of *Faith and Impiety in Revolutionary Mexico* (Palgrave Macmillan, 2007). He is currently completing a manuscript on independent Catholicisms in Mexico and coediting (with Marta Eugenia Garcia Ugarte and Pablo Serrano Alvarez) a volume on the regional history of Catholicism in nineteenth- and twentieth-century Mexico.

Jason H. Dormady (PhD, University of California, Santa Barbara) is an associate professor of history at Central Washington University where he teaches courses on Mexico, Latin America, and world history. He is the author of *Primitive Revolution: Restorationist Religion and the Idea of the Mexican Revolution, 1940–1968* (UNM Press, 2011). He is also the author of "'Disobedience, rebelliousness . . . and discontent': Parishioner / Clerical Disputes in Tepalcingo, Morelos, 1937–1946" (2014) and "Mennonite Colonization in Mexico and the Pendulum of Modernization, 1920–2013" (2014).

Daniel Herman (PhD, University of California, Berkeley) is a professor of history at Central Washington University. His specialties include the American West, American cultural history, and American Indian history. His most recent book—*Rim Country Exodus: A Story of Conquest, Renewal, and Race in the Making* (Tucson: University of Arizona Press, 2012)—won the Labriola Center National American Indian Book Award and the Charles Redd Center-Phi Alpha Theta Book Award in Western History.

Barbara Jones Brown (MA, University of Utah) is an independent scholar and sits on the board of directors of the Mormon History Association. She served as content editor for Oxford University Press's 2008 *Massacre at*

Mountain Meadows and is currently working in the same capacity on a sequel to that book. She is a team member of the Mormon Women's History initiative and recently completed a biography of Lorna Call Alder, a child of a polygamous family living in Mexico during the Revolution of 1910.

Brandon Morgan (PhD, University of New Mexico) currently teaches Latin American and borderlands history at Central New Mexico Community College and online at Western New Mexico University. In addition to teaching, he is working on revisions to his dissertation manuscript, "Columbus, New Mexico, and Palomas, Chihuahua: Transnational Landscapes of Violence, 1888–1930." Recent publications include "Columbus, New Mexico: The Creation of a Border Place Myth, 1888–1916" (2014) and "From Brutal Ally to Humble Believer: Mormon Colonists' Image of Pancho Villa" (2010).

Stuart Parker (PhD, University of Toronto) is a historian, activist, and socialist politician based in Vancouver, BC. Since completing his postdoctoral work at Brigham Young University, he has maintained a diverse research portfolio, including articles in *Sport and Society* and the *Journal of Mormon History*. His dissertation—"History Through Seer Stones: Mormon Historical Thought 1890–2010"— is currently under contract with Greg Kofford Books as *History Through Seer Stones: A Hundred Years of Mormon Pasts*. A commentator on political, religious, and cultural issues, Parker appears regularly on Canada's Space Channel and the CTS Christian TV Network and serves as founding president of Los Altos Institute.

Elisa Pulido (PhD candidate, Claremont Graduate University) is a historian of Christianity and the religions of North America. She is a contributor of a chapter on Mormon women and missions for *Mormon Women Have Their Say: Essays from the Claremont Oral History Project* (Greg Kofford Books, 2013).

George R. Ryskamp (JD, Brigham Young University) is a professor of history at Brigham Young University, specializing in Southern European and Latin American family history. He is the author of "Colonial Spanish Borderland Research" in *The Source: A Guidebook to American Genealogy* (Ancestry Publishing, 2006) as well as *Finding Your Hispanic Roots* (Genealogical Publishing Company, 1997). He is a fellow of the Utah Genealogical Association, a *miembro académico* of the Academia Americana de Genealogía, and a corresponding member of the Academia Real Matritense de Genealogía y Heráldica. Additionally, he has served as a member of the Advisory Council of the New England Historic Genealogical Society.

Bill Smith (PhD, Washington State University) is a clinical professor and the director of the Martin Institute and Program in International Studies at the University of Idaho. His main research and teaching activities are directed toward causes of war and the conditions necessary for peace in the international system.

Jared M. Tamez (PhD student, University of Texas at El Paso) studies Latin American and US-Mexico borderlands history. He has published on race and Mormonism in the *Utah Historical Quarterly* and the *Journal of Mormon History*. His dissertation will examine the Mormon colonies in northern Mexico as a borderlands community in the late nineteenth and early twentieth centuries. He is the cofounder of the academic blog Borderlands History (www.borderlandshistory.org).

Index

Page numbers in italic text indicate illustrations.